California's
Wilderness Areas

THE COMPLETE GUIDE

VOLUME 2
THE DESERTS

TEXT AND
PHOTOGRAPHY BY
GEORGE WUERTHNER

WESTCLIFFE PUBLISHERS

Joshua tree frames Jumbo Rocks, Joshua Tree National Park.

Table of Contents

4

Table of Contents

Colorado Desert Subregion

ISBN: 1-56579-282-3

PHOTOGRAPHY AND TEXT COPYRIGHT: George Wuerthner, 1998. All rights reserved.

PRODUCTION MANAGER: Harlene Finn, Westcliffe Publishers

EDITOR: Cat Ohala

DESIGN AND PRODUCTION: Rebecca Finkel; F + P Graphic Design, Boulder, CO

PUBLISHED BY: Westcliffe Publishers, Inc.
PO Box 1261
Englewood, Colorado 80150

PRINTED IN: Hong Kong through World Print, Ltd.

LIBRARY OF CONGRESS CATALOGING-IN-PUBLICATION DATA

Wuerthner, George.
The complete guide to California's wilderness areas / text and photography by George Wuerthner.
p. cm.
Includes index.
Contents: v. 1. Mountains and coastal ranges
ISBN: 1-56579-233-5
1. Wilderness areas—California—Guidebooks.
2. Natural history—California—Guidebooks. 3. Trails —California—Guidebooks. 4. Hiking—California— Guidebooks. I. Title
QH76.5.C2W84 1997   97-6015
508.794—dc21   CIP
Volume 2, ISBN: 1-56579-282-3

PLEASE NOTE:
Risk is always a factor in backcountry travel. Many of the activities described in this book can be dangerous, especially when weather is adverse or unpredictable, and when unforeseen events or conditions create a hazardous situation. Readers should be aware that conditions in the desert are more variable than in other regions. A severe storm may wash out roads, turning a formerly passable road into a riverbed. New roads are continually being established by off-road vehicle enthusiasts and may complicate directions or may not appear on maps. As there are almost no trails in most desert wildernesses, hike descriptions are only suggested routes and do not necessarily represent the best or only route. The author has done his best to provide the reader with accurate information about backcountry travel, as well as to point out some of its potential hazards. It is the responsibility of the users of this guide to learn the necessary skills for safe backcountry travel and to exercise caution in potentially hazardous areas. The author and publisher disclaim any liability for injury or other damage caused by backcountry traveling, mountain biking, or performing any other activity described in this book.

For more information about other fine books and calendars from Westcliffe Publishers, please call your local bookstore, contact us at 1-800-523-3692, or write for our free color catalog.

COVER CAPTION:
Sand dunes, Stovepipe Wells, Death Valley National Park.

The Saline Valley Road drops into the Saline Valley of Death Valley National Park. The steep escarpment of the Inyo Mountains is on the right.

Acknowledgments

In researching this book I was assisted by several Bureau of Land Management (BLM) and Park Service workers. In particular, Chris Roholt, BLM Wilderness Coordinator for the California Desert, offered much encouragement, and Jim Eaton of the California Wilderness Coalition provided historical context to the California Wilderness debate.

California Wilderness Areas

Volume 1: Mountains and Coastal Ranges
Northeast: The Cascades to the Great Basin
Northwest: The North Coast Ranges and
Klamath–Siskiyou Mountains
Sierra Nevada: The Northern, Central, and
Southern Sierras
South Coastal Ranges: The Santa Lucia,
Diablo, and Sierra Madre Mountains
Southern California: The Transverse
and Peninsula Ranges

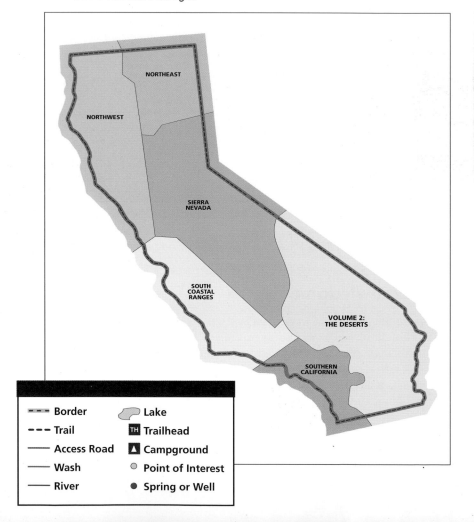

▬▬▬ Border	🖙 Lake
▬ ▬ ▬ Trail	**TH** Trailhead
─── Access Road	▲ Campground
─── Wash	○ Point of Interest
─── River	● Spring or Well

Volume 2: The Deserts

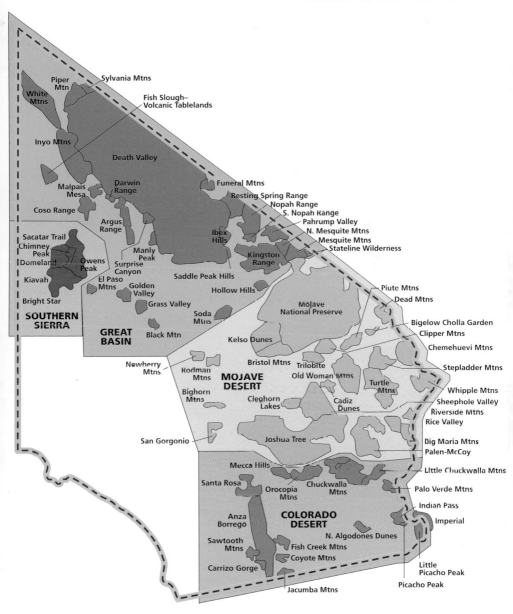

Piper Mtn
Sylvania Mtns
White Mtns
Fish Slough–Volcanic Tablelands
Inyo Mtns
Death Valley
Malpais Mesa
Darwin Range
Funeral Mtns
Resting Spring Range
Nopah Range
S. Nopah Range
Coso Range
Pahrump Valley
Argus Range
N. Mesquite Mtns
Ibex Hills
Mesquite Mtns
Stateline Wilderness
Sacatar Trail
Chimney Peak
Manly Peak
Kingston Range
Domeland
Owens Peak
Surprise Canyon
Saddle Peak Hills
Kiavah
El Paso Mtns
Golden Valley
Hollow Hills
Piute Mtns
Bright Star
Grass Valley
Dead Mtns
Mojave National Preserve
SOUTHERN SIERRA
Soda Mtns
Bigelow Cholla Garden
GREAT BASIN
Black Mtn
Clipper Mtns
Kelso Dunes
Chemehuevi Mtns
Newberry Mtns
Bristol Mtns
Trilobite
Stepladder Mtns
Rodman Mtns
MOJAVE DESERT
Old Woman Mtns
Turtle Mtns
Whipple Mtns
Bighorn Mtns
Cleghorn Lakes
Cadiz Dunes
Sheephole Valley
Riverside Mtns
Rice Valley
San Gorgonio
Joshua Tree
Big Maria Mtns
Palen-McCoy
Mecca Hills
Little Chuckwalla Mtns
Santa Rosa
Chuckwalla Mtns
Palo Verde Mtns
Orocopia Mtns
Indian Pass
Anza Borrego
COLORADO DESERT
Imperial
Sawtooth Mtns
N. Algodones Dunes
Fish Creek Mtns
Coyote Mtns
Little Picacho Peak
Carrizo Gorge
Picacho Peak
Jacumba Mtns

Introduction

California—The Wilderness State

California is unique. There is no other place on earth like it. There are 1,200 miles of coastline, 32 million acres of forest, 21 million acres of desert, and mountains almost everywhere except the Central Valley. Despite being the most populous state in the nation, California possesses a surprising amount of wildlands.

The reason for this apparent contradiction has to do with how people are distributed across the face of the land. Although 15 million people call the urban cities of southern California their home, much of the nearby California desert is essentially uninhabited. Although there are millions living around the greater San Francisco Bay area, much of northern California has a population density lower than Montana.

There are surprisingly few lights when you drive up the northern part of the Central Valley at night. The population density is actually quite sparse. This doesn't mean, however, that the landscape is untouched. The Central Valley is little more than a factory farm these days. Humans may not live everywhere, but there are few places we haven't domesticated to one degree or another. Logging, farming, ranching, road building, off-road vehicle (ORV) use—all have altered the natural landscape significantly.

Nevertheless, there are some parts of the state that are relatively "pristine," by which I mean these areas are largely unaltered by modern human modification. I call them wildlands to denote their lack of human manipulation. Most of California's wildlands exist by chance, not by design. They are the lands that lacked significant mineralization, or were too steep, too dry, or too rugged to invite human exploitation.

Still, despite this happenstance, few other states can claim to approach California in terms of the amount of acreage under legal protection as wilderness. Some 13.8 million acres of the state's federal lands are legally designated wilderness, and close to a million acres of state lands are also protected by a similar legal mandate. By comparison, Montana (a state that many assume to be far less developed) only boasts 3.4 million acres protected as wilderness. In fact, there are more acres of designated wilderness in Death Valley National Park (one wilderness area) than in the combined acreage of all the designated wilderness areas in the entire state of Oregon, with its 38 wilderness areas! In addition, the second largest roadless complex in the nation outside of Alaska—some 2.8 million acres—is found in California's High Sierra.

California easily claims the title *wilderness state*—and no part of California has a greater concentration of wildlands than its deserts.

What Makes a Desert?

Although we may not ordinarily think of California as a desert state, arid lands occupy 28 percent of the state. Two factors account for the state's deserts: global weather patterns and mountains. Globally there is a wide band of deserts located between 15 and 30 degrees north and south of the equator. Southern California, at 32 degrees north latitude, straddles the northern edge of this worldwide desert

Moonrise seen from Pacific Crest Trail in Kiavah Wilderness.

zone. The arid conditions are created when the air, heated at the equator, rises. This warm, moist air circulates north and south—away from the equator—gradually cooling and losing much of its moisture. This moisture falls to the earth and supports the tropical rain forests located on either side of the equator. As this cool but dry air continues to move north and south of the equator, it begins to sink and dominate the lands near the Tropic of Cancer and the Tropic of Capricorn. As the air descends, these air masses are warmed and therefore able to hold more moisture, practically sucking the land dry in these regions.

Exacerbating this global weather pattern is the tendency for strong, subtropical Pacific high-pressure systems to develop and park themselves off the California coast all summer. These Pacific "highs" draw cool (and hence), dry air off the ocean and on to the shore, creating fog along the coast but clear, dry weather inland. In winter, the jet stream shifts southward, bringing cyclonic storms from the Gulf of Alaska in the Pacific Northwest and sometimes further south into northern California. These storms result in copious amounts of winter precipitation. Occasionally these winter storms penetrate southern California and bring winter moisture to the desert. This alternating wet winter/dry summer weather pattern is known as a Mediterranean climate.

Adding to the natural aridity of this global desert belt is the rain shadow effect, which is due to the presence of mountains. All of California's desert regions lay east of the mountain barrier created by the Cascades, and the Sierra Nevada, Transverse, and Peninsula Ranges. Air masses coming off the Pacific Ocean encounter the high peaks of the Santa Rosa Range, the San Jacinto Range, the San Bernardino Mountains, the San Gabriel Range, the Sierra Nevada, and the Cascades, where they cool and drop most of their moisture on the western slope. When these air masses clear the mountain barrier, they descend the eastern slope and absorb moisture as they warm. The end result is some of the driest conditions in the world. For instance, Death Valley (several mountain ranges east of the Sierra Nevada) is one of the most arid places on earth, yet it is only 200 miles from the ocean.

By definition, deserts receive less than 10 inches of precipitation. Some would also add the qualifier that desert areas are regions with high evaporation rates. By such definitions, San Diego, San Bernardino, Bakersfield, and much of what is now lush farmland in the Central Valley might be considered desert, were it not for irrigation. However most people would agree that the southeastern corner of the state harbors most of California's desert. Indio, for example, receives a mere 3.2 inches of annual precipitation. But due to the arid climate and high temperatures, Indio's potential evaporation rate is exceedingly high, to which any urban dweller trying to maintain a green lawn can attest. Some idea of just how much water could evaporate is indicated by the annual evaporation from the Salton Sea just to the south. Approximately 12 feet of water is evaporated from the surface of the sea per year. In other words, just to maintain current water levels, there needs to be an input of 12 feet of precipitation a year. Clearly this is not the case. The Salton Sea would have disappeared years ago were it not for the input of irrigation runoff from the farmland surrounding it.

Although 10 inches is the *maximum* precipitation criteria for an area to meet the "desert" classification, much of the California desert gets considerably less than 10 inches of precipitation. Death Valley, for instance, averages only 1.8 inches of precipitation a year. Bishop (in Owens Valley) and Barstow (in the Mojave Desert) are lush by comparison, receiving more than 5.5 inches and 4.0 inches of annual precipitation respectively.

However, it is not just limited precipitation that defines a desert; it is also the variability in precipitation. In some cases a single, large storm can dump the equivalent of the entire yearly amount of precipitation, whereas at the other extreme no rain or snow may fall for months or even years. Bagdad, in the Mojave Desert, once went two years and one month without a single record of measurable precipitation! Drought is the norm, not the exception, in desert areas.

Aridity is a common denominator in all deserts and it affects many aspects of the desert environment. Not only is evaporation increased, but temperature changes are more extreme. Cloud cover and high humidity both moderate temperature changes because water can hold a lot of latent heat. But in the dry, clear desert, air temperatures fluctuate significantly on a daily basis. As anyone who has spent time in the desert can attest, once the sun sets the temperature drops considerably. Up to 90 percent of the heat absorbed by the earth during the day may be reradiated back into space during the night. A 50°F spread between the high and low temperatures in a typical day is not unusual. The temperature extremes lead to greater air circulation. As a rule, desert regions tend to be windy regions. Winds are generated by differential heating of air masses. Hot air rises and cool air sinks to create breezy conditions. Wind increases evaporation, exacerbating the already dry conditions found in desert regions.

Despite these hostile conditions, California's deserts are full of an amazing array of well-adapted plants and animals, including 1,836 species of plants, 94 mammals, 420 species of birds, and 40 species of fish. However, deserts are places of limited productivity. Compared with other major ecosystems, deserts have a lower overall biomass of both plants and animals.

California's Three Deserts—The Great Basin, the Mojave, and the Colorado

The elevation of California's desert regions varies from below sea level to as high as 8,000 feet, giving rise to three general regimes: cold, warm, and hot deserts. Traditionally geographers have given these regions more formalized names—the Great Basin, the Mojave, and the Colorado.

THE GREAT BASIN DESERT

The most northern and coldest of California's three desert areas is the Great Basin Desert. Although the name implies a low, wide valley, most of the Great Basin region is mountainous and of generally high elevation.

The Great Basin Desert is the largest desert region in the United States. It covers most of Nevada, parts of eastern Oregon, southern Idaho, western Wyoming, and northern and western Utah. Within California, the Great Basin Desert lies east of the Cascades and the Sierra Nevada from the Oregon border south as far as the Lone Pine area in Owens Valley.

The Great Basin Desert is within the Basin and Range Province. It is a region with internal drainage. No rivers run to the sea except for the Pit River in northeastern California. The Basin and Range Province is based on a geologic definition—an area where mountains and valleys are created.

California's Great Basin Desert is typically divided into two geomorphologic subsets based on geology: the Modoc Plateau and the Basin and Range Province. The Modoc Plateau, a nearly level plain with an elevation between 4,000 and 5,000 feet, lies in northeastern California and was formed by large lava flows that spread across much of eastern Oregon, southern Idaho, and adjacent areas between 25 million years ago and the present. Some minor volcanic flows have occurred in the region within historic times.

The Basin and Range Province is dominated by high mountains that are separated by wide valleys or basins. The alternating pattern of mountains and wide intermontane basins marches in regular sequence from eastern California across Nevada all the way to the Rockies. Mountain ranges found in California's portion of the Basin and Range include the Warner Mountains, Sweetwater Range, White Mountains, Inyo Range, Saline Range, Last Chance Range, Cottonwood Mountains, and the Panamint Mountains.

The Basin and Range Province is a region of the earth's crust that is gradually stretching apart. Most of the mountains were uplifted along faults, and the intervening valleys dropped. This faulting is still ongoing, as the numerous earthquakes in the region attest. These fault blocks are much as 100 miles long and 15 to 20 miles wide. The fault-block basin-and-range pattern is seen easily in the traverse from Owens Valley by Lone Pine to Death Valley. Owens Valley is separated from Panamint Valley by the White-Inyo, Coso, and Argus Ranges. The Panamint Range then separates the Panamint Valley and Death Valley. Just beyond Death Valley lie the Grapevine, Funeral, and Black Mountains. All of these ranges are uplifted fault-block masses.

Many of the valleys in the Great Basin Desert are relatively level. They are, in fact, the bottoms of ancient lakes. During the last Ice Age, a time of greater moisture and overall cooler temperatures, giant lakes occupied many of the Great Basin valleys. Great Salt Lake, Pyramid Lake, and Humboldt Lake are all relict water bodies of much larger glacial lakes. In California, giant lakes occupied a number of valleys east of the Sierra Nevada. For instance, Owens Lake near Lone Pine was much larger and it overflowed into the China Lake Valley, and then to the east by Trona to create Searles Lake, which in turn overflowed into the Panamint Valley and ultimately Death Valley, creating Lake Manly. As recent as 5,000 years ago, Lake Manly still covered the floor of Death Valley. The California desert has more than 50 major playas that are reminders of these Ice Age lakes.

Owens Valley is one of the most spectacular examples of basin-and-range geomorphology. The lofty Sierra Nevada rises up to the west, while the White-Inyo Range walls in the eastern border. More than 100 miles long and 10 miles wide, the valley extends south from Bishop to Owens Lake in the south. Not all of the glacial lakes have disappeared entirely due to climatic change. Owens Lake, south of Lone Pine, was a fairly large water body as late as 1900, with steam paddle wheelers plying its waters. Water diversions of the Owens River for Los Angeles have all but dried up the lake.

Reeds along Mojave River, Afton Canyon, California desert.

Anyone who has spent time in the Great Basin can attest to the cold, snowy winters. Temperatures below 0°F are not unusual, and some of the coldest temperatures in California have been recorded in this region. Summers by contrast are warm to hot, and except for an occasional thunderstorm, are generally dry. Most plant growth occurs in the spring while soils are still moist—prior to the drought and heat of summer.

Sagebrush is one of the characteristic plants that covers hundreds of square miles of the intermontane West, giving rise to the notion of a sagebrush ocean. Although there are more than a dozen species of sagebrush (and even more subspecies), the dominant form of sagebrush in the Great Basin Desert is Great Basin big sage, or *Artemesia tridentata tridentata* (or *tri tri* as some botanists lovingly call it). Great Basin sagebrush is a surprisingly long-lived species, with some individuals living for as long as 800 years. Other shrubs associated with the Great Basin Desert include rabbitbrush, hopsage, and saltbush.

Prior to the advent of widespread livestock grazing, most sagebrush communities had a lush understory of perennial native grasses including bluebunch wheatgrass, Great Basin wild rye, and Idaho fescue. Some of these grass species live more than 100 years. Such long life is necessary in this arid climate, where conditions for successful seed germination and establishment are unpredictable and varied.

The introduction of livestock to the Great Basin and other California deserts was the ecological equivalent of dropping a nuclear bomb. As one Nevada biologist put it, livestock grazing didn't just degrade desert ecosystems, it *shattered* them. Unfortunately domestic livestock grazing is still a widespread, ongoing activity on public and private lands in the region.

Unlike the Great Plains of the central United States, most of the Great Basin as well as other desert regions of California did not have large herds of grazing animals. There were no bison, no elk, and antelope were present but not abundant. As a consequence, native vegetation never had to develop a tolerance for heavy grazing and trampling. The repeated grazing of these native grasses by domestic livestock reduced root systems and often removed the annual seed crop. Trampling and soil compaction also reduced water infiltration, compounding the already arid conditions. Hooves destroyed soil algal crusts, which are common in desert regions. These crusts grew between the bunchgrass and promoted mulch-reducing evaporation (hence, loss of soil moisture) while enriching the soil with nitrogen—an essential nutrient that is often in short supply in desert regions. In the past, algal crusts also prevented the establishment of other plants, particularly annuals like the invasive cheatgrass—an exotic grass that now covers much of the Great Basin. Since cheatgrass greens up earlier than native grasses, it rapidly depletes soil moisture and "cheats" other grasses out of water. This intensifies drought conditions for native grasses.

For more than a century, native grasses have been extirpated from most sagebrush communities. The end result is a depauperate plant community and a loss to the overall biologic productivity of this ecosystem.

The decline in native grasses has had another ecological effect. In the past, grasses helped to support wildfires, which were relatively common in the Great Basin, at least at the higher elevations. Most ecologists view periodic wildfires as a positive ecological process. Wildfires recycle nutrients, kill pathogens in the soil, and create a patchy mosaic of plant distribution and age classes. Fires also limited the distribution of trees in some places. As a result of heavy grazing, wildfires burn less frequently.

In the Great Basin Desert, dwarf forests of single-leaf pinyon pine and Utah juniper grow, usually at elevations higher than 5,000 feet. The distribution of these forests has expanded as a result of reduced wildfire occurrence. At the highest elevations in some desert mountain ranges grow forests of Jeffrey pine, bristlecone pine, white fir, and aspen.

THE MOJAVE DESERT

South of the Great Basin lies the Mojave Desert. The Mojave is named for its dominant drainage system—the Mojave River. The "river" originates on the eastern slope of the San Bernardino Mountains then flows east, only occasionally appearing above ground before disappearing altogether in the desert south of Baker. During glacial periods, the Mojave River was a more significant water source and it drained northward into Death Valley. A number of large glacial lakes occupied the lower valleys of the Mojave Desert region, and sands from those ancient lakes now comprise the large dunes seen at Kelso Dunes and elsewhere in the area.

Although most of the Mojave Desert lies in California, small portions of it lap over into southern Nevada and adjacent parts of Arizona. Within California the Mojave Desert is wedge shaped, with a narrow apex to the west near Antelope Valley, spreading to more than 200 miles wide at the Arizona border. The Mojave Desert lies north and east of the Transverse mountain ranges like the San Gabriel Range and the San Bernardino Mountains, north of the mountains of Joshua Tree National Park, and south of the Sierra Nevada and Death Valley National Park.

Dozens of mountain ranges poke up through the alluvium that covers much of the region, including the Eagle Mountains, Sheephole Mountains, New York Mountains, Clark Mountains, Old Woman Mountains, Providence Mountains, and many others. Both the Mojave National Preserve as well as most of Joshua Tree National Park are within the Mojave Desert. Like the Great Basin to the north, Ice Age lakes once covered parts of this region, including the Harper, Manix, and Mojave glacial lakes.

In many respects the Mojave Desert resembles the Great Basin, however there are some differences that warrant a separate classification. Geologically, basins—not mountain ranges—seem to dominate the Mojave Desert, particularly to the west near Antelope Valley, Palmdale, and the surrounding vicinity. Overall, the Mojave Desert is lower in elevation than the Great Basin, generally between 2,000 and 4,000 feet in elevation, and hence is warmer. Joshua tree, with its shaggy bark and picturesque branching habit, is the signature plant of higher elevations of this desert. Beneath Joshua tree "forests" grow shrubs like blackbrush, shadscale, and four-wing saltbush. Grasses include James' galleta grass and needle-and-thread grass.

More common at lower elevations is creosote bush. This shrub cloaks the basins and flats with a monotonous green veneer, accounting for as much as 70 percent of the vegetative cover of the Mojave Desert. With small, narrow, leafy leaves and numerous branches emulating from a root crown, creosote bush is so abundant that even if you don't know one plant from another, if you called every waist-high green bush encountered in the Mojave Desert a creosote bush, you'll probably be right most of the time.

Creosote bush is one of the most successful desert plants, and is widely distributed from California to Texas and far down into Mexico. Branches of creosote bush will sometimes take root, creating genetically identical clones. Some biologists believe that cloning has created some creosote groups that may be as old as 11,000 years, making them the oldest plants on earth.

Besides creosote bush, other shrubs found in the Mojave Desert include burrobush and brittlebush. Brittlebush has beautiful clusters of large yellow flowers that in late winter (when in flower) often make the plant look like a giant golden pumpkin.

Due to the warmer temperatures, cactus are far more abundant in the Mojave Desert than the colder Great Basin. Some 20 species are known, including silver cholla, beavertail, and cottontop.

Like the Great Basin, the Mojave Desert is dominated by winter precipitation. Much of it comes as rain, but snow is common at higher elevations. However, unlike the Great Basin, the generally warmer and lower elevations of the Mojave Desert permit plant growth during the winter months when moisture is most abundant. A rich flora of annual flowers known as winter ephemerals grow in the Mojave Desert. Most of these species germinate in late fall if more than an inch of precipitation has fallen. They grow slowly during the colder winter months, then complete their life cycle in the spring before the onset of summer drought and heat.

THE COLORADO DESERT

The Colorado Desert contains the lowest and often hottest parts of California. Named for the Colorado River, which marks its eastern boundary in California, the Colorado Desert lies south of the San Bernardino Mountains and east of the Peninsula Ranges, and extends into adjacent parts of Mexico and Arizona. It includes the Coachella Valley, Imperial Valley, and Salton Sink. Most of the area is at or below sea level, with the Salton Sea at the lowest point.

The San Andreas Fault delineates much of the western border of the Colorado Desert, and as a rule the mountains have been rising as the valleys have dropped, creating steep mountains such as the Santa Rosa Range and the San Jacinto Range west and south of Palm Springs. Other mountain ranges within the Colorado Desert include the Jacumba Mountains, the Coyote Mountains, the Palo Verde Mountains, and the Orocopia and Chocolate Mountains. Anza Borrego Desert State Park is the largest protected area within the Colorado Desert.

The Salton Sea lies in the center of the Colorado Desert with a surface level about 240 feet below sea level. The "sea" didn't exist prior to 1905. High water caused an irrigation canal to break, and water flowed into the Salton Trough depression. Irrigation runoff continues to fill the basin, making it the largest body of water in the state of California.

The Salton Sea isn't the first body of water to occupy this region. Clays deposited in ancient lakes have eroded into badlands common throughout the basin today. As little as 500 years ago, a huge lake that geologists call Lake Cahuilla filled the basin, covering 2,000 square miles. Old shorelines more than 200 feet above the current "sea" surface are still plainly visible on the eastern slope of the Santa Rosa Mountains.

Hikers in badlands near Zabrinski Point, Death Valley National Park.

Winds have captured much of the sand from these ancient lakes and moved it westward. In the southeastern corner of the Colorado Desert lies one of the largest dune complexes in the United States. The Algodones Dunes stretch more than 50 miles north to south and are up to 6 miles wide.

Winter precipitation is the norm; however, up to 30 to 40 percent of the annual precipitation occurs during the summer, primarily as thunderstorms. In some years the Colorado Desert receives the greatest amount of summer precipitation of any part of the state. As a consequence, the Colorado Desert can support plant growth in both winter and summer. It is by far the "richest" desert in terms of plant communities, and has an abundance of cacti, shrubs, and small trees.

The Colorado Desert is actually a subset of the larger Sonoran Desert. The Sonoran Desert, with its saguaro cactus, is what most people conjure up when they think of desert. Although a few saguaro cacti do cross into California near the Arizona border, on the whole, large columnar cacti like the saguaro are rare in the Colorado Desert. Nevertheless, there are still more species of cacti found here than in any of the other desert regions in California.

The grayish smoke tree, a member of the pea family of legumes that grows along desert washes, and the whiplike ocotillo are both indicator species of the Colorado Desert. Other plant species found in the Colorado Desert include palo verde, ironwood, California fan palm, desert agave, chuparosa, jojoba, and honey mesquite. Cactus species include jumping cholla, pincushion cactus, and California barrel cactus. Grasses include big galleta and Indian ricegrass.

What This Book Covers

This is not your typical guidebook for trails or recreational opportunities. Although trails for a few major parks are described, most of the California desert is trailless. This is true wilderness in a physical sense—you are on your own, without even a preexisting trail to influence your explorations. However, what this book does provide is a narrative of each wilderness and basic information regarding the size, elevation, location, appropriate maps, and the agencies that administer it. These data are followed by a description of the major attributes and physical features of the wilderness area, such as geology, major plant communities, and historic information. Bear in mind that most of these descriptions are brief. These areas remained wildlands largely because they were bypassed by modern humanity. They are still largely unknown landscapes. Lastly, directions are provided for the easiest access to some portion of the wilderness where one might begin hiking.

The scope of this book includes all existing federally designated wilderness areas in the California desert as designated by the 1994 California Desert Protection Act, as well as a few undesignated but significant roadless lands that could be added to the wilderness system eventually. Also described is the Anza Borrego Desert State Park, because it is one of the more significant protected desert areas, and to leave it out of a discussion of desert wildlands seems inappropriate.

The focus of this book is California's desert region. For those of you interested in the rest of the state's wilderness areas, please obtain the companion book, *California's Wilderness Areas: The Complete Guide, Volume 1—Mountains and Coastal Ranges* (Englewood, CO: Westcliffe Publishers, 1997).

Given the scope and breadth of the subject, not all areas receive equal treatment. Emphasis is placed on the national park units since they are among the largest wildland complexes, as well as the most accessible. Rather than organize these wildernesses in alphabetical order, I assumed that most people using this book would be visiting a specific geographic region. If you are visiting Death Valley National Park, it is more useful to read about other wildlands in that immediate region than to have to flip back and forth through the book to find all the wilderness areas in the immediate vicinity of Death Valley. Therefore I have grouped the wilderness areas by biogeographic subregions: the southern Sierra, the Great Basin Desert, the Mojave Desert, and the Colorado Desert subregions. All but the southern Sierra are anchored by a major state or national park. For instance, the Colorado Desert subregion includes Anza Borrego Desert State Park.

To make it easier for someone new to the California desert to locate a subregion, human landmarks like interstate highways are often used as the major division between subregions. Since nature is not nearly as neat as the way we characterize natural communities in books, in reality some of the wilderness areas included in one region might fit better under a different subregion. For example, the Whipple, Turtle, Big Maria, and other mountains near the Colorado River are included within the Mojave Desert subregion even though they are more like areas in the Colorado Desert subregion biologically. However, in the interest of brevity and simplicity, I sometimes fudged a bit to make areas fit political-topographical boundaries.

What Does a Wilderness Designation Do?

The passage of the Wilderness Act in 1964 institutionalized an idea—that maintaining some of our natural landscape in an undeveloped condition had a value to humanity equal to using that landscape for consumptive purposes. As written, the Act seeks to preserve for posterity an "enduring resource" of wilderness on those federal lands that are essentially "untrammeled" or undeveloped. As defined by the Act, these are lands that "generally appear to have been affected primarily by the forces of nature, with the imprint of man's work substantially unnoticeable." Thus lands that are heavily logged, mined, and developed usually do not qualify as wilderness. However, minor intrusions such as dams, fencing for livestock, cabins for administration purposes or recreational use, and even previously developed areas such as mining or logging camps that have largely reverted to a more natural condition can be found in designated wilderness areas. In particular, old mining ruins are ubiquitous and abundant in many California desert wilderness regions.

In addition to natural appearance, other qualities that an area must possess to be designated as wilderness include some opportunities for solitude and unconfined recreation; and a minimum size of 5,000 acres (exceptions are made for smaller areas that may be adjacent to larger wildland complexes). Wilderness areas may also preserve features that are of historic, geologic, or ecological significance.

To maintain these qualities, activities like timber harvest, road building, mining, motorized vehicle use, and even some modern recreational activities like mountain biking are not permitted. However, a few existing commercial activities are allowed, such as livestock grazing and outfitting. Unless otherwise prohibited by other agency mandates, recreational uses like fishing, cross-country skiing, canoeing, hiking, and camping are recognized as legitimate wilderness uses. But the most important "use" of wilderness is protection of watersheds, biologic diversity, ecological processes, and scenic qualities.

It is important to note that Congress does not "create" wilderness any more than a weather bureau creates a sunny day. All Congress can do is recognize the existing qualities of the landscape and decide to maintain those landscape features in an undeveloped state. Wilderness designation is thus a generous act, giving future generations the opportunity to know something of the earth's natural landscape.

The History of Wilderness Protection

Depending on how the word is used, "wilderness" can have several meanings. Throughout the book I use the term "Wilderness" (with a capital *W*) for formally named congressionally designated wilderness areas (such as the Argus Range Wilderness, the Inyo Mountain Wilderness, and so forth), whereas "wilderness" (with a lowercase *w*) implies undeveloped landscapes that have no formal legislative protection, but have wildland characteristics.

Formally designated wildernesses require an act of Congress under the guidelines set forth under the 1964 Wilderness Act. Congress passed the Act to provide permanent protection for federal wildlands. Earlier preservation efforts were aimed toward protecting other resources, such as geologic, biologic, and scenic oddities or what one writer termed "freaks of nature." For example, the designation of Yellowstone National Park in 1872 was done primarily to protect the region's abundance of hot springs and geysers. Nothing was mentioned about protecting wilderness. Similarly, Yosemite was declared a park to preserve its scenic grandeur. Although certainly Sierra Club founder, John Muir, was primarily interested in advocating protection for the Sierra and elsewhere to preserve wildland qualities, this was not the dominant philosophy guiding most early park designations.

Formal recognition for protection of large landscapes in a primitive and undeveloped condition did not occur until 1924, when the National Forest Service set aside the headwaters of the Gila River in New Mexico as a wilderness. This administrative decision, small though the area may have been, signaled a change in the nation's collective philosophy. For more than 300 years Americans made a conscious effort to "tame" the wilderness. We sought to protect civilization, not wildlands. To be sure, even in 1924 the majority of people considered it desirable to extend development to every corner of the globe, but at least a few individuals and groups were now asking that some scattered remnants of wildland be preserved for future generations and for nature itself.

The philosophical roots of the wilderness protection concept can be traced back to Henry David Thoreau who wrote in his essays on Walden Pond that "a town is saved, no more by the men and women in it than the woods and swamps that surround it" (New York: Knopf, 1992). John Muir continued this tradition, ceaselessly advocating for preservation of the Sierra Nevada and protection from logging, mining, and livestock grazing.

The first direct effort to set aside land from development to maintain its wildland qualities occurred in 1919. Arthur Carhart, a Forest Service landscape architect, was sent to Trappers Lake in Colorado to survey the area for a proposed summer home recreational development. His original recommendation for Trappers Lake only involved a small amount of land, and it appears that initially Carhart did not have the vision to see the need for landscapewide preservation. After seeing the site, Carhart decided that maintaining its natural condition was far more valuable than ringing the lake with cabins. In his memorandum to his superiors, Carhart recommended against any development. Within a few years he began to advocate protection of natural areas for their wilderness qualities.

While working for the Forest Service, Carhart met up with another early wilderness advocate—Aldo Leopold. Leopold was then assistant forester in Albuquerque, New Mexico. Author of the now classic book *A Sand County Almanac* (New York: Ballantine Books, 1966), Leopold was thinking along similar lines as Carhart, however he had already acquired a landscapewide vision. Very early in his career, Leopold recognized that the preservation of large, roadless areas was the only way to protect wildlands. In 1921 he outlined these ideas in an essay "The Wilderness and Its Place in Forest Recreation Policy," published in the *Journal of Forestry*. In part, due to Leopold's encouragement, the Forest Service set aside a half-million-acre tract in New Mexico as the Gila Wilderness.

Although merely a bureaucratic decision that carried no weight of law, the creation of the Gila Wilderness captured the imagination of others in the Forest Service. In 1926 an agency inventory of its holdings revealed that there were 74 areas

Two-and-a-half-year-old Summer Wuerthner strides up the Wild Rose Peak Trail with her mother behind her; Panamint Range, Death Valley National Park.

totaling 55 million acres where no roads existed and none were as yet planned. The largest roadless area was 7 million acres. This led to the designation of other Forest Service lands as primitive areas under its L-20 regulations implemented in 1929. L-20 regulations permitted the chief of the Forest Service to withdraw roadless lands from development schemes. Eventually 72 primitive areas were established within the 10 western states. The main purpose was "to maintain primitive conditions of transportation, subsistence, habitation, and environment to the fullest degree…with a view to conserving the values of such areas for purposes of public education and recreation."

Primitive area status offered no real long-term protection since such designation was purely administrative and could be reversed by any succeeding Forest Service chief. Nevertheless, many of California's currently designated wilderness areas were originally set aside as primitive areas or future incantations of the same concept. California wilderness areas that were once primitive areas include portions of what is now the San Rafael Wilderness, John Muir Wilderness, Domeland Wilderness, Ventana Wilderness, Trinity Alps Wilderness, plus many others.

Throughout the 1930s the Forest Service added to the acreage of lands that were to be protected in an undeveloped state, setting aside many additional primitive areas. One of the most ardent proponents of primitive area establishment was an energetic Forest Service employee named Bob Marshall. In 1936 Marshall published an article outlining the results of a study he had done of the remaining roadless lands left in the continental United States. He found 48 forested, roadless areas in excess of 300,000 acres, plus another 29 desert areas that were 500,000 acres or larger, identifying many of the areas that are today among California's largest wilderness areas.

Realizing that outside political pressure was necessary to ensure protection of wildlands, Marshall, along with other like-minded conservationists including Aldo Leopold, Olaus Murie, Robert Sterling Yard, Harvey Broome, and Benton Mackaye, founded the Wilderness Society in 1935. The group's goal was to establish a nationwide system of federally protected wildlands. From its beginnings, Marshall not only provided great energy and enthusiasm for the organization, but also funded the fledgling group with his significant inherited wealth. It was a real blow to the Society and the wilderness movement when Marshall died unexpectedly of a heart attack in 1939 at the early age of 38.

Nevertheless, the idea of a nationwide wilderness system prevailed. Howard Zahniser, who became executive director of the Wilderness Society in 1945, recognized that some systematic way of protecting wildlands that went beyond the Forest Service's regulations was necessary. In 1956 he penned the first version of what would become the Wilderness Act, and Senator Hubert Humphrey of Minnesota introduced the bill into Congress in 1957. The bill called for the establishment of a nationwide wilderness system on all suitable federal lands including those managed by the National Park Service, the US Fish and Wildlife Service, as well as the National Forest Service. (The original bill omitted Bureau of Land Management [BLM] lands from consideration.) The Wilderness Act only required policy change, not the establishment of a new agency, and thus required no additional funds. The law required federally designated lands to be managed to retain their primitive character. Consequently, activities such as motorized vehicle access, road building, and logging were not permitted.

Then, as now, western commercial extractive interests rallied against the bill, arguing that withdrawing even a tiny percentage of the West from potential development would destroy western economic opportunities. The bill was also opposed by the Forest Service and the Park Service, both of which saw it as potentially hamstringing their own development designs and plans. Opposition was strong, and the bill was revised 66 times before it finally passed in both houses of Congress. President Lyndon Johnson signed it into law in September 1964. However, in making its way through the political process, a number of concessions were made to ensure its passage. Mineral and oil exploration were given a 20-year grace period to give ample opportunity for these industries to find and develop new deposits. In addition, livestock grazing was specifically permitted to continue in designated wilderness to reduce opposition from that quarter. These concessions would come back to haunt conservationists in the ensuing years. In particular, livestock grazing continues to be the single greatest source of environmental degradation on western lands, especially in desert regions.

The Wilderness Act immediately granted wilderness protection to 54 areas totaling 9.1 million acres. This included such California wilderness areas as the Hoover, John Muir, Marble Mountain, San Gorgonio, San Gabriel, South Warner, Domeland, Cucamonga, and Minarets (now Ansel Adams). In addition, another 5 million acres of primitive areas were to be reviewed for potential permanent protection as designated wilderness.

After passage of the Act, the federal agencies were to recommend additional areas for inclusion within the National Wilderness Preservation System. A number of new wilderness areas in California came about in the years following passage of the Act including the Ventana Wilderness, Desolation Wilderness, and San Rafael Wilderness. The latter was established in 1968 and became the first new addition to the National Wilderness Preservation System. However, designation of many of the larger wildlands was stalled by agency resistance to change.

In 1972 the Forest Service embarked on its Roadless Area Review Evaluation, or what became known as RARE I. The agency was supposed to determine which lands had wilderness qualities, but the results seemed to be more of a review of which lands had little commercial value. Two years later the agency released its results, calling for protection of 12.3 million acres out of a possible 56 million. The results were disappointing to conservationists, who thought that too many areas deserving recognition were left out of the recommendations. The Sierra Club filed suit against the Forest Service, barring it from developing any roadless areas without first doing an environmental impact statement as required by the National Environmental Protection Act passed by Congress in 1969.

To comply, the Forest Service went back to the drawing board and did a second Roadless Area Review Evaluation, or RARE II. As before, a small percentage of the roadless lands—15 million acres—was recommended for wilderness. In California, 6 million acres were identified as roadless, but only 900,000 acres were recommended by the agency as suitable for addition to the National Wilderness Preservation System. The state of California sued the Forest Service, claiming it had done a rushed and incomplete job.

In 1982 a federal court of appeals ruled in the state's favor in the case of California vs. Block that the RARE II environmental impact statements were inadequate. Until a more detailed study of each area was conducted, the Forest Service could not develop or otherwise compromise the wildland quality of RARE II lands. This effectively blocked development of 47 California roadless areas.

In the meantime, several other laws affected wilderness designation, particularly with regard to BLM roadless lands. In 1976 Congress passed the Federal Land Policy and Management Act, which mandated that the BLM review areas without roads under its management, select wilderness study areas, and make recommendations about potential new wilderness to Congress by 1991. New BLM areas were slowly added to the wilderness system, usually small parcels of lands adjacent to existing or new Forest Service or National Park Service wilderness areas.

In the meantime, public pressure to designate additional wilderness acres continued, and citizens began working for additional wilderness designation outside of agency recommendation. In 1984, 21 statewide wilderness bills were passed by Congress, establishing more than 8 million acres of new wilderness areas. In California this effort culminated in the California Wilderness Act of 1984. The bill established 23 new wilderness areas in the state, including the Dick Smith, South Sierra, Trinity Alps, Siskiyou, and Carson-Iceberg Wilderness areas. Additions to 15 other existing national forest wildernesses included expansion of the Domeland, Marble Mountain, Mokelumne, Ansel Adams, and Yolla-Bolly-Middle Eel Wildernesses. In addition, two new national park wildernesses were established that covered major portions of Yosemite, Kings Canyon, and Sequoia National Parks. The bill also declared 83 miles of the Tuolumne River as Wild and Scenic, and established the Mono Basin National Scenic Area.

Increasingly, desert lovers were casting their eyes on California's undeveloped arid lands and looking to protect them under the Wilderness Act as well. Momentum for protection of California's BLM lands accelerated after Congress passed the Arizona Desert Wilderness Act in 1990, which designated 1.1 million acres of BLM lands and another 1.3 million acres of National Wildlife Refuge lands as wilderness.

The next major wilderness designation occurred with the passage of the California Desert Bill in 1994. This bill was the largest addition to the National Wilderness Preservation System outside of the Alaska Lands Bill of 1980. The California Desert Bill established 69 new BLM wilderness areas (three of which shared borders with new Forest Service wilderness) totaling 3.5 million acres, 95,000 acres of Forest Service wilderness, 4 million acres of National Park Service wilderness in three national park areas, and 9,000 acres in two national wildlife refuges for a total of 7.6 million acres of new wilderness protection in California. The bill also enlarged Joshua Tree National Monument and Death Valley National Monument by placing some adjacent BLM lands under Park Service management, and upgraded them to national park status. In addition, lands originally managed by the BLM as the East Mojave Scenic Area were redesignated the Mojave National Preserve and were placed under National Park Service jurisdiction.

Passage of the California Desert Bill raised the total designated federal wilderness in the state to 129 units covering 13,971,548 acres, or approximately 13 percent of the entire state. California now has the second (after Alaska) greatest area protected as wilderness in the entire nation, and the greatest number of wilderness areas in the country.

Petroglyphs near Corn Springs, Chuckwalla Mountains.

Nevertheless, the California Desert Protection Act also released nearly a million acres of roadless lands that had wildland qualities from further protection as potential wilderness. In addition, it did not address the fate of other roadless lands in the state. For example, there are millions of acres of National Forest Service lands that remain open to development, including more than 200,000 acres in the White Mountains. Plus the BLM manages lands in other parts of California that could qualify as wilderness, particularly in northern California. In total, depending on how you draw the boundaries, as much as another 4 million acres in California may qualify as wilderness. Clearly, formal protection of California's federal wildlands is not yet over.

In addition to federal lands, California protects a sizable amount of state lands, and its state park system is among the largest and most diverse in the nation. A few of its larger state parks are also managed for wilderness values, largely following the same management philosophy found on federal Wilderness areas. By far the largest state wilderness is found in the 600,000-acre Anza Borrego Desert State Park. Some 12 units encompassing 63 percent of the park are designated as wilderness.

Undoubtedly, even after the fate of most of the larger roadless areas is determined, new legislation will seek to preserve the ecological integrity of California's wildlands. The new science of conservation biology recognizes that habitat fragmentation poses one of the greatest threats to long-term preservation of biologic and ecological processes. Biodiversity is more than protecting or sustaining a few token individuals of any species. Real biodiversity protection requires long-term viability of breeding populations. In addition, the evolutionary processes that shape and influence species must be maintained. Thus, reestablishing wildfire or maintaining predation from large carnivores like the mountain lion is as critical to biodiversity preservation as maintaining populations of rare species like the California condor or Stephen's kangaroo rat.

Eventually California may become a state ribboned by roads and freeways, with islands of urban and agricultural development set within a sea of wildlands. Such a vision is not really impractical from a biologic and ecological perspective, although mustering the needed political support for such a transformation may still be decades away. Hopefully this book will act as both a guide and inspiration to those who wish to pursue such a vision.

The History of the California Desert Protection Act

The bills that eventually authorized the California Desert Protection Act—Senate Bill 21 (S.21) and House Resolution 518 (H.R.518)—were introduced early in the second session of the 103rd Congress. Senator Feinstein authored S.21 and Representative Lehman introduced H.R.518. Lawmakers amended both bills as they moved through the legislative process, modifying some parts of the bill substantially from the original versions championed by environmentalists. According to Jim Eaton of the California Wilderness Coalition, a silver lining in the legislative process that eventually led to the passage of the California Desert Protection Act was that most of the congressional discussion focused on the proposed Mojave National Park. As a consequence, there was almost no scrutiny or modification made to all the other BLM wilderness proposals that were also included in the bill, which were passed into law virtually unchanged from the way environmentalists had originally proposed them.

After its introduction, Feinstein's S.21 stayed in the Senate Energy and Natural Resources Committee until October 1993. During this time more than 150 changes were made before it finally passed out of committee. Several major concessions were made to appease conservatives, property rights advocates, ORV enthusiasts, and the military. These included keeping some roads open, excluding Lanfair Valley from the proposed Mojave National Park (leaving a 276,000-acre gap in the middle of the proposed park), and altering language that restricted the military's right to overflight of protected areas. The bill passed out of committee on October 5, 1993, with a vote of 13 to 7 in favor of the measure.

From committee, Feinstein's significantly altered bill went to the Senate floor where lawmakers debated it and eventually passed it by a significant margin. Yet to gain passage in the Senate, further concessions to resource exploiters were made. Amendments added included a provision to allow grazing in perpetuity on all park lands. (Typically when new parks are established grazing is terminated immediately or sometimes phased out over a period of years—one way or another the cows are sent home.) With these new concessions, the Senate passed the legislation on April 13, 1994, by a vote of 69 to 29 in support of the bill. The bill now headed back to the House for consideration.

On August 27th, the House began consideration of the Senate's work by amending an earlier desert protection bill (H.R.518) to reflect closely the wording of S.21. The House generally followed S.21 but modified a few parts of the legislation. The amount of land in Lanfair Valley to be excluded from the proposed Mojave National Park was reduced to only 40,000 acres. In addition, the House version called for the removal of active mines in park boundaries.

The bill languished in the House for months. Additional amendments were added and H.R.518 was slowly weakened. Near the end of this struggle, the National Rifle Association managed to achieve a provision for hunting in the park; mining interests were able to get additional mineral-rich lands "removed" from the park; and property rights advocates passed an amendment that disallowed consideration of endangered species when assessing property value. Finally, after escaping an amendment that would have delayed creation of the park for several decades, the bill passed out of the House on October 4th by a vote of 283 to 140 and headed for a joint House-Senate conference.

Despite widespread public support of no hunting in the new park, the conference committee downgraded the status of Mojave National Park to Mojave National Preserve to permit sport hunting, kept the provision that permitted livestock grazing forever, and expanded the mileage of ORV roads. By now almost everyone was exhausted from the struggle. Within the next 48 hours both Houses agreed to the committee's report. The compromised product was signed into law by President Bill Clinton.

Exploring the Desert

Driving in the Desert

You don't need a four-wheel-drive (4wd) high-clearance (high ground clearance) vehicle to access most of the wilderness areas described in this book. I explored all of these areas using only a two-wheel-drive (2wd) vehicle. Admittedly there were times when I had to park my vehicle and walk, when someone in a 4wd vehicle would have kept going, but common sense dictates that you err on the side of safety when you travel in remote desert country. In any case, many California desert wildlands are immediately adjacent to paved highways. In these instances, find a place to park off the road then begin your hike. In particular, all of the national parks and Anza Borrego Desert State Park all have good, paved highway access to numerous hiking areas. First-time desert hikers might wish to start their explorations in the parks.

However, not all wilderness areas are accessible by paved roads, and even if they are, you may wish to explore another part of the wilderness that is only reachable by driving on gravel or dirt roads. If this is the case, there are some considerations to keep in mind. The best advice is to go slowly and stop before you get into an irreversible position. This includes avoiding sandy washes that might have loose sand pockets, or proceeding up steep hills and rocky roads without first scouting the area. You don't want to find yourself halfway up a steep hill without enough power to gain the top, and be forced to back down a narrow rocky road. To get yourself into such a fix is easier to do than you might think, since many of the roads in desert areas were created by miners with bulldozers who often took the most direct route up a slope. Old mining roads tend to be exceedingly narrow and have a steeper grade than many cars and trucks can climb.

When I get to a questionable road, I stop and walk ahead to inspect it. I always look for potential places to park or turn around. If the road is so poor that you can't go forward, chances are that few other people can travel it either, so the road becomes a nice, wide "hiking trail."

Since the vast majority of people don't own 4wd vehicles, another option to gain access without having to walk miles on old roads is to use a mountain bike. I carry a mountain bike on a good bike rack that hooks to the back of my vehicle, and I use it whenever the road gets too rough for my small pickup. Bear in mind that mountain bikes don't work well on loose, sandy tracks, so they aren't a good option in washes.

In addition to providing access, riding a mountain bike on desert back roads is enjoyable in and of itself. Keep in mind that many old roads and "ways" lace the desert wilderness areas. In many instances these roads were closed on wilderness designation and are now supposed to be used only for nonmotorized, nonmechanical access. So when you reach the wilderness boundaries, hide your bike and then walk, even if the "road" continues.

Even with the best care and caution, there are going to be times when you run into trouble, and it's best to be self-equipped so you can extract yourself from the situation. To this end, *always carry plenty of water.* If you have trouble, you want to be able to have enough water to meet your needs for more than a day or so.

Beyond carrying water, several other items are mandatory and should always be in your car, particularly if you venture off a paved road. These items include a good jack and a good spare tire or two. Also, I always carry a couple of cans of tire inflator, which fills small punctures and inflates a tire enough so you can drive to a town to get the tire changed. Even if you have a spare tire, you never know when you might get two flats while on the same road. It's happened to me—twice. With the cans of tire inflator, I was still able to get to a town under my own power and have the tires repaired.

I also carry a small collapsing camp shovel, a chunk of two-by-four, and a piece of carpet. These items are useful if you happen to get stuck in loose sand. I use the board to provide a firm, secure surface for the car jack, and use the shovel to dig out the tire. After jacking up the vehicle, place the carpet under the drive wheel for traction. Often this will be enough to get you out of a sand trap—if you're not too far into it. You may also want to carry a tow chain or rope for a second vehicle to pull you out of a bad spot.

Low-impact Camping and Travel

Because of the extreme fragility of desert soils, and the slim margin for additional stress under which most desert plants and animals live, all desert visitors have an even greater responsibility to practice low-impact camping and travel techniques. The desert environment is slow to heal from abuse. Tank tracks in the California desert from General Patton's World War II desert training sessions are still clearly visible more than 50 years after they were made. The ruins of old mining operations, many of them dating from the turn of the century, are still largely intact. Litter and refuse do not decompose rapidly as in more humid regions.

The fragility of desert environments is heightened by the presence of microscopic soil coverings known as cyptogramic crusts. These crusts are critical to desert landscapes. Crusts act like a mulch and help to seal in soil moisture. They take atmospheric nitrogen and transfer it to the soil in a manner usable for plant growth. By capping the soil, these crusts prevent the invasion of exotic weedy species. When dry, these crusts are extremely fragile, and even walking on them can destroy this cover. The advent of domestic livestock grazing destroyed much of the cyptogramic cover over large areas of the West; nevertheless, desert visitors should avoid adding to the destruction by adhering to the following guidelines.

1. Whenever possible, walk on preexisting trails and roads. Where there are no trails—a common condition in much of the California desert—hikers should concentrate travel to sites where cyptogramic crusts aren't common, such as in desert washes and on rocky ridges. If you are in a group, walk single file as much as possible to avoid disturbing soils more than necessary.

2. When driving, use preexisting roads and established access routes. Avoid establishing new tracks or routes.

3. When camping, use preexisting campsites or choose sites that are either bare rock or sandy desert washes.

Other Considerations

Avoid camping near water sources and springs. Maintain a quarter-mile distance if possible. In the desert environment, water is critical to many wildlife species, and human presence near a spring may preclude its use by sensitive wildlife like bighorn sheep and other animals.

Due to the limited biologic productivity of desert regions, campfires are probably not an option in most regions. Use a camp stove whenever possible. If you must have a campfire or have brought wood from other regions, limit placement of the campfire to existing fire rings or build fires in sandy washes where future floods will remove all traces of previous fires.

Remove all trash. In particular, remember that aluminum doesn't burn. Putting an aluminum container in a fire will not destroy it. When leaving a campsite, pick up all trash—even the trash left by others. Leave the desert in better condition than you found it.

Bury all human waste in the ground 6 to 8 inches deep.

Safety Matters

The desert is a beautiful region, but it is also an unforgiving environment. Humans are not particularly well adapted for life in the desert. The margin for error for our bodies is even slimmer than it is for many of the desert's plants and animals. Unlike popular National Park and Forest Service wilderness areas, the likelihood of encountering another person in the desert is extremely remote. In researching this book I never encountered another hiker, except on a few National Park Service nature trails, and I seldom even passed another vehicle once I left the major highway.

To have both a safe and enjoyable trip, all travelers to the desert should consider the following advice. First of all, plan your trip. Tell a responsible person, preferably a relative or close friend, your general location and planned itinerary. Remember that unlike popular National Park Service backcountry areas, you may not be able to count on outside help to happen along. If you are injured or hurt, you will be on your own. When you leave your vehicle, place a note inside (obviously not in the windshield for potential thieves to read) that indicates your proposed hiking route and how long you plan to be gone, and date the note.

Take a compass and map with you. For better or worse, most California desert areas are not more than a day's hike from a major road—providing you walk in the right direction. If you have time to wait out the heat of the day, it's often not a bad idea to travel at night when temperatures are cooler. In addition, it's often possible to orient your travels by observing car headlights (which may indicate a busy road) or by locating the lights of a community or other small settlement.

Water and Heat

Water is the single limiting factor in the desert. Although there is more water in some mountain ranges than you might suspect, most of these streams and springs are seasonal, and are not reliable water sources. In addition, some water sources are polluted by livestock or burros, and therefore are of questionable purity. Of course, if you have a choice between drinking polluted water and dying of thirst, take the polluted water. Nevertheless, it's wise to purify all water you encounter unless it's flowing directly from a spring.

Due to the uncertainty of desert water resources, the best advice is to make sure you have plenty with you. I always carry a minimum of 5 gallons in my vehicle anytime I travel in the desert. For day hikes I carry no less than 3 quarts of water, and I drink it often. The hotter the day, the more water you should drink. At a temperature of 120°F (a not uncommon temperature in California's desert regions during the summer), a person will die in one day if he has no water. Avoid hiking in midday sun. If lost or injured, try to travel at night when humidity is higher and water needs are reduced.

The ability to withstand heat stress is related to the body's ability to eliminate heat through sweating. That is why it's easier to tolerate high heat in a dry environment than in a humid one. All things being equal, for every two-degree rise in air temperature, 40 grams of sweat per hour will result. If exposed to the direct rays of the sun, this water loss may increase fivefold. In a dry environment when the temperature is between 110 and 115°F, adults may sweat 2 to 3 gallons of water out of their body in a single day. Interestingly, women usually tolerate heat slightly better than men, and begin sweating at higher temperatures.

If dehydration continues beyond a 10-percent water loss of bodily fluids, most people suffer from heat exhaustion. They collapse and break out in a sweat. This reaction effectively stops exercise, reducing the heat load on the heart, and sweating helps to remove heat before lethal internal temperatures are reached. More serious is heat stroke. During a heat stroke the body's automatic sweating mechanism fails, and internal heat builds rapidly, often to the lethal point if immediate medical aid is not received.

It is obvious that traveling in desert environments during the hotter times of the year is a serious matter and is not to be taken lightly. It is advisable to remember that only "mad dogs and Englishmen go out in the noonday sun"—and both die if it's too hot. Follow the habits of desert-dwelling animals, who are largely active in early morning and evening when temperatures are lower and humidity is higher. Limit your activity to those time periods. During the hottest part of the day, stay in the shade with a cool drink if possible.

Keep your head and body covered as much for protection against sunburn as for protection against the sun's heating effects. Wear a hat with a brim and wear light, loose-fitting cotton clothing. As much as it may seem illogical to maintain a clothing cover in hot weather, loose clothing can reduce evaporation rates by reducing water loss to wind. Of course this only works if temperatures are not extreme, since sweating is necessary to reduce heat loads below lethal conditions.

It seems odd to other hikers that I've met, but I sometimes use an umbrella when hiking on a hot, sunny day—not to protect me from rain but to provide shade. There are small collapsible umbrellas that fit handily into a daypack. I carry an umbrella, which is preferable to wearing a hat, since air can circulate around my head, helping to reduce my heat load while still protecting my upper body from the direct rays of the sun. Studies have shown that shading skin from direct sunlight can reduce skin temperature by as much as 30 to 40°F.

As much as possible try to avoid close contact with the ground. The earth has a tremendous ability to absorb heat. Temperatures on or immediately above the ground can be as much as 60 or 70°F hotter than the air temperature. A ground temperature of 201°F was once recorded in Death Valley—that's nearly hot enough to boil water! When resting, try to elevate yourself off the ground. Even raising yourself a few feet away from the ground can reduce the heat load on the body significantly.

Other Essentials

Even if you are going for a short day hike, it's important to carry a few other items besides water. The clear desert air makes protection from the sun more critical than in other regions. Be sure to carry sunscreen and a hat or umbrella. In addition it's not a bad idea to have a flashlight with extra batteries, a first aid kit, extra clothes in case you have to rough it overnight, a knife, and matches.

Maps

Obtaining good up-to-date maps of the desert region is difficult. New "ways" are pioneered each year by ORVs, adding to the confusion of all travelers attempting to find their way through the region. I found that the best maps for navigating the California desert are available from the American Automobile Association (AAA), particularly the office located in southern California (2601 South Figueroa Street, Los Angeles, CA 90007; 714-850-5015). The maps are also available directly from any of the club outlets located in El Centro, Ridgecrest, Blythe, Indian Wells, and Palm Springs, and are often sold in the national park visitor centers. In addition, your local AAA office should be able to order these maps for you.

The AAA maps show the boundaries of all new wilderness areas, plus all important access roads including dirt, gravel, and in some cases jeep trails. If you stick to the roads shown on these maps you should be able to negotiate the desert with a minimum of hazard and trouble.

The maps needed to cover most of the California desert region include Kern County, Imperial County, San Diego County, Riverside County, and San Bernardino County. In addition, the AAA produces a map specifically for the east side of the Sierra Nevada and Owens Valley, as well as Death Valley National Park. Both of these maps also show the location and access to BLM wilderness areas and other public lands.

To negotiate BLM routes it helps to have copies of the BLM's Desert Access Guide maps. I found these maps somewhat difficult to read, but they do show numbered BLM travel routes. Sometimes knowing which numbered road to follow is critical to getting to your destination. These maps cover the entire 25-million-acre California desert, however they were printed prior to the passage of the California Desert Protection Act and thus do not show the boundaries of new BLM wilderness areas and national park units. Nevertheless, for general navigation in the desert they can be quite useful if combined with the AAA maps. At the time of this writing, the Desert Access Guide series is scheduled to be replaced with new maps that show greater detail and delineate the boundaries of the new wilderness units.

The BLM also publishes a *BLM Wilderness Areas Maps and Information Guide,* which has maps that indicate the borders of all new wilderness areas and describe the access routes. For information about the guide, contact the BLM, California Desert District Office, 6221 Box Springs Boulevard, Riverside, CA 92507; 909-697-5200.

In addition to the BLM's Desert Access Guide series, there are topographical maps available for each of the major park areas. Contact the natural history associations for each park to obtain the most current maps and other information.

Anza Borrego Desert Natural History Association
PO Box 310
Borrego Springs, CA 92004
619-767-3052

Death Valley Natural History Association and Mojave National Preserve
PO Box 188
Death Valley, CA 92328
760-786-3285

Joshua Tree National Park Association
74485 National Park Drive
Twentynine Palms, CA 92277
760-367-1488

OTHER SOURCES INCLUDE THE FOLLOWING:
Anza Borrego State Park
A 1994 Anza Borrego Region Recreation Map is available from Earthwalk Press. A series of eight 15-minute maps covering the entire park is available from the Anza Borrego Desert Natural History Association.
Death Valley National Park
A 1996 Death Valley National Park topographic map is available from Trails Illustrated. A 1996 Death Valley National Park topographical map is available from Tom Harrison Maps, 415-456 7940. A map of Death Valley National Park is published by the AAA-Automobile Club of Southern California.
Joshua Tree National Park
A 1996 Joshua Tree National Park topographic map is available from Trails Illustrated.
Mojave National Preserve
A 1996 Mojave National Preserve topographical map is available from Tom Harrison Maps, 415-456-7940. The BLM Desert Access Guide maps for Needles, the Providence Mountains, and the New York Mountains cover the new preserve.

Abbreviations

There are a number of abbreviations used throughout this book, including

AAA	American Automobile Association
ACEC	Area of Critical Environmental Concern
BLM	Bureau of Land Management
BP	before present
4wd	four-wheel drive
Hwy	highway
I	interstate
ORV	off-road vehicle
Rte	route
2wd	two-wheel drive

Basalt flow at Amboy Crater, which erupted as recently as a thousand years ago.

Geology of the California Desert

The California desert is shaped by large geologic forces, such as the movement of continental plates over millions of years, as well as ongoing geologic/geomorphologic changes as recent as the last flash flood. In one sense, the geologic processes that created the desert landscape can be thought of as a house—the large-scale geologic forces create the foundation and structure, and the geomorphologic changes rearrange the furniture in the rooms.

Plate tectonics is the driving force behind California's landscape development. The earth's crust is made up of large, moveable plates that are in continuous motion. These plates "float" on top of the more liquid layers of the earth's mantle. Convection currents, resulting from temperature differences within the earth's layers, drive the movement of the plates. These plates collide, break up, and sometimes unite to form new configurations, similar to ice floes in a river that mingle, fuse, or move on. At one time, what we now know as North America was joined with Europe, Africa, and South America in a supercontinent called Pangea. When North America broke away from these continental plates, it drifted north and west to its current position, and the rift between the plates formed the Atlantic Ocean. The North American plate continues to drift westward at a rate of about 1 inch per year.

The stresses induced by collision with other plates creates faults or breaks in the earth's crust. These breaks are physically manifested as earthquakes, which mark the uplift of mountains and the dropping of valleys. Weak points along these major structural breaks in the earth's crust provide an easy outlet for molten rock from within the earth to rise to the surface and erupt as volcanoes.

The theory of plate tectonics explains why high mountains are located along the western United States. Since these mountains influence the formation of deserts due to their rain shadow effect, one could infer that plate tectonics accounts for California's deserts. Plate tectonics also accounts for the bewildering array of rocks found among California's mountains. Some mountain ranges consist of sediments that were once on the sea bottom and were uplifted over millennia to create present-day mountains. Other rocks were created by the outflow of volcanoes. Still others are the result of long burial and pressure deep in the earth that changed sedimentary and volcanic rock into new forms called metamorphic rock. The differences in rock type, hardness, and the degree to which they have been crushed, twisted, and pulverized by ongoing tectonic movement affects the way erosion proceeds, and influences the resulting landforms and vegetation.

Most mountains in the California desert are the result of faulting. Faulting occurs when two pieces of the earth's crust move up, down, or sideways relative to one another. The precipitous slope of the Panamint Range, Inyo Range, San Jacinto Mountains, and other mountains of the region are all fault-induced ranges. The intervening valleys are typically blocks of earth that have slid down relative to the upthrusted mountains. Death Valley, for example, is one such valley that owes its existence to faulting. Two giant faults—the San Andreas and Garlock Faults—define the Mojave Desert.

The faulting that defines the Basin and Range Province is due to stretching of the earth's surface. This stretching—up to 150 miles of extension—has resulted in numerous faults and a thinning of the earth's crust. This thinning provides an easy route for magma, located deep in the earth, to reach the earth's crust, and is one reason for the numerous hot springs, volcanoes, basaltic flows, and cinder cones found throughout the desert region.

All rocks can be categorized into three major types—igneous, sedimentary, and metamorphic—based on their origin. When rocks melt to form magma, and later cool, they are known as igneous rock. Igneous rock is further subdivided into two major subsets: plutonic and volcanic. Plutonic rock is formed when magma cools slowly deep in the earth, allowing for the formation of large crystals. Later, such rocks may be exposed at the surface by erosion. Granitic rocks, a kind of plutonic rock, are common in the California desert. To a geologist, the term granite is very specific, and refers to only one kind of rock within the granite "family." The term granite, however, is also used as a catch-all phrase for all kinds of granitic rocks, of which there is a huge variety. The Sierra Nevada is perhaps the best known example of a huge block of granitic rock that was later uplifted and exposed by erosion. Granite also makes up the rocks exposed in the Little San Bernardino Mountains in Joshua Tree National Park, the Santa Rosa Mountains in Anza Borrego Desert State Park, and numerous other desert ranges, including the four Granite Mountains scattered about the region.

If the same molten material forces its way to the surface to flow or erupt, it is known as volcanic rock. Cooling rapidly at the surface, such rocks are fine grained. Basalt, rhyolite, and obsidian are all examples of volcanic rock. Many desert ranges are dominated by volcanic rock, including the Newberry Mountains, the Coso Range, the Argus Range, and the Chocolate Mountains, to name a few.

The chemical composition of the molten material as well as the amount of gas embedded in it when it is erupted, determines its qualities. Small fragments of volcanic dust thrown high into the sky will settle back to earth to form a rock known as tuff. Tuff is a common volcanic rock in many parts of the California desert. For example, tuff comprises a large part of the Volcanic Tablelands near Bishop. If the particles of rock are larger, they are called cinders. Their heavier weight means the rocks are not thrown as far during eruptions and they fall to earth near the site of the volcano to create cinder cones. There are many examples of cinder cones in the California desert, including Little Ubehebe Crater in Death Valley, Amboy Crater near Amboy, and the cinder cones just east of Kelbaker Road south of Baker in the Mojave National Preserve.

Sedimentary rock is formed by the accumulation of sand, mud, pebbles, and other rock fragments eroded by wind, water, or chemical action, deposited over time in layers. Sandstone and shale are examples of sedimentary rock formed when rock particles are deposited in oceans or dry land and later harden into stone due to the pressure of additional rock deposition. Sedimentary rock is the major repository for fossils, as well as hydrocarbons like oil, coal, and natural gas. As previously mentioned, metamorphic rock is created when existing rock is altered due to heat and pressure.

As remarkable as it may sound, water is the chief geologic agent at work in most desert regions. A raindrop falling on bare ground dislodges soil particles. When this happens on a slope, the result is gradual downhill movement. The sparse vegetation found in desert regions provides little protective cover from water erosion.

Violent rainstorms often occur in the desert, resulting in flash floods. These sudden deluges rapidly erode unvegetated slopes and stream banks. Frequently the water will undercut the sides of steams, steepen the sides, and fill the channel with sediment. The resulting land forms are termed box canyons. Sediment-rich flood waters race down mountain canyons and, on reaching the foot of the slope, lose their velocity and deposit most of their suspended sediment to create alluvial fans at the base of the slope. As sediments accumulate, the channel shifts laterally across the fan. Gradually, over time, the fan grows larger and larger. In many desert regions, alluvial fans coalesce to form what are called pediments. Eventually the pediments partially bury mountains in deep deposits, exposing only a few of the higher peaks.

On steeper slopes, particularly those made of clay and other impermeable materials, the water from cloudbursts rapidly run off, creating numerous narrow ravines parallel to each other known as badlands topography. The badlands near Mecca Hills outside of Indio are one example of this kind of topography.

Sometimes floodwater running off nearby mountains reaches the floor of the basin. In some instances it may pool to create a shallow lake with no outlet. Such lakes eventually succumb to the desert sun, and dry up to create a flat, salt-encrusted lake bed known as a playa. The floor of Death Valley contains a playa. Streams wash in dissolved minerals, which are left behind when the lake dries up. Hence, many playas are rich in minerals like sodium, borax, and potassium. Searles Lake near Ridgecrest is one such playa that is mined for its minerals.

In the nearly treeless desert, with its powerful gales, wind erosion is a significant geologic force. There are two kinds of erosional processes associated with wind: deflation (or the removal of rock particles by wind) and abrasion (when particles carried by wind grind away at other rock surfaces). Of the two, deflation is by far the most important wind-eroding force in the desert. Desert pavement is the term for flat, wind-scoured desert surfaces. This pavement has most of the finer dust and sand removed by wind, leaving behind the coarser, heavier stones.

One of the most conspicuous desert features resulting from wind deflation is the sand dune. Sand dunes are created when powerful winds eddy and swirl, or when sand particles are driven by powerful prevailing winds to lift particles off the ground. These particles bounce along in a looping manner, never far from the ground. Repeated over and over, this sand movement gradually creates the waves of sand that we know as dunes. Although we commonly associate sand dunes with desert regions, they are relatively rare in the California desert. The best example of sand dunes in this region is the Algodones Dunes.

Desert Plants

Adaptation to Desert Conditions

Desert environments impose severe limitations on plants and animals. The lack of moisture, unpredictable nature of rainfall, short growing seasons, and extremes in temperature all create inhospitable conditions for most organisms. For those species, however, that have adapted to these conditions, the desert is not only home, but a very good home indeed. No one can deny that creosote bush, which covers millions of acres of California's desert, isn't thriving—in spite of the limitations imposed by the environment.

Each species of plant adopts different strategies to cope with its environment. Some plants avoid "desert" conditions altogether. For example, plants living along streams, such as cottonwood trees, are not really "desert" plants. They use water lavishly, but they are restricted to growing only in places where water is readily available to roots throughout the growing season.

Many flowers, particularly ephemerals or annuals, are drought evaders. They only grow when there is sufficient moisture. In the California desert, ephemerals make up 40 percent of the plant species, whereas typically they only comprise 10 to 15 percent of most ecosystems. Ephemerals have various mechanisms that ensure germination and development only after sufficient water has soaked the soil. Some flower seeds are coated with a chemical inhibitor that prevents germination until enough water has soaked the seed to carry away the inhibiting chemicals and, not coincidentally, to guarantee a good chance of growing to seed set before running out of soil moisture.

In the California desert most ephemerals have adapted to growing in winter, since this is the season when rain and snow are most likely to occur. Ephemerals are also able to photosynthesize faster than most other plants, completing their growth in an abridged time frame.

Temperature plays a role in seed germination. The seeds of many plants will not germinate if desert temperatures are too high, thus avoiding chance germination as a result of the occasional, rare summer thunderstorm.

Grasses exhibit drought avoidance tactics similar to flowers. Most grasses "green up" after a wet season, produce seeds, and then allow the exposed grass to die and go dormant during the dry period. At the onset of dormancy, most of the valuable nutrients in the exposed plant are relocated to the root system, where they are stored for future growth. Not surprisingly the root systems of perennial grasses are huge, with the majority of the plant located underground. Many grass plants live 100 years or more and can survive a number of years of drought simply by entering dormancy.

Some grasses, particularly those found in desert regions, have a special adaptation to living in a hot, dry environment. This adaptation, known as C4 photosynthesis, allows these plants to continue to thrive at higher temperatures. Most plants are C3 photosynthesizers, and their rate of photosynthesis actually declines when temperatures exceed 80°F. Another advantage of "C4 plants" is that they are capable of closing their stomata (the openings in the leaves through which plants "breathe") during photosynthesis. This is a real advantage since closed stomata reduces water loss.

The desert can bloom if it receives enough moisture.

A variation of the C4 process is crassulacean acid metabolism. Plants using crassulacean acid metabolic processes can conduct photosynthesis at night, when humidity is higher and water loss is decreased, using stored carbon dioxide and water. Many leaf succulents use this process.

Most desert plants deal with drought by minimizing water loss or needs. Cacti are a good example of plants that use this strategy. Cacti have lost their leaves—a source of great water loss for most plants—and have replaced them with thorns, which are really modified leaves. Instead of leaves, cacti use their green chlorophyll-filled stems for photosynthesis.

Cacti also have the ability to store water gathered during wet periods, for use during dry periods. Such plants are known as succulents. Succulents include cacti, yucca, and agave. All these water-storing plants tend to grow in coarse soils such as mountain slopes where water runs off rapidly. Under these conditions, the ability to capture water, store it, and continue growing is a huge life-sustaining advantage.

The spindly ocotillo is another drought evader. It grows leaves after a major rainfall and then drops them when drought conditions return. An ocotillo may grow several sets of leaves in a single growing season, depending on moisture availability.

Evergreen shrubs like the ubiquitous creosote bush demonstrate another means of coping with drought. This plant possesses small leaves coated with a waxy surface that reduces water loss. The small leaf size also helps to prevent heat stress—a problem for plants with large leaf surfaces like the cottonwood, which must consume a tremendous amount of water to promote evaporative cooling. Furthermore, creosote has a huge root system that spreads out from the plant to capture any available soil moisture. Creosote also has the ability to tolerate long periods of drought without perishing.

Sagebrush, common at higher elevations in the Great Basin, is another drought-tolerant shrub. It, like the creosote bush, has deep, widespread roots. It also produces several different kinds of leaves in the course of the year. Larger, less efficient leaves sprout when water is abundant, then are gradually replaced by smaller leaves, which are more parsimonious with water as soils dry out.

Overgrazing

When grasslands are grazed during the growing season, a shift occurs in the plant's priorities. The plant cannot survive without food, and it needs to continue photosynthesis, so it quickly replaces the lost leaves with new growth. To grow new leaves, however, the grass must transfer energy from its roots. Most grasses can tolerate an occasional cropping without suffering serious consequences. However, if forced to transfer energy and nutrients from its roots repeatedly to produce new leaves, little will be left to replace or expand the root system.

The repeated and frequent cropping, year after year, by cattle creates overgrazed range lands. Unlike wild herbivores whose numbers fluctuate in response to natural events like drought, disease, and other environmental factors, cattle numbers are typically maintained at more or less the same level year after year, irrespective of weather or other events. In drought years, preferred grasses will be cropped over and over again. Subjected repeatedly to grazing for a number of years, the plant's root system shrinks, the grass is unable to recover, and the plant dies.

Major Plant Communities

CREOSOTE BUSH

By far, the most widespread and dominant plant in the California desert is creosote bush. If you guessed that the name of every waist-high, spindly, regularly spaced evergreen shrub you saw growing across the flats and bajadas of the Mojave and Colorado Deserts was creosote bush, you'd probably be right nine times out of ten. Creosote bush covers more than 21 million acres of California—an area the size of the state of Maine.

Despite the ability of mature creosote bush to withstand greater water stress than any other known plant, young seedlings are susceptible to both water stress and heat. Creosote bush requires a minimum of three to five years of moist, cool conditions for successful establishment. Such climatic conditions are relatively infrequent in the California desert, hence there are few creosote seedlings.

This is not as great a disadvantage for creosote as it might appear, since the plant is long lived. A creosote bush is able to produce genetic clones from its root stock. A circle of younger plants will develop from the root stock of the parent plant, creating clones as old as 3,000 years. A creosote bush in Johnson Valley has been dated at 11,700 years—a record age. Another clone in Arizona was found to be 18,000 years old! Records like these have forced some biologists to argue that creosote bush, not bristlecone pine, is the oldest living thing on earth.

As the plants mature, they develop a widespread root system. Creosote stands take on a regularly spaced, almost orchardlike appearance, with few or no other plants growing among them. This is due to its tremendous ability to absorb rapidly any moisture that infiltrates the soil, leaving nothing for other plants.

SAGEBRUSH

While creosote bush dominates the warmer, lower elevations of the California desert, sagebrush is clearly the dominant plant cover over most of the Great Basin, and is indicative of this region. There are many different species of sagebrush, but the most common is Great Basin big sage (*Artemisia tridentata tridentata*), affectionately called *tri tri* by sagebrush aficionados. *Artemesia tridentata* has several subspecies including Wyoming big sage (*Artemisia tridentata wyomingensis*) and mountain big sage (*Artemisia tridentata vaseyana*). Between the three of them, these species of sagebrush cloak most of the well-drained soil sites in the Great Basin.

Sagebrush tends to have deep roots that are designed to absorb water that has soaked into the soil. This complements the Great Basin Desert climate perfectly because this region is dominated by winter precipitation, primarily snow, which then melts slowly and percolates into the root zone of sagebrush.

Sagebrush also has small linear leaves, which reduce heat stress and water loss. The grayish appearance of the leaves is due to tiny hairs that further inhibit the rapid evaporation of moisture from the leaf surface.

Growing in juxtaposition to sagebrush are numerous other plants. In presettlement days, native perennial grasses such as bluebunch wheatgrass (*Agropyron spicatum*) and Idaho fescue (*Fescue idahoensis*) were common. They competed with sagebrush for water by tapping into the soil moisture at shallow and mid depths. Although these grasses were long lived, repeated grazing by domestic livestock led to a reduction in grass root systems and seed production. With their smaller roots, these grasses could no longer compete against the seedlings of sagebrush, which were largely ignored by cattle. Grasses were grazed, sagebrush was not.

Grasses can tolerate occasional fire and, indeed, they thrive on it. Since most fires only occur during drought years or after grasses have set seed and gone dormant, fires seldom damaged the roots, where most of the nutritional reserves are stored. After a burn, the plant sends up fresh new leaves from its roots. Sagebrush, however, cannot sprout from its roots. It takes 20 to 30 years to recolonize a site by seed after a burn. The continual mixture of burns and recolonization created a grassland-sagebrush mosaic over much of the Great Basin that today has been replaced by a sagebrush monoculture. Now most native perennial grasses are relegated to cliff sides and mesa tops where cattle can't graze.

Other shrub communities common in the desert include blackbrush. It typically grows on alluvial fans and rocky slopes at higher elevations of the Great Basin and Mojave Deserts. Like sagebrush, blackbrush loses its leaves as drought progresses, until there is just a small number of green leaves in the center of the plant. These leaves are somewhat shaded by the bare stems around them, helping to reduce water stress and loss.

At lower elevations, particularly on alkaline soils, grow various species of shadscale, saltbush, desert holly, and winter fat. Winter fat gets its name from the ability of domestic sheep to put on fat by consuming this plant during the winter months. These plants have the ability to excrete salt, permitting them to survive on highly salt-laden soils.

JOSHUA TREE

Joshua tree tends to grow on gentle sandy slopes at higher elevations where snow falls. Its distribution generally coincides with the boundaries of the Mojave Desert. Damage to the growing terminal points of the limb cause the plant's branches to fork, resulting in the odd shapes that characterize these plants.

CACTUS SHRUB

The lower, hotter Colorado Desert has a different assemblage of shrubs and plants growing on its slopes. Cacti are to the Colorado Desert what Joshua tree are to the Mojave Desert—an indicator plant community.

Cacti evolved in tropical regions and gradually adapted to arid conditions. These adaptations allowed them to expand northward and to colonize the developing deserts of North America. Common forms of cacti in the California desert include prickly pear, cholla, hedgehog, barrel, and beavertail.

Most cacti produce beautiful flowers and large fruit. The fruit is consumed by a wide variety of animals who then shed the seeds in their feces, ensuring seed distribution. One cactus, the teddy bear cholla, so named for its dense covering of spines that makes some people think the cactus should be hugged like a teddy bear, is capable of sprouting roots from broken fragments of the stalk. Pieces of cholla cactus drop to the ground and then stick to the fur of passing rodents, coyotes, deer, and even people's clothing. These bits of cholla are then deposited some distance from the parent plant and take root.

DESERT WASH WOODLAND

The desert wash woodland is common in the Mojave Desert, but reaches its greatest diversity in the Colorado Desert. Species common along washes include mesquite, palo verde, smoke tree, ironwood, and desert willow. Most of these plants are winter deciduous and possess small pinnate leaves that help to reduce heat stress and water loss. Ironwood, however, is evergreen.

Most of these plants require seed scarification for germination. The hard seed coats are cracked after being tumbled in streams during floods. This ensures adequate water for the seeds. After germination, these plants put most of their energy into root development. A mesquite root can grow as much as 4 inches a day!

RIPARIAN WOODLANDS

In the streams that border the higher mountains of the Sierra Nevada, the Peninsula Ranges, and the higher parts of the Great Basin (such as the Panamint Range), a riparian woodland—replete with Fremont cottonwood and black willow—borders waterways. These plants are only associated with permanent water sources.

In a few special locations in the Colorado Desert one may encounter a California fan palm oasis. The fan palm is a tropical plant that managed to migrate northward. It barely survives in a few widely dispersed palm oases. Fires actually promote palm survival. By removing competing vegetation, fires permit palms to obtain more water. In addition, palm seedlings require open, bare, mineral-rich soil to germinate and establish themselves. Most palm groves are burned by vandals with no regard for the survival of the palm, but in this instance, their actions are probably not detrimental.

WOODLANDS

At higher elevations, particularly in the Great Basin and to a more limited degree in the Mojave, grow woodlands of juniper and pinyon pine. These shrubby-looking trees reach 20 to 30 feet in height. The pinyon pine produces a large edible nut called a pinyon nut that was relished by native Americans as well as many wildlife species.

Growing at the highest elevations, one may find forests of Jeffrey pine, ponderosa pine, red fir, limber pine, and bristlecone pine. Jeffrey pine, ponderosa pine, and red fir are associated with the southern Sierra Nevada, and parts of the San Bernardino and Santa Rosa Ranges, whereas limber pine and bristlecone pine are typical Great Basin species. Most of these species of pine and juniper are long lived and survive drought by sheer tenacity. Of these species, red fir is more dependent on regular moisture and is found only where winter snow is common.

Southern Sierra Subregion

The Sierra Nevada is one of the defining features of California. It is a spectacular, glacier-carved massive uplift of granitic rock 400 miles long and up to 75 miles wide. In Owens Valley the eastern scarp of the range rises more than 11,000 feet, culminating in the lofty heights of Mount Whitney—the highest peak in the nation outside of Alaska.

Most of the precipitation occurs in winter; less than 3 percent of the annual precipitation comes in summer. As a result, the Sierras are essentially a "desert" during the growing season. Were it not for its high, snow-trapping peaks, most of the range could not support trees, meadows, and rivers.

South of Mount Whitney, the overall elevation of the Sierra Nevada drops significantly—to the point that snow accumulations in winter melt quickly in the spring, and desertlike conditions prevail. The Sierras officially end at Walker Pass; however, although the name changes to the Scodie Mountains, geologically it is still the same range. South of Walker Pass the landscape tends to appear undeniably like the desert, stretching eastward to Nevada.

The desertlike conditions apply only to the lower elevations of the south-ernmost portion of the range, where cholla cactus and Joshua tree grow. Higher elevations support more diverse vegetation than areas further east, including forests of aspen, white and red fir, ponderosa pine, and Jeffrey pine, along with the more ubiquitous pinyon pine and juniper. When people think about recreation in this area they typically think of the Southern Sierra's high peaks or perhaps the cliffs that border the Yosemite Valley. Nevertheless, the very southernmost portion of the range has its own attributes, one of which is the opportunity to hike in the southern range year round. There is a host of designated wilder-nesses in the Southern Sierra that were created by the 1994 California Desert Protection Act. These include the Owens Peak, Chimney Peak, Domeland, Bright Star, Sacatar Trail, and Kiavah Wildernesses.

The rugged, steep slopes of Owens Peak Wilderness at the southern end of the Sierra Nevada.

Bright Star Wilderness

Joshua tree along Kelso Canyon Creek, Bright Star Wilderness.

LOCATION: Kern County; 26 miles southwest of Ridgecrest, California

SIZE: 9,520 acres

ELEVATION RANGE: 3,300 to 5,500 feet

ADMINISTRATION: BLM Ridgecrest Resource Area Office

MAPS: Desert Access Guide Jawbone/Dove Springs #5; AAA Kern County

With a name as lovely as Bright Star Wilderness, how can you go wrong? And it is, indeed, quite beautiful. Part of the Piute Mountains (a southern extension of the Sierra Nevada Range south of Lake Isabella), the wilderness surrounds Kelso Peak and its associated drainages. The Piute Mountains roadless area of the Sequoia National Forest forms the contiguous western boundary of this area, making the entire area part of a larger wilderness complex.

The higher elevations are cloaked in juniper and pinyon pine, whereas Joshua tree is common at lower elevations. Granite outcrops similar to those found at Joshua Tree National Park abound.

ACCESS

The wilderness is reached by taking Highway (Hwy) 178 east from Lake Isabella, then south for approximately

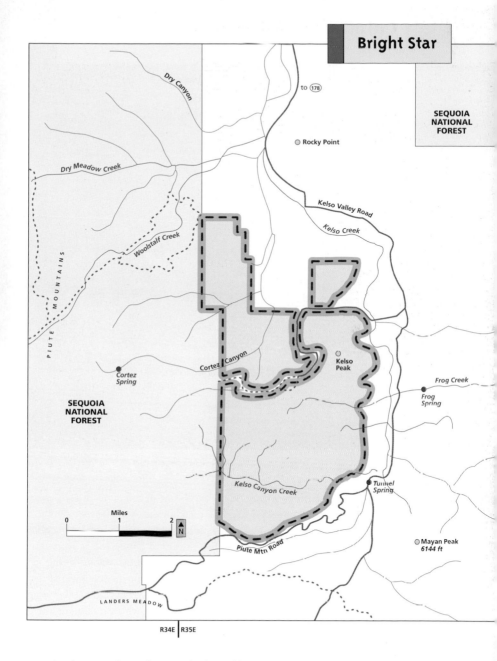

16 miles on Kelso Valley Road. The wilderness is west of the road. There are no formal trails in the BLM portion of the Piute Mountains. All hiking is cross country. Bright Star or Cortez Canyons offers the best access. A popular destination is the scramble up 5,090-foot Kelso Peak, accessible directly from Kelso Creek Road. In winter, expect snow at higher elevations.

2 Chimney Peak Wilderness

Rabbitbrush frames the granitic, domed surface of Chimney Peak Wilderness. Pinyon pine is the most common tree here.

LOCATION: Tulare County; 20 miles northwest of Ridgecrest, California

SIZE: 13,700 acres

ELEVATION RANGE: 6,000 to 8,035 feet

ADMINISTRATION: BLM Caliente Resource Area Office

MAP: Sequoia National Forest

Chimney Peak Wilderness is one of several wilderness areas that protect the southern end of the Sierra Nevada. Dome-shaped Chimney Peak Wilderness is part of the larger rolling plateau that continues westward to Domeland Wilderness. Lower elevations are cloaked in sagebrush, rabbitbrush, and grasses, and pinyon pine and juniper cover most of the higher elevations. The faint remains of the old Sacatar wagon trail cross the area. Chimney Creek, which runs along the edge of the wilderness, supports trout.

ACCESS

You can reach the wilderness from Canebrake Road off Hwy 178 or from Nine Mile Canyon Road near Kennedy Meadows off Hwy 395. The only formal trail is a section of the Pacific Crest Trail, which crosses 8 miles of the wilderness just south and west of Chimney Peak.

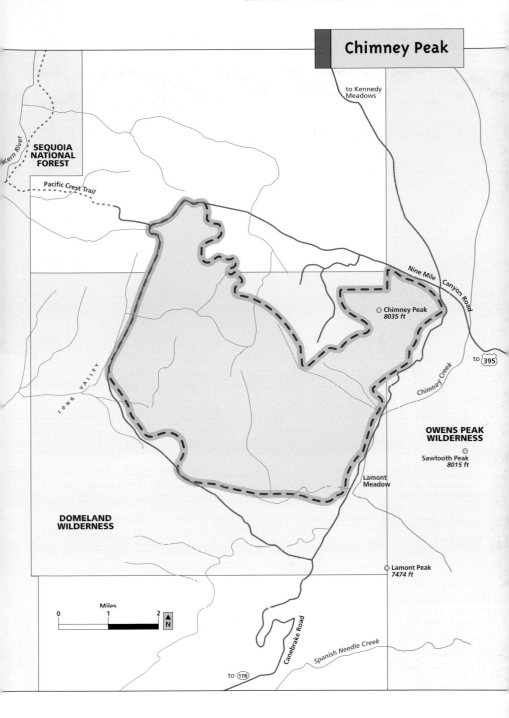

Chimney Peak

to Kennedy
Meadows

Kern River

SEQUOIA
NATIONAL
FOREST

Pacific Crest Trail

Nine Mile Canyon Road

○ Chimney Peak
8035 ft

Chimney Creek

to (395)

LONG VALLEY

OWENS PEAK
WILDERNESS

○ Sawtooth Peak
8015 ft

Lamont
Meadow

DOMELAND
WILDERNESS

○ Lamont Peak
7474 ft

Miles
0   1   2

N

Canebrake Road

Spanish Needle Creek

to (178)

3 Domeland Wilderness

Riparian vegetation, including cottonwood, along the South Fork of the Kern, a Wild and Scenic River that flows through Domeland Wilderness. Pilot Knob is the high peak in the background.

LOCATION:
Tulare-Kern Counties;
25 miles northwest of
Ridgecrest, California

SIZE: 130,986 acres

ELEVATION RANGE:
3,000 to 9,730 feet

ADMINISTRATION:
Sequoia National Forest
and BLM Caliente
Resource Area Office

MAPS: Forest Service
Domeland Wilderness
and Sequoia National
Forest

Domeland Wilderness is the southernmost wilderness in the Sierra Nevada. Scanning Domeland Wilderness from a high vantage point reminds one somewhat of a drier Yosemite high country. Granitic domes, rocky outcrops, and rolling terrain covered with small meadows; and dry sagebrush uplands cloaked in juniper, pinyon pine, and Jeffrey pine are all drained by the South Fork of the Kern. Elevations range from 3,000 to 9,730 feet. The South Fork of the Kern runs the length of the wilderness and is a designated Wild and Scenic River. Below Rockhouse Meadow, the South Fork enters a steep, granitic gorge that has no trail access for 15 miles.

Although granitic bedrock dominates the wilderness, volcanic outcrops occur between Taylor and Manter Creeks, and a basalt flow is evident in Dark Canyon near the northwest border. The South Fork of the Kern River forms its southern border, while Kennedy Meadows-Nine Mile Canyon Road lies to the north.

The area lies at a transition zone between the arid eastern Sierra and the wetter western edge of the range. Jeffrey pine is the most common tree, but there are black oak along the western edge of the wilderness, and pinyon pine dominates the drier eastern side. Scattered lodgepole pine and red fir also occur. One of the largest concentrations of *Nolina parryi*, a giant yucca that attains heights of 15 feet, is found here.

Along the western border of Domeland Wilderness lies the Sirretta Peak wilderness study area, which if designated would add significantly to the size and biologic value of the wilderness. The top of Sirretta Peak is part of the Twisselmann Botanical area. This 859-acre area encompasses the summit and slopes of 9,978-foot Sirretta Peak. Sirretta Peak is the most southerly known range for foxtail pine in the Sierra. In addition, limber pine as well as nine other plant species also reach their southernmost known distribution in this same area.

Bald Mountain Botanical Area lies just north of the wilderness. Composed of metasedimentary rock, the soils hold moisture better than the surrounding granitic material, hence the mountain is home to more kinds of plants than surrounding areas, including limber pine and the endemic Bald Mountain potentilla, which is found nowhere else. A lookout was built atop the mountain in 1951 and it offers fine views southward into the wilderness.

Despite its biologic value, federal agencies managing these lands seem to treat the wilderness more like a cow pasture than a nationally significant wildland and botanical reserve. And it's not just the plants that are suffering. According to the California Department of Fish and Game, severe degradation of riparian areas and meadows continues to threaten fisheries and other wildlife.

As a consequence of aridity as well as its lower elevation compared with the High Sierra, Domeland Wilderness offers the best year-round access to a Sierra Nevada wilderness. Solitude is easily achieved, particularly if you avoid the Pacific Crest Trail and Manter Meadow.

ACCESS

Unlike most desert wildernesses, Domeland Wilderness has real trails. The best access is from Hwy 178. Follow Canebrake Road and Chimney Peak Scenic Byway to Long Valley Campground.

DAY HIKE: LONG VALLEY HIKE

One-way length:	3 miles
Low and high elevations:	4,800 to 5,270 feet
Difficulty:	moderate

This hike takes you into Domeland Wilderness to the South Fork of the Kern Wild and Scenic River in the heart of the wilderness. The trail begins at the BLM's Long Valley Campground. The hike begins at the far end of the campground, which is set in a grove of large Jeffrey pine. If possible, tank up on water in the campground because the scourge of southern California wilderness areas—cows—usually have trampled and polluted the water downstream. The trail basically follows Long Valley Creek to the river, occasionally switching from side to side as the creek pinches off the trail, forcing a crossing to the opposite bank. There are a few narrow gorges where you may have to negotiate your way around an occasional slab of granite beside the creek.

OVERNIGHT HIKE: MANTER/WOODPECKER LOOP TRAIL

One-way length:	24 miles
Low and high elevations:	6,600 to 8,250 feet
Difficulty:	strenuous

This is a good two- to three-day backpacking trip that gets you into the heart of Domeland Wilderness. When other trails further north are still under snow, this trip is usually negotiable as early as late May or early June.

The trailhead is on the western side of the wilderness. From Kernville drive toward Sherman Pass on Forest Service Road 22S05. By Burton Camp you turn south (right) on Poison Meadow Road (22S12) and follow signs for Horse Meadow/Big Meadow. Just a few miles beyond Horse Meadow Campground there is a left-hand fork to Forest Service Road 23S07, which will take you the rest of the way to the parking area.

From the parking area, where your trip will end, walk the road along Big Meadow south about 1 mile to Manter Trailhead on the left (east). Take Manter Trail approximately 3 miles to Manter Meadow, then follow Woodpecker Trail (34E08) north to its junction with Rockhouse Basin Trail (35E16), where you turn west to Woodpecker Meadow and Trout Creek. Trout Creek is reputed to be good fishing. From Woodpecker Meadow head west and then south to Sirretta Peak and Sirretta Pass. The peak is a scramble. From the pass continue southwest down to Cannell Trail (33E32), where you bear right and head south about 1 mile to the parking area.

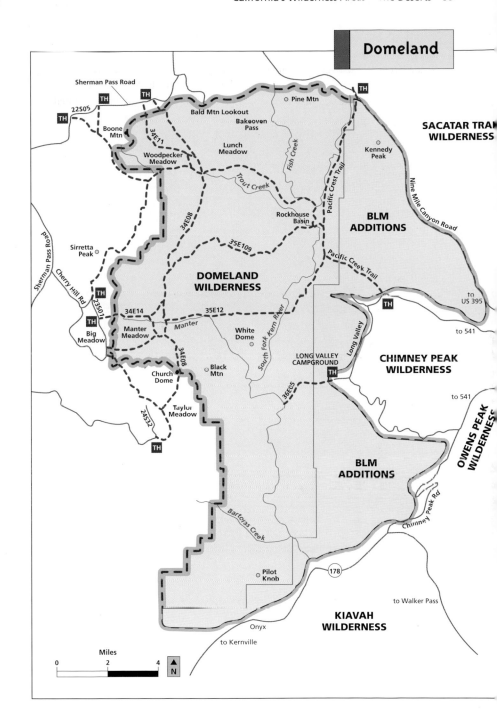

Domeland

Sherman Pass Road

TH
TH

22S05

TH

Boone
Mtn

34E71

Woodpecker
Meadow

Pine Mtn

TH

Bald Mtn Lookout

Bakeoven
Pass

Lunch
Meadow

Fish Creek

Kennedy
Peak

Trout Creek

Pacific Crest Trail

SACATAR TRAI
WILDERNESS

Nine Mile Canyon Road

Sirretta
Peak

34E08

Rockhouse
Basin

35E109

Sherman Pass Road

Cherry Hill Rd

23S01

TH

34E14

TH

Big
Meadow

TH

Manter
Meadow

Church
Dome

24S32

Taylor
Meadow

TH

DOMELAND
WILDERNESS

35E12

Manter

White
Dome

34E08

Black
Mtn

South Fork Kern River

BLM
ADDITIONS

Pacific Creek Trail

to
US 395

to 541

TH

Long Valley

LONG VALLEY
CAMPGROUND

TH

36E05

CHIMNEY PEAK
WILDERNESS

to 541

OWENS PEAK
WILDERNESS

BLM
ADDITIONS

Bartolas Creek

Pilot
Knob

178

Chimney Peak Rd

to Walker Pass

Onyx

to Kernville

KIAVAH
WILDERNESS

Miles

0   2   4

N

4 Kiavah Wilderness

Scodie Mountains along the Pacific Crest Trail near Skinner Peak, Kiavah Wilderness.

LOCATION: Kern County; 15 miles west of Ridgecrest, California

SIZE: 88,290 acres

ELEVATION RANGE: 3,000 to 7,096 feet

ADMINISTRATION: BLM Ridgecrest Resource Area Office, Sequoia National Forest Cannell Meadow Ranger District

MAPS: Desert Access Guide Ridgecrest #4, Jawbone/Dove Springs #5; Sequoia National Forest; AAA Kern County

Kiavah Wilderness, along with several other wilderness areas designated by the California Desert Bill, seems less like a desert than a mountain upland. Encompassing the Scodie Mountains, a rolling southern extension of the Sierra Nevada, most of Kiavah Wilderness is administered by the Sequoia National Forest. The lower flanks of the mountains, however, are managed by the BLM. The highest summit is 7,096-foot Cathie's Peak.

The Scodie Mountains lie at the transition zone between the Mojave Desert and the Sierra Nevada. Desert species like creosote bush, Joshua tree, and shadscale grow here, as well as more typical Sierran species like digger pine and canyon oak, and pinyon and juniper woodlands are also in evidence.

Kiavah

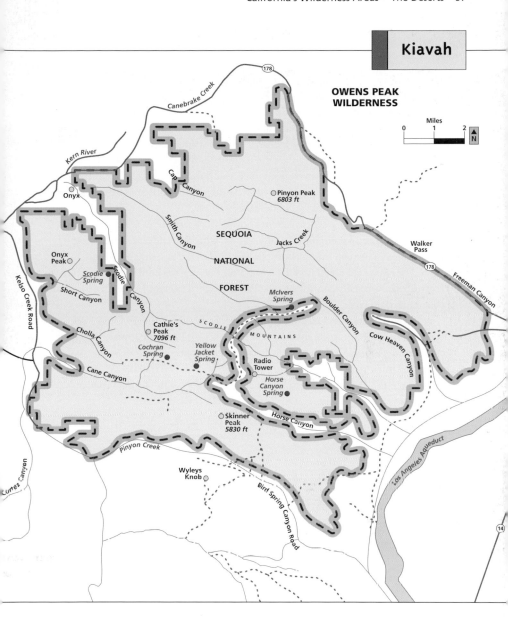

OWENS PEAK WILDERNESS

Miles

0   1   2

N

ACCESS

There are two basic ways to access Kiavah Wilderness: (1) Travel east from Lake Isabella on Hwy 178 to the tiny community of Onyx, and the wilderness lies due south or (2) turn off Hwy 395 near Inyokern and go west 16 miles to Walker Pass. The wilderness lies just south of the pass.

Unlike most desert wildernesses, Kiavah Wilderness does have a few trails. Paved Hwy 178 forms the northern border of the wilderness and provides access to the Pacific Crest Trail, which crosses the highway at Walker Pass. Hikers can enter the wilderness by traveling south from the pass on the Pacific Crest Trail. You can also access the Pacific Crest Trail from Bird Springs Canyon Road at Bird Springs Pass on the southern edge of the wilderness.

A road winds up Horse Canyon at the southeastern corner of the wilderness for more than 9 miles into the mountains, with the wilderness bounding it on both sides. The road intersects the Pacific Crest Trail at a microwave site.

Another trail off Kelso Creek Road on the western border follows Cholla Canyon and eventually connects to the Pacific Crest Trail and Horse Canyon Road at the microwave site.

Kelso Creek Road also provides access for another hike up Onyx Peak. To get there, go south from Hwy 127 on Kelso Creek Road for approximately 3 miles to the entrance of Short Canyon, where you should park. It is approximately 3.5 miles to the summit. You can follow an old jeep trail up the canyon and to the northeast before heading out cross country for the summit, which provides a grand view of the South Fork of the Kern River Valley.

Owens Peak Wilderness 5

Lamont Spires in Owens Peak Wilderness.

Owens Peak Wilderness takes in the eastern slope of the Sierra Nevada, rising up to jagged, granite spires cloaked in Jeffrey pine and white fir. Some of the more technically challenging climbs in the Southern Sierra are found here, and names like Spanish Needles, Sawtooth Peak, and Lamont Spires give some indication of the rugged features of the area. Twenty-two miles of the Pacific Crest Trail traverse the area south to north, providing access to the high country.

Expect snow in the winter, nevertheless this is a wilderness that is accessible nearly year round. Due to its generally high elevation, the crest of the wilderness is probably more enjoyable in the spring, summer, and fall than in the dead of winter, although midsummer can be very warm.

This wilderness has more water than most "desert ranges," with springs and even perennial streams. As a consequence there is riparian vegetation like cottonwood and

LOCATION: Kern, Tulare, and Inyo Counties; 15 miles northwest of Ridgecrest, California

SIZE: 74,640 acres

ELEVATION RANGE: 3,000 to 8,453 feet

ADMINISTRATION: BLM Ridgecrest Resource Area Office

MAPS: Desert Access Guide Ridgecrest #4; AAA Kern County

willow. At the transition zone from the Sierra Nevada to the desert, Owens Peak Wilderness supports pinyon pine, oak, white fir, incense cedar, ponderosa pine, and limber pine. At the same time, a healthy forest of Joshua tree grows near Walker Pass on the southern edge of the wilderness.

ACCESS

The wilderness lies north of Hwy 178 at Walker Pass where a trailhead for the Pacific Crest Trail is located. Other access points include canyons off Hwy 395, including Indian Wells Canyon, Sand Canyon, Grapevine Canyon, and Short Canyon.

Except for the Pacific Crest Trail, there are no other formal trails in this wilderness, although a number of "use" trails have developed in and near the more popular canyons and peaks.

A good day-hike destination is the steep 1.6-mile (2,800-foot elevation gain) climb to the summit of Owens Peak from Indian Wells Canyon. A "use" trail departs from the end of the road and passes up the north side of the canyon to the crest, where you can follow a ridge north-northwest through a woodland to the summit. The views from the top are unrestricted and expansive.

Another good day hike (8.8 miles round-trip) is the climb up 7,215-foot Morris Peak. To reach the summit, take the Pacific Crest Trail approximately 4 miles north of Walker Pass until you see an obvious saddle on the crest. Head for the saddle, then climb the southwest slope of the mountain to the top.

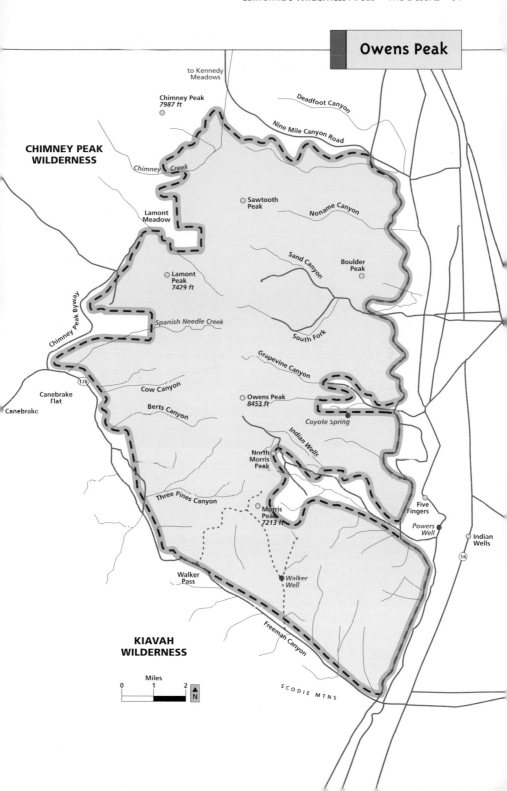

Owens Peak

to Kennedy Meadows

Chimney Peak
7987 ft

Deadfoot Canyon

Nine Mile Canyon Road

**CHIMNEY PEAK
WILDERNESS**

Chimney Creek

Lamont
Meadow

Sawtooth
Peak

Noname Canyon

Sand Canyon

Boulder
Peak

Lamont
Peak
7429 ft

Chimney Peak Byway

Spanish Needle Creek

South Fork

Grapevine Canyon

1/8

Cow Canyon

Canebrake
Flat

Canebrake

Berts Canyon

Owens Peak
8453 ft

Coyote Spring

Indian Wells

North
Morris
Peak

Three Pines Canyon

Morris
Peak
7213 ft

Five
Fingers

Powers
Well

Indian
Wells

14

Walker
Pass

Walker
Well

**KIAVAH
WILDERNESS**

Freeman Canyon

S C O D I E   M T N S

Miles
0   1   2

N

6 Sacatar Trail Wilderness

Riparian habitat in canyon along Sacatar Trail, Sacatar Trail Wilderness.

LOCATION: Inyo and Tulare Counties; 20 miles northwest of Ridgecrest, California

SIZE: 51,900 acres

ELEVATION RANGE: 3,000 to 7,800 feet

ADMINISTRATION: BLM Ridgecrest Resource Area Office

MAPS: Desert Access Guide Panamint #2, Ridgecrest #4

The rocky granitic ridges of Sacatar Trail Wilderness take in the eastern slope of the southern Sierra Nevada, rising to nearly 8,000 feet. This area is seldom snow covered—at least not the lower elevations—and it offers some great fall, winter, and spring hiking opportunities, particularly for those anxious to get into the Sierras early in the season. Summers may be a bit warm.

The area boasts meadows, sagebrush, and pinyon and juniper woodlands, and even pockets of ponderosa pine and red fir are found at higher elevations. Springs are abundant. In particular, Deer Spring supports 4 acres of riparian meadow. Unfortunately, many of these riparian areas have been severely trampled by domestic livestock. Cottonwood, wild grape, and willow line many of the canyons. Nine Mile Canyon phacelia, an annual lavender flower recommended for endangered species protection, grows here.

Wildlife include deer, black bear, cottontail rabbit, mountain lion, coyote, bobcat, and other species typically associated with the Sierra Nevada.

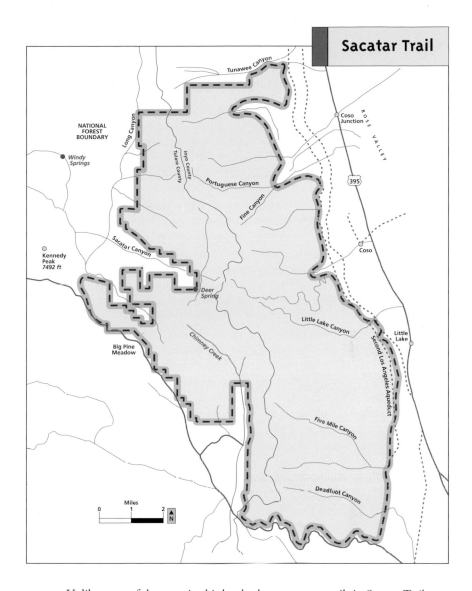

Sacatar Trail

Unlike most of the areas in this book, there are some trails in Sacatar Trail Wilderness. In particular an old "road," known as the Sacatar Trail, climbs the steep face of the Sierra Nevada and offers outstanding views of Rose Valley and beyond. The trail eventually crosses the eastern divide of the range to Sacatar Canyon near Kennedy Meadows. This trail has roots even more ancient than the pre-automobile era. It was used as a major travel corridor for native Americans crossing the Sierra Nevada. Hike this trail and you will be traveling the path that humans have used for generations.

ACCESS

Take Hwy 395 north of Inyokern. Dirt roads lead from Hwy 395 across the Los Angeles Aqueduct to canyons leading to the wilderness, including the Portuguese, Lewis, and Tunawee Canyons.

Great Basin Desert Subregion

Of California's three major deserts, the Great Basin is the most northern and the coldest. The Great Basin was named by explorer John Fremont for its internal drainage. Except for the Pit River in northern California, the Great Basin has no rivers that run to the sea.

The Great Basin is the largest major desert region in the United States, stretching from the Sierra Nevada eastward to the Wasatch Range of Utah. It takes in parts of western Utah, southern Idaho, southeastern Oregon, and nearly all of Nevada. The Great Basin Desert occupies two major regions in California. It overlaps into northeastern California east of the Cascades, including the Modoc Plateau, but reaches its greatest extent in California east of the southern Sierra Nevada.

Like most natural systems, there are no neat, clearly defined edges on the landscape where the Great Basin Desert ends and, say, the Mojave Desert begins. For the purposes of this book, the wildlands of the Great Basin are found east of the Sierra Nevada, south of Mono Lake, and north of Interstate 15 (I-15). Death Valley National Park is the largest wildland in this region, but in many instances the lower elevations in the southern part of the region could easily be considered part of the Mojave Desert.

The overwhelming geographic feature of the Great Basin is its basin-and-range configuration of north-south mountains and valleys stretching from the Sierra Nevada east to the Wasatch Front. The basin-and-range pattern is a consequence of the extension or the stretching of the earth's surface due to tectonic forces.

The Great Basin is sometimes called a "cold" desert—and for good reason. Temperatures can drop well below 0°F. Nearly all the precipitation comes in winter, although summer thunderstorms do occur. Most plant growth occurs in the spring when soil moisture is high and temperatures are more moderate.

The dominant vegetation across the Great Basin is sagebrush. At one time perennial grasslands were a major component of this region, however grazing by domestic livestock has altered the original vegetative cover dramatically. At higher elevations grow woodlands of pinyon and

Dawn on Inyo Mountains from Saline Valley, Death Valley National Park.

juniper. Occasionally, if the mountains are high enough, there are forests of limber pine, aspen, bristlecone pine, and other species. Due to the cool temperatures, cacti are rare in this desert.

As a general rule, most of the wildlands within the Great Basin are at higher elevations than desert areas further south. Some of the highest peaks exceed 10,000 feet, and White Mountain Peak in the White Mountains tops 14,000 feet. This is really the only part of the California desert that is tolerable in summer. Indeed, some of the highest areas are largely inaccessible due to snow the rest of the year.

7 Argus Range Wilderness

View from Argus Range Wilderness looking across Panamint Valley to Panamint Range.

LOCATION: San Bernardino County; just south of Panamint Springs and directly west of Death Valley National Park; 48 miles from Ridgecrest, California

SIZE: 74,890 acres

ELEVATION RANGE: 2,800 to 7,500 feet

ADMINISTRATION: BLM Ridgecrest Resource Area Office

MAPS: Desert Access Guide Panamint #2, Ridgecrest #4; AAA Death Valley National Park

Located on the western side of the Panamint Valley, the Argus Range is a long, narrow range directly west of Death Valley National Park. Some 28 miles of the range crest have been protected within the wilderness, however, nowhere is the wilderness more than 5 miles wide. Dissected by numerous canyons and steep slopes, the area supports a creosote bush and cactus plant community at lower elevations, with pinyon and juniper woodlands near the range crest. A relict bighorn sheep herd existed here at one time, and some 18 additional sheep were reintroduced in 1988.

Evidence of past native American cultural use consists of prehistoric stone tool flakes and rock shelters found in several locations. The area was traditionally used for spring and summer food gathering by Shoshone-Paiute bands. In addition, the area around Lookout Mountain-Maturango Peak was occasionally used for the collection of pinyon pine nuts.

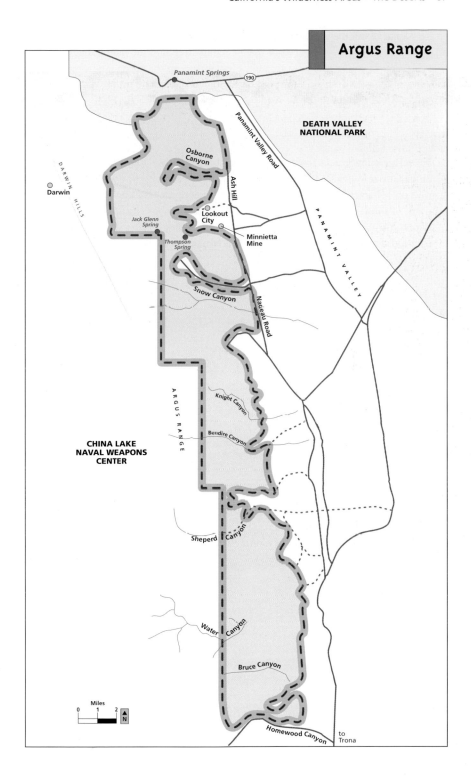

Argus Range

Panamint Springs

190

DEATH VALLEY
NATIONAL PARK

Panamint Valley Road

Osborne
Canyon

Ash Hill

DARWIN HILLS

Darwin

Jack Glenn
Spring

Lookout
City

Minnietta
Mine

Thompson
Spring

PANAMINT VALLEY

Snow Canyon

Nadeau Road

ARGUS RANGE

Knight Canyon

Bendire Canyon

CHINA LAKE
NAVAL WEAPONS
CENTER

Sheperd Canyon

Water Canyon

Bruce Canyon

Miles
0   1   2
N

Homewood Canyon

to
Trona

Signs of mining activity are abundant. Osborne, Thompson, and Snow Canyons all provide access via old mining roads that penetrate deep into the mountains.

Water is scarce and there are only a few springs in the entire range, making long overnight treks difficult. However, there is good day hiking up the canyons along now-closed, old mining trails and roads.

ACCESS

From Panamint Springs Resort go east a few miles on Hwy 190 then turn south on Panamint Valley Road. Travel 8 miles south of Panamint Springs then turn west on Minietta Road. Go 4 miles to the intersection of Nadeau Road. Go either north or south on this road and take any number of poor vehicle "tracks" back to the edge of the wilderness. Some of these roads might be better walked or ridden on a mountain bike unless you have a 4wd vehicle.

Black Mountain Wilderness 8

Basalt boulder frames Black Mountain,
Black Mountain Wilderness.

Black Mountain Wilderness is a plateau of exposed basalt rising as much as 1,900 feet above the surrounding lowlands. The rise from Harper Valley and Black Canyon is abrupt, but more gentle on other sides of the plateau. There are sweeping vistas from the rolling surface of the plateau. Raven, hawk, and eagle are frequently sighted gliding on the wing.

The entire area figured prominently in local native American mythology, and there are spectacular rock art sites within the wilderness. Along the southeastern corner are some sand dunes that create a sharp color contrast between the black volcanic rock and the lighter sand grains. The western boundary of the area is delineated by Black Canyon Road, and the eastern border is formed by Opal Road. The state-listed Mojave ground squirrel is found in the area.

LOCATION: San Bernardino County; 13 miles northwest of Barstow, California

SIZE: 13,940 acres

ELEVATION RANGE: 2,000 to 3,900 feet

ADMINISTRATION: BLM Barstow Resource Area Office

MAPS: Desert Access Guide Red Mountain #7; AAA San Bernardino County

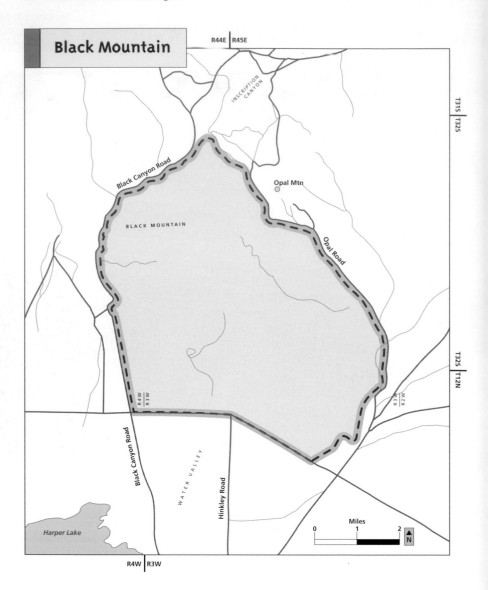

Black Mountain

R44E | R45E

T31S | T32S

INSCRIPTION CANYON

Black Canyon Road

Opal Mtn

BLACK MOUNTAIN

Opal Road

T32S | T12N

R 4 W | R 3 W

R 3 W | R 2 W

Black Canyon Road

WATER VALLEY

Hinkley Road

Harper Lake

Miles
0   1   2
N

R4W | R3W

ACCESS

The best access to this wilderness is to drive north from Hinkley on Hwy 58. Take Hinkley Road due north until it dead ends on the wilderness boundary. Park and hike north from the road.

Coso Range Wilderness 9

Joshua tree, Joshua Flat, Coso Range Wilderness.

Coso Range Wilderness takes in the northern end of the Coso Range—a volcanic upland just south of Owens Lake. Great views of the Sierra Nevada are possible from within the wilderness, particularly at Joshua Flat. Joshua Flat, an interior valley near the southern border of the wilderness, is named for the outstanding forest of Joshua tree that grows there. Sagebrush and pinyon pine are also present. Colorful Vermillion Canyon on the western edge of the wilderness is highly scenic. As a consequence of its overall higher elevation compared with most desert wilderness areas, Coso Range Wilderness is somewhat cooler in the summer than most areas of the California desert. Nevertheless, the best hiking season is spring and fall. Numerous archeological sites, rock art, and other evidence of native American use can be found.

LOCATION: Inyo County; 12 miles west of Darwin and 6 miles northeast of Olancha, California

SIZE: 50,520 acres

ELEVATION RANGE: 4,000 to 7,492 feet

ADMINISTRATION: BLM Ridgecrest Resource Area Office

MAP: Desert Access Guide Panamint #2

Coso Range

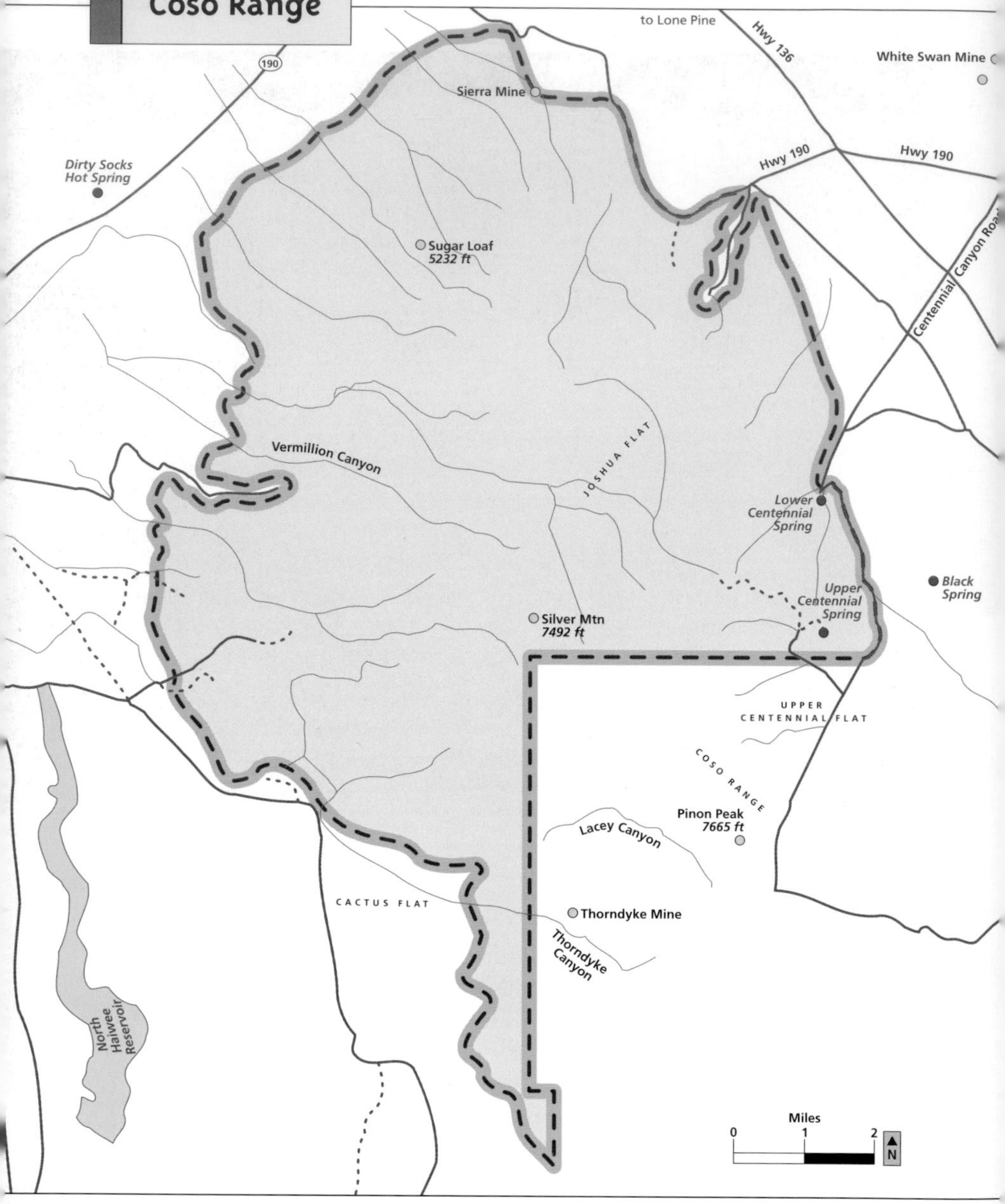

to Lone Pine

Hwy 136

White Swan Mine

190

Sierra Mine

Hwy 190

Hwy 190

Dirty Socks
Hot Spring

Centennial Canyon Road

Sugar Loaf
5232 ft

Vermillion Canyon

JOSHUA FLAT

Lower
Centennial
Spring

Upper
Centennial
Spring

Black
Spring

Silver Mtn
7492 ft

UPPER
CENTENNIAL FLAT

COSO RANGE

Lacey Canyon

Pinon Peak
7665 ft

CACTUS FLAT

Thorndyke Mine

Thorndyke
Canyon

North
Haiwee
Reservoir

Miles

0   1   2

N

ACCESS

The best approach to the east side of the wilderness is from Hwy 190. A number
of 4wd roads approach the wilderness boundary. Centennial Canyon on the eastern
edge of the wilderness is the best trailhead. To access the west side of the wilderness, drive 1 mile south of Olancha and take a dirt road that heads east 7 miles to
Vermillion Canyon. Hike to the wilderness boundary.

Darwin Falls Wilderness 10

Towards Darwin Falls Wilderness.

Darwin Falls Wilderness doesn't contain its namesake waterfall, which is now in Death Valley National Park immediately adjacent to the wilderness. It does, however, contain the headwaters and drainage area for the falls. The terrain of this compact 3-mile-wide by 5-mile-long wildland consists of rolling volcanic upland known locally as the Darwin Plateau. The plateau is covered with Joshua tree. The highest elevations exceed 5,000 feet, so the area may be snow-covered in winter, but relatively cooler in summer than surrounding desert areas. The best time to hike here is in the spring, when wildflowers may be in bloom.

    The town of Darwin and the wilderness area are both named for Darwin French, who explored the area in the 1860s. Silver and lead deposits led to the establishment of the town in 1875, and Darwin became the center for the New Coso Mining District. Today Darwin is a quasi-ghost town with only a few year-round residents.

LOCATION: Inyo County; 3 miles north of Darwin, California

SIZE: 8,600 acres

ELEVATION RANGE: 2,300 to 5,400 feet

ADMINISTRATION: BLM Ridgecrest Resource Area Office

MAP: Desert Access Guide Panamint #2

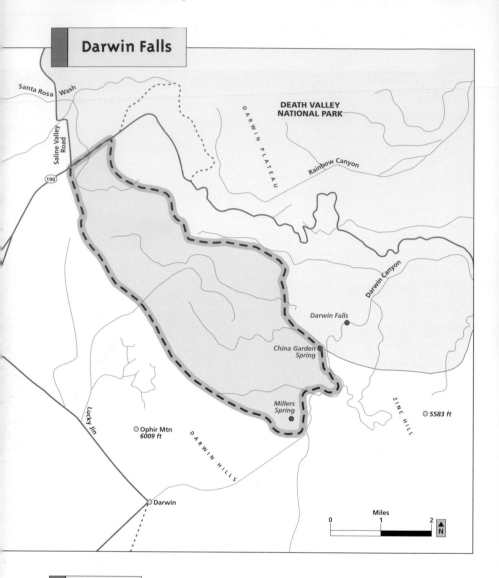

Darwin Falls

Santa Rosa Wash

Saline Valley Road

190

DEATH VALLEY NATIONAL PARK

DARWIN PLATEAU

Rainbow Canyon

Darwin Canyon

Darwin Falls

China Garden Spring

Millers Spring

ZINC HILL

○ 5583 ft

○ Ophir Mtn 6009 ft

DARWIN HILLS

Lucky Jin

○ Darwin

Miles
0   1   2
N

ACCESS

Hwy 190 forms the border for 1 mile on the northern end of the wilderness. This part of the wilderness is reached by traveling east on Hwy 190. Just a quarter-mile past the turn to the north heading to Saline Valley, begin looking for a place to park. The wilderness lies to the south of the highway. Hiking the plateau is merely a matter of getting out and following your nose across the open terrain. Great views of the Sierra Nevada high peaks are possible from some parts of the plateau. For those who want to experience the splashing sound of water in the desert and view lush riparian vegetation, a hike to Darwin Falls is memorable. The falls are accessed by hiking from the signed Darwin Canyon Road several miles off Hwy 190 just west of Panamint Springs.

Death Valley National Park II

Sand dunes at Stovepipe Wells, Death Valley National Park.

Death Valley is one of the newest national parks in the country. It was designated a national monument in 1933, but only recently was enlarged and upgraded to national park status in 1994. Its global significance was recognized when it was designated a Biosphere Reserve in 1984.

Death Valley itself is a large desert trough nearly surrounded by mountains. It is nestled between the Amargosa Range on the east, which includes the Black, the Funeral, and the Grapevine Mountains; and the Panamint Range on the west, which includes the Cottonwood Mountains. The Owlshead Mountains rise at the southern end of the park and the Last Chance Range and Sylvania Mountains border the northern end.

Death Valley is a place of superlatives. Its size alone gives it distinction. Running more than 50 miles southwest to northeast and more than 200 miles northwest to southeast, it is the largest national park in the contiguous United States.

LOCATION: Inyo County; adjacent to the California-Nevada border, 150 miles northeast of Los Angeles, California

SIZE: 3.4 million total acres (3.1 million acres of designated wilderness)

ELEVATION RANGE: 282 feet below sea level to 11,049 feet

ADMINISTRATION: Death Valley National Park

MAPS: Desert Access Guide Death Valley National Park; AAA Death Valley National Park

Within its boundaries are 3.4 million total acres, with 3.1 million acres of designated wilderness. There are actually more acres of designated wilderness in Death Valley National Park than wilderness found in the entire state of Oregon. Within its boundaries there are 10 named mountain ranges and some very large valleys, including the park's namesake—Death Valley. The floor of Death Valley is several hundred feet below sea level, whereas Telescope Peak in the adjacent Panamint Range rises to 11,049 feet, making the total elevation difference more than 2 miles—one of the greatest ranges in elevation in the entire country.

Death Valley is also one of the driest and hottest places in the United States, if not the world. A record temperature of 134°F in the shade was recorded there in July 1913, and in 1972 when the air temperature was 128°F, a ground temperature of 201°F was recorded, which is nearly hot enough to boil water. The high temperatures are a consequence of the low elevation, and the reflection and radiation of heat into the air caused by the surrounding mountains. Cool air descending from the mountains compresses the rising warm air from the valley, trapping it close to the ground, where additional heating takes place. Even the nighttime low in the summer can be 90°F! Ironically, Death Valley can also be a very cold place, with lows in the teens recorded in the valley and more frigid temperatures experienced in the higher basins.

Death Valley only averages 1.8 inches of precipitation a year, and in some years as little as a half-inch of precipitation has fallen from the sky. Even in "really wet" years, no more than 4.5 inches has been recorded. By contrast, Tucson in the Sonoran Desert receives almost 12 inches of moisture a year.

The extreme aridity of Death Valley is partially a consequence of the high wall of mountains to the west. Air masses from the Pacific Ocean must first climb over the lofty heights of the Sierra Nevada, including Mount Whitney (the highest summit in the lower 48 states). In rising over this barrier, moisture in the atmosphere cools and falls as snow and rain, leaving the air mass much drier east of the Sierras than on the western slope of the range. But before any rain-bearing clouds reach Death Valley, they have to negotiate several other high ranges, including the Inyo Range, the Argus Range, and the Panamint Range. By the time air masses reach Death Valley, nearly all of the moisture has been wrung from them.

Beyond these dubious superlatives as hottest, driest, steepest, lowest, and other topographical and climatic factors, Death Valley has one more claim to fame—it is one of the largest wilderness areas in the lower 48 states. The amount of designated wilderness in the park is larger than the state of Connecticut. It is not, however, a single continuous piece of roadless land. The 3.1 million acres of wilderness is the collective figure for the designated wilderness within the park. Death Valley National Park Wilderness consists of a number of smaller roadless parcels separated by dirt and paved roads. Nevertheless, this wildland is still the largest protected desert environment in the country, and when considered within the context of the adjacent designated wilderness that fringes the park on many sides, this is one of the greatest wildland complexes in the nation.

HISTORY

Despite its climatic extremes, Death Valley has been visited by people for the past 7,000 years. The most recent native Americans to call Death Valley home were members of the Shoshone tribe who occupied the area during the past 1,000 years. The frugality of life in such an austere place limited the number of people who could exist there to little more than a few widely roaming family groups who eked out an existence that most would hardly call more than bare survival. Jedediah Smith, an American trapper who became the first European-American to traverse the Great Basin, described the Shoshone as "the most miserable objects in creation." Smith, no doubt, suffered from a Eurocentric perspective, but there's no mistaking that life in places like Death Valley left few excesses for frills.

Despite their lack of material wealth, the Shoshone demonstrated an amazing adaptability to a harsh land. The fact that they could survive in a place where most of us today would die without our technological support systems is a remarkable testimony to their skill as foragers and hunters. They did not possess permanent homes, but migrated with the seasons and availability of food resources. They spent their winters in the valley and moved to higher, cooler elevations in the summer. Staples of their diet included mesquite beans, pinyon nuts, beavertail cactus fruit, insects, and the occasional jackrabbit or bighorn sheep.

Pinyon nuts are derived from the pinecones of the pinyon pine that grow on the higher slopes of the desert ranges such as the Panamint and Inyo Mountains. Indian women would work in teams, shaking the cones from the trees, then gathering them in baskets and carting them off to a roasting area. The cones were cooked until the scales cracked open revealing the large seed inside. This was collected, roasted further, then either eaten or ground to make a thin soup or flour. It took a dozen women all day to gather a single bushel of seeds. To gather enough pinyon nuts to feed a large family group must have required a tremendous amount of work.

Hunting the sparse wildlife of the region required cooperative efforts as well. Almost anything living was eaten, including lizards, snakes, pack rats, kangaroo rats, ground squirrels, and mice. Many of these were gathered in cooperative hunting ventures. Jackrabbits were a particularly popular game animal, not only for their meat but for their fur, which the natives used to make blankets. Jackrabbit populations vary from year to year, and in some years there are tremendous numbers of them. In such years the Shoshone would gather in larger bands to conduct cooperative rabbit drives. Jackrabbits were driven ahead of brush beaters toward some natural constriction where other hunters waited with sticks to club the animals to death.

Cooperative drives were also used to hunt bighorn sheep. Sheep tend to be found in rugged terrain, but also follow traditional game trails. Once a herd of bighorns was located, most of the tribe would rush the sheep to frighten them toward the hunters waiting in ambush behind stone blinds.

In the late 1700s and 1800s, horse meat became a more common addition to the diet. The Shoshone would raid the outlying Spanish outposts by Los Angeles and drive horses back to the desert where they would be eaten, not ridden.

The Shoshone survived in their desert stronghold for years without any encroachment from white settlers. No one wanted Death Valley, and no one purposely ventured there. It was not until 1849 that the first European-Americans wandered into the valley, and they were not looking to find it. And as soon as they found it, they couldn't wait to leave. These fortune hunters, traveling as part of a wagon train of gold seekers heading to California to pluck gold from the streams, took a "short-cut" to the gold fields, which required crossing the deserts of southern Nevada and California. This group consisted of four families and some unmarried men known as the Jayhawkers. The steep up-and-down terrain, combined with the lack of food and water for their stock, began to take a toll on their draft animals. Nearly all the oxen hauling the wagons died. The pace slowed to a crawl and supplies ran low. Eventually the group splintered, each going their own way. One family went alone and made it out of the valley with their wagon intact. The Jayhawkers burned their wagons near Stovepipe Wells and left the valley by way of Towne Pass, while a third group moved on to Bennett's Well south of Furnace Creek. By now there was just one wagon left in the entire group, and only a few exhausted oxen left to haul it. The party decided to halt at Bennett's Well. They were in no immediate danger since they had water and a few animals they could kill, but they were desperate to find a way out of the valley. Convinced that the Spanish settlements of Los Angeles were just beyond the next range of mountains, the party decided to send several of the youngest men—William Manly and John Rogers—ahead to obtain food and help. (Both men had peaks subsequently named for them in the Panamint Range.)

The men had trouble finding a way out of the valley, but finally located a pass to the south and eventually made a grueling journey across the desert to the Spanish settlements on the outskirts of Los Angeles. With fresh horses and supplies, they raced back to Death Valley hoping to save the rest of the families. Twenty-one days after they had left their comrades, they returned to Bennett's Well. Some of the stragglers waiting there had abandoned hope that help would arrive and had set out on their own hoping to reach Los Angeles. At least one of these gold seekers, Captain Culverwell, died in the valley. Because of this death and the hardships endured, one of the female members of the rescued party bestowed the valley's infamous name upon it. On ascending a ridge, with a final look back at the valley, she is reported to have exclaimed, "Goodbye, Death Valley." The name stuck.

The next wave of humanity to invade Death Valley was the miners. As the story goes, one of the Jayhawkers on his way out of the valley picked up a sliver of silver, which he used to fashion a new gun sight for his rifle. But with supplies short, he had no time to explore the area for more traces of the ore. Once the party arrived in Los Angeles the silver find was now inflated to a rich ore deposit, triggering a minor flood of prospectors to the region looking for the Lost Gunsight Mine. Like the Lost Dutchman Mine in Arizona's Superstition Mountains, and other lost mines in the West, no one has yet rediscovered the reported ore deposit.

Despite some prospecting activity, no real mining occurred until a silver discovery was made in the Panamint Range in 1873. Like so many other rich mineral discoveries in the West, Chance played an important role. Reportedly the silver lode was found by a band of thieves who had robbed a Wells Fargo stage express box loaded with silver bullion. They had gone up Surprise Canyon in the Panamints to evade pursuing law enforcement officers. While waiting in the canyon, one of the thieves found a vein of silver ore. The discovery created a dilemma for

Looking down Little Hunter Canyon in the Inyo Mountains Wilderness to Slaine Valley within Death Valley National Park.

the bandits. The silver ore was potentially worth far more than the silver bullion they had taken from the stage; but if they went into town to file their claim, they risked being arrested for the stage robbery.

As the story goes, one of the robbers was an acquaintance of Nevada Senator William Stewart. This robber left the Panamints, went to Nevada, contacted the Senator, and showed him the rich ore deposits. The Senator wasn't adverse to profiting as a consequence of his connections. For a large share of the ore deposit, Stewart arranged a payback settlement with the Wells Fargo Company so the bandits could file their claim. Once the mining claims were officially recorded, the rush to the Panamints was on. Within a year, Panamint City (as the new settlement was called) boasted more than 1,000 people, a newspaper, and plenty of saloons. (A man gets mighty thirsty working out in the desert.)

Although some silver was produced, eventually, like most mining ventures, the boom of Panamint City turned to bust. By the 1880s Panamint City was largely a ghost town. Nevertheless, new mineral discoveries, including gold, silver, lead, and copper, continued to attract prospectors and miners to the region. Other mining ventures and short-lived towns included Skidoo, Harrisburg, Goldbelt, Leadfield, Choride City, and others. Most of these towns were established in the late 1800s and early 1900s. Given the high transportation costs and isolation of work in the region, few of the mines were profitable. One exception was the mines at Skidoo in the Panamint Range. Between 1906 and 1917 some six million dollars in gold were taken from the mines.

The most valuable mineral to come out of Death Valley was not gold or silver, but a whitish, powdery product we know as borax. In 1881, Aaron Winters gathered some borax from Death Valley from a site north of Furnace Creek now known as the Harmony Borax Works. Winters sold his claim to William Coleman, a San Francisco mine developer, for $20,000. Coleman hired Chinese laborers to gather the mineral, which loosely covered the ground in the vicinity of the Borax Works. This raw material was boiled in giant metal vats and was precipitated out on rods suspended in the liquid. Once the borax was collected, Coleman still had to get it to market. He solved his transportation problem with the development of 20-mule-team wagon trains. The huge wagons, with 7-foot wheels, were able to hold 10 tons of the mineral. The journey to the nearest railhead at Mojave took 10 days. Even with these difficult transportation costs, the mining operation was profitable for a while, until borax sources closer to the rail line were discovered. The 20-mule-train story would have faded into history were it not for its popularization in the TV show *Death Valley Days*.

In 1933, President Herbert Hoover created Death Valley National Monument by executive decree. Monuments, unlike national parks (which require an act of Congress), can be established by presidential order. In 1937, President Franklin Roosevelt expanded the monument by adding lands in adjacent Nevada. In 1952, 40 acres in Nevada surrounding Devil's Hole were added to the monument. Devil's Hole is a deep, clear spring and the only known home for the Devil's Hole pupfish. In 1976 Congress passed the Mining in the Parks Act, which had a direct consequence for Death Valley. The new law closed all national park units, including Death Valley, to new mining claims. When the new law was enacted, thousands of claims covered the park; today, less than 200 remain valid.

In 1984, Death Valley was incorporated as part of the Mojave and Colorado Biosphere Reserve, a designation that recognizes areas with globally significant resources. Death Valley finally achieved national park status when the California Desert Protection Act was signed into law by President Bill Clinton in 1994. The act not only upgraded the status of the area by giving it national park recognition, but it expanded the old borders of the existing national monument by more than a million acres and designated 95 percent of the park as wilderness under the 1964 Wilderness Act.

GEOLOGY

With little vegetation to hide the geologic structure, Death Valley is an open geology book for those with the skills to read nature's text. The oldest rocks exposed in Death Valley are crystalline basement rocks, primarily gneiss and schist that were originally laid down as volcanic deposits some 1.7 billion years ago. These rocks have been changed by heat and pressure, so they little resemble their original components. In

Playa in Panamint Valley below Panamint Range, Death Valley National Park.

most of the California desert these rocks are buried deep beneath overlying sediments, but the great amount of faulting and uplift in the Death Valley area has permitted erosion to strip away more of the overburden than in other areas, exposing these rocks at the surface. The best place to see exposure of these basement rocks is in the Panamint and Black Mountains.

Covering these basement rocks in most places are sedimentary marine deposits known collectively as the Pahrump Group. These deposits include limestone and dolomite, which precipitated out of a warm sea approximately 1.4 billion years ago.

Other depositions occurred, but the greatest number of rock formations in Death Valley were deposited during the Paleozoic era between 570 and 325 million years ago. Rocks of this era—mostly shale, limestone, and sandstone—make up the eastern slope of the Panamints, southern Funeral Mountains, Cottonwood Mountains, Grapevine Mountains, and Last Chance Range.

Then a shift in plate tectonics brought the long period of deposition to a close. During this time an oceanic plate began to be subducted under the North American plate. A long line of volcanoes (similar to the Cascades in today's Pacific Northwest) developed along the western margin of the continent. Molten rock rose along fractures in the earth's mantle to become embedded among the overlying rock formations. This rock cooled to form granitic intrusions (plutons), like those now exposed in the Sierra Nevada. These intrusions also occurred in the Death Valley region and are exposed in a few locations within the park, including Hunter Mountain in the Cottonwood Range (you pass through this granitic exposure on the road to Saline Valley), in the upper Hanaupah and upper Warm Spring Canyons in the Panamints, and around Skidoo Canyon also in the Panamints. The granitic exposures in Death Valley are relatively young. For instance, the Hunter Mountain pluton was intruded about 165 million years ago. Since gold and other minerals are often associated with such intrusions, it is not surprising that the mining operations at Skidoo and Harrisburg were focused along the margins of another granitic pluton.

The major geologic event shaping Death Valley's features was the gradual extension of the Basin and Range Province by plate tectonic forces, which began about 25 million years ago. Land along the San Andreas Fault began to rotate relative to the rest of the continent and began sliding to the northwest. This caused spreading of the earth's surface in the Basin and Range Province, and created the north-south alignment of mountain ranges from California to Utah. Blocks of the earth's crust rose as mountains, while the valleys dropped (technically called grabens) in succession. Today there is a procession of uplifted mountains and down-dropped valleys from the Sierra Nevada all the way to the Wasatch Range in Utah. Beginning with Owens Valley at the base of the Sierra Nevada, you have the Inyo-White Mountains and then the Saline and Panamint Valleys, followed by the Panamint-Cottonwood Mountains and then Death Valley, and the Grapevine-Funeral-Black Mountains, and so it goes across the entire Basin and Range Province all the way to the Rockies. The Panamint Range, for instance, has moved 50 miles westward from a position adjacent to the Nopah Range. As this extension pulled the earth's crust apart, and uplift accelerated erosion of the mountains, sediments filled the valleys. In Death Valley, sediments washed down from the mountains (often into lakes that filled the valley during wetter climatic periods). Some of these sediments have subsequently been uplifted and eroded, and form the badlands we see today—for example, at Zabrinski Point. Then about four million years ago, uplift of the Panamint Mountains accelerated. At the same time, the mountains were tipped eastward, deepening the valley in the process. Even though the Panamints rise some 2 miles above the valley floor, rapid erosion of the range as it rose has filled the valley with 9,000 feet of sediment.

During the Pleistocene Ice Age, which began about two million years ago and has only recently ended or is experiencing an interlude, precipitation increased over the region. Death Valley was filled by a succession of lakes that alternatively filled the valley then dried up with changing climatic conditions. The last glacial lake was 600 feet deep and stretched for 100 miles along what is today Death Valley. This water body, known as Lake Manly, dried up about 11,000 years ago. As little as 2,000 years ago, water again covered Death Valley with a shallow lake some 30 feet deep. The salts that cover the Devil's Golf Course and other salt pans in the valley are carbonates, sulfates, and chlorides that were precipitated from the water of these drying lakes.

FAUNA AND FLORA

More than 1,000 plant species are recorded for Death Valley National Park. Such species diversity isn't surprising if you consider the significant altitudinal differences between the highest peaks and the deepest valleys, which create a wide variety of habitats and microsites.

One surprising aspect of Death Valley is that it doesn't support an abundance of cacti. Only 15 species of cacti are reported for the park, and most are relatively rare. The most common are beavertail, prickly pear, and cottontop (a kind of barrel cactus). The most widespread plant is probably creosote bush. This evergreen shrub covers the slopes, alluvial fans, and valley floors throughout the park up to an elevation of about 5,000 to 6,000 feet. It is the most common shrub in the Panamint Valley, Death Valley, Saline Valley, and other lower elevations of the park. At higher elevations you find sagebrush and Joshua tree. Sagebrush in particular is strongly associated with the Great Basin Desert. Most of the higher valleys, such as around Skidoo and Wildrose Canyons, are covered with sagebrush. Joshua tree is relatively rare in the park and is best viewed in the Nelson Range along the road to Saline Valley. Between 6,000 and 9,000 feet you encounter woodlands of pinyon pine and juniper. For instance, the Panamint Range has a good forest component comprised largely of these tree species. Finally, at the highest elevations grow forests of limber pine and bristlecone pine. These are found primarily in the Panamint Range. Along water sources are dependent species like cattails, willows, cottonwood, and sometimes mesquite grows where the water table is high, such as the playa basin near Stovepipe Wells.

Although most of the plants found in Death Valley are widespread and common throughout the California desert, there are 19 endemics found nowhere else but in this region. These include Eureka Dunes evening primrose, Panamint daisy, Death Valley sagebrush, and Panamint monkeyflower.

Wildlife that call the park home include six species of fish, five species of amphibians, 36 species of reptiles, several hundred species of birds, and 51 species of mammals. Fish include endemics such as the Salt Creek pupfish, Cotton Marsh pupfish, Saratoga pupfish, and Devil's Hole pupfish. Most of these fish are threatened and endangered because their habitats are so restricted.

Of the snakes, the most common are the gopher snake, king snake, banded shovel-nosed snake, and the red racer. Rattlesnakes include the Panamint rattlesnake, sidewinder, and Mojave rattler.

Death Valley is not a birding paradise. Most birds are just passing through during their migratory flights. Nevertheless, you might see Gambel quail, raven, turkey vulture, canyon wren, and hummingbird.

You're not likely to see most of the mammals because they are generally active at night, and most are small rodents. Nevertheless, if you are lucky you may see bighorn sheep, mule deer, coyote, kit fox, and jackrabbit. You may also see wild burros. The burros compete with native species for water, food, and space. Since the National Park Service mandate is to protect native species, removal of the burros has been an ongoing, never-ending project. Between 1939 and 1969, the National Park Service removed more than 3,600 burros from the park. Then another burro removal program that began in 1983 eliminated more than 5,700 burros from the park during a five-year period. Burros are again on the rebound, drifting into the park from adjacent BLM lands.

ACCESS

United States (US) Rte (Rte) 395 passes west of Death Valley and connects with California Rte 178 at Inyokern and Rte 190 at Olancha, both of which enter the park from the west. I-15 passes to the southeast of Death Valley and connects with Rte 127 at Baker, California. Drive 60 miles north then turn left on Rte 178 just past Shoshone, or drive 20 miles further north to Death Valley Junction and turn left on California Rte 190 to enter the park.

US Rte 95 passes north-south through Nevada, east of the park, and connects with Nevada Rte 267 at Scotty's Junction, Rte 373 at Amargosa Valley, and Rte 374 at Beatty, all of which lead to the park from the east. From Las Vegas, Nevada, Rte 160 leads to Pahrump, where a left on Nevada Rte 132 (which becomes California Rte 190 at the state line) leads to Furnace Creek through Death Valley Junction.

CAMPING

The park has nine campgrounds. Three are open all year (Furnace Creek, Mesquite Spring, and Wildrose), three are open October to April (Texas Spring, Sunset, and Stovepipe Wells), and three other campgrounds are open April to

Panamint Dunes in Panamint Valley and Panamint Range from Mill Canyon, Death Valley National Park.

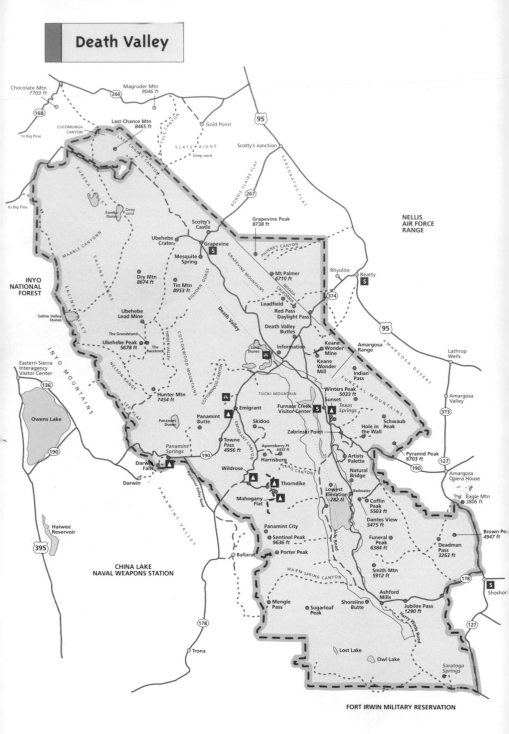

Death Valley

Chocolate Mtn
7703 ft

Magruder Mtn
9046 ft

266

168

to Big Pine

CUCOMUNGA CANYON

Last Chance Mtn
8465 ft

Gold Point

95

Scotty's Junction

SLATE RIDGE

Deep sand

LAST CHANCE CANYON

TULE CANYON

EUREKA VALLEY

BONNIE CLAIRE FLAT

267

SARCOBATUS FLAT

to Big Pine

Eureka Dunes

Deep sand

Scotty's Castle

Grapevine Peak
8738 ft

NELLIS
AIR FORCE
RANGE

Ubehebe Crater

Grapevine
S

MARBLE CANYON

Mesquite Spring

PHINNEY CANYON

Dry Mtn
8674 ft

Tin Mtn
8953 ft

GRAPEVINE MOUNTAINS

Mt Palmer
6710 ft

Rhyolite

Beatty
S

INYO
NATIONAL
FOREST

SALINE RANGE

BIGHORN GORGE

374

NEVADA CALIFORNIA

Saline Valley Dunes

Ubehebe Lead Mine

Leadfield

Red Pass
Daylight Pass

SALINE VALLEY

The Grandstand

Death Valley

Death Valley Buttes

95

Ubehebe Peak
5678 ft

The Racetrack

HIDDEN VALLEY

COTTONWOOD MOUNTAINS

Sand Dunes

Information

Keane Wonder Mine

Amargosa Range

AMARGOSA DESERT

Lathrop Wells

INYO MOUNTAINS

Eastern Sierra Interagency Visitor Center

NELSON RANGE

Keane Wonder Mill

Indian Pass

136

Hunter Mtn
7454 ft

LEE FLAT

TUCKI MOUNTAIN

Winters Peak
5033 ft

Sunset

FUNERAL MOUNTAINS

Amargosa Valley

373

Owens Lake

Panamint Dunes

Panamint Butte

Emigrant

Skidoo

Furnace Creek Visitor Center
S

Texas Springs

Schwaub Peak

Hole in the Wall

Zabrinski Point

190

Towne Pass
4956 ft

EMIGRANT CANYON

Aguereberry Pt
6433 ft

Harrisburg

TRAIL CANYON

Artists Palette

Pyramid Peak
6703 ft

127

Darwin Falls

Panamint Springs

190

Wildrose

Natural Bridge

190

Amargosa Opera House

Darwin

PANAMINT VALLEY

Panamint Valley Road

Thorndike

Lowest Elevation
-282 ft

Badwater

Coffin Peak
5503 ft

Eagle Mtn
3806 ft

Haiwee Reservoir

Mahogany Flat

Dantes View
5475 ft

Brown Pe
4947 ft

395

CHINA LAKE
NAVAL WEAPONS STATION

WARM SPRING CANYON

Panamint City

Side Road

Sentinel Peak
9636 ft

Porter Peak

Funeral Peak
6384 ft

Deadman Pass
3263 ft

Ballarat

Smith Mtn
5912 ft

178

S

Shoshor

Ashford Mills

Trona

178

Mengle Pass

Sugarloaf Peak

Shoreline Butte

Jubilee Pass
1290 ft

Harry Wade Road

127

Lost Lake

Owl Lake

Saratoga Springs

FORT IRWIN MILITARY RESERVATION

☐ Sea Level Elevation

October (Emigrant, Thorndike, and Mahogany). For information write for the folder *Camping in Death Valley* (the address for Death Valley National Park is listed in Appendix A, For Further Information).

EMIGRANT CAMPGROUND 10 sites open April through October. Water, tables, flush toilets. No fires. Located on the western side of park at the fork of Rtes 190 and 178; elevation 2,100 feet. No fee.

FURNACE CREEK CAMPGROUND 136 sites open year round. Tables, water, flush toilets, fireplaces, and sanitary station. Located just north of the visitor center on Rte 190; elevation 196 feet below sea level. Fee.

MAHOGANY FLAT CAMPGROUND 10 sites open March through November. Tables, fireplaces, pit toilets. Located at the western extreme of the park east of Rte 178; elevation 8,200 feet; 4wd recommended. No fee.

MESQUITE SPRING CAMPGROUND 30 sites open year round. Water, flush toilets, tables, fireplaces, sanitary station. Located at the far northern end of the park just west of Rte 267; elevation 1,800 feet. Fee.

STOVEPIPE WELLS CAMPGROUND 200 sites open October through April. Water, flush and pit toilets, sanitary station. No fires. Located just north of Stovepipe Wells off Rte 190; elevation sea level. Fee.

SUNSET CAMPGROUND 1,000 sites open October through April. Water, flush and pit toilets, sanitary station. No fires. Located just south of the visitor center off Rte 190; elevation 190 feet below sea level. Fee.

TEXAS SPRING CAMPGROUND 92 sites open October through April. Tables, water, flush and pit toilets, fireplaces, sanitary station. Located just south of the visitor center off Rte 190; elevation sea level. Fee.

THORNDIKE CAMPGROUND 8 sites open March through November. Tables, fireplaces, pit toilets. Located at the extreme western edge of the park east of Rte 178; elevation 7,500 feet; 4wd recommended. No fee.

WILDROSE CAMPGROUND 30 sites open year round. Water (available April through November), tables, fireplaces, pit toilets. Located at the extreme western edge of the park just off Rte 178; elevation 4,100 feet. No fee.

Primitive camping is allowed in many backcountry areas. Generally, camping is allowed 1 mile back from the main paved or unpaved roads and no closer than 0.25 mile to water sources. Most abandoned mining areas are restricted to day-use only. Check for restrictions with rangers at the visitor center. To get information about the park write to Death Valley National Park, PO Box 579, Death Valley, CA 92328 or call (760)-760-2331.

HIKING

Remember to carry 1 gallon of water per person per day as a minimum. Do not rely on the springs shown on maps for water. Many are either dry or have been contaminated by burros.

There are only two maintained hiking trails in the entire park: Wildrose and Telescope Peaks. Since both are at relatively high elevations in the Panamint Range, they are the only hikes recommended during the hot days of summer. The rest of the suggested hikes are cross-country routes. Mileage can be deceiving, so allow plenty of time for these trips. A good topographic map is handy to have. Most hikes in Death Valley, as in most of the California desert, are day hikes; however, many of the following suggested hikes can be turned into multiday hikes if sufficient water is carried or cached in advance. At present, permits are not required for either day hiking or overnight camping in the park.

DAY HIKE: WILDROSE—PANAMINT RANGE

One-way length:	4.2 miles
Low and high elevations:	6,870 to 9,064 feet
Difficulty:	moderate

The trail up Wildrose Peak is one of two maintained paths in the park. It is a well-marked and easily followed path. Bear in mind, however, that it climbs more than 2,200 feet in 4 miles.

There are terrific views along much of the route, so even if you don't make it to the top of the peak you will be well rewarded for your efforts. The summit itself is treeless and offers a 360-degree panoramic vista. Winds can be extreme on the top, so be prepared with adequate protective clothing.

To find the trailhead from Stovepipe Wells, take Hwy 190 to Emigrant Junction. Turn south (left) and continue 20.9 miles to Wildrose Junction. Turn east onto Mahogany Flat Road and drive 7.1 miles to Charcoal Kilns parking area and trailhead.

After examining the kilns (which were constructed in 1877 to produce charcoal for use in mining smelters across the valley in the Argus Range), find the trail that is located at the western end of the line of kilns. The trail climbs quickly to a lovely view in about 0.25 mile and provides a good panoramic view of the Panamint Valley and the Argus Range beyond. Continue up a wooded draw, passing many old stumps that remain preserved by the dry desert air more than 100 years after loggers cut the trees to feed the kilns. In 1.8 miles you reach a saddle on the crest of the Panamint Range—and the first views of Death Valley. Here the trail turns north and follows the ridge. At 2.9 miles you reach a second saddle with more great views. The trail drops slightly, with a switchback up a ridge to the peak. The views from the summit are expansive. Telescope Peak rises to the south, and range after range marches off toward the horizon to the east.

DAY HIKE: TELESCOPE PEAK—PANAMINT RANGE

One-way length: 7 miles
Low and high elevations: 8,133 to 11,048 feet
Difficulty: strenuous

Telescope Peak (elevation 11,048 feet) is the crown of Death Valley National Park and one of the highest peaks in the entire California desert. Rising directly from the salt pans in Death Valley more than 2 miles straight up, the peak has one of the steepest gradients of any in the West. Only three other mountains have a greater relief: Mt. Rainier in Washington, and Mount McKinley and Mount Fairweather in Alaska. Twisted, ancient bristlecone pine adorn the higher portions of the peak. The trail to the summit is one of two maintained paths in the park.

To reach the trailhead from Stovepipe Wells, head west on Hwy 190 to Emigrant Junction. Turn south (left) on Emigrant Canyon Road. Travel 20.9 miles to Wildrose Junction. Turn east (left) on to Mahogany Flat Road. Travel past several campgrounds and the charcoal kilns for 8.7 miles to the parking area. The last 1.6 miles are steep, narrow, and rough. Those with low-clearance cars (low ground clearance) may wish to leave their vehicles at the charcoal kilns and walk from there. This would add another 3.2 round-trip miles to the total miles of the hike, so it's best to start early in the day.

From the Mahogany Flat Trailhead, the trail passes through a pinyon and juniper forest as it climbs at an average eight-percent grade toward Rogers Peak. The trail reaches Arcane Meadows in a saddle (elevation 9,620 feet) 2.6 miles from the trailhead. From the saddle, the trail winds around Bennett Peak to another saddle 4.3 miles further on. Beyond Bennett Peak, the trail follows the crest and offers great views of Jail Canyon and the South Fork of Hanaupah Canyon. The last mile or so passes many photogenic bristlecone pine, which will keep your mind off the steep switchbacks you must climb before reaching the top of the peak. Once on top, enjoy the view, which includes the Sierra Nevada to the west and the Spring Mountains in Nevada to the east.

DAY HIKE: DARWINS FALLS—ARGUS RANGE

One way length: 0.8 mile
Low and high elevations: 2,360 to 2,500 feet
Difficulty: easy

Ferns, lush riparian vegetation, bird song, and the trickling sound of falling water all set the hike to Darwin Falls apart from most "desert" hikes. The 25-foot falls are not booming (there's not enough water for that), but the thin stream that cascades down the rock face is still a refreshing sight amid the harsh desert landscape.

Darwin Falls was formerly managed by the BLM but is now part of Death Valley National Park as a result of the 1994 desert bill expansion of the park. The BLM's Darwin Falls Wilderness is immediately west of this area, but ironically doesn't include its namesake falls. Water from China Garden Spring sustains the falls and provides the water for the Panamint Springs Resort.

To reach the trailhead, go 1.1 miles west of Panamint Springs on Hwy 190. There is a signed dirt road heading west (left) that leads up a wash for 2.6 miles to a turnoff to the trailhead. The road to the parking area is rocky but passable in a 2wd vehicle if driven carefully. The hike starts at a barricade designed to keep ORVs from going up the canyon.

From the parking area just walk up the wash, jumping the small creek now and again. In a third of a mile or so, the canyon narrows and the trail becomes more defined as it winds through the willows and other thick vegetation. As you get closer to the falls, there are smooth rock ledges that must be negotiated. The path leads to a small sandy spot beside a cattail-rimmed pool.

There is a higher 140-foot waterfall that is seldom visited about a quarter-mile further upstream. To reach it, climb up the slick, smooth canyon walls on the south side of the stream next to the lower falls and follow a "use" trail upstream and through willows to another pool and waterfall. Return the way you came.

DAY HIKE: FALL CANYON—GRAPEVINE MOUNTAINS
One-way length: 3 miles
Low and high elevations: 950 to 2,170 feet
Difficulty: moderate

The narrow, winding passage of Fall Canyon may remind you of the slot canyons of the Colorado Plateau. The 2.5-mile hike up to a dry waterfall is relatively easy. For the more adventurous who are willing and able to climb around this obstacle, the upper canyon offers a potential overnight excursion.

Fall Canyon is just north of Titus Canyon. To find the trailhead, drive north 15 miles from the junction of Hwy 190 and Scotty's Castle Road (Hwy 267) to the eastern (right) turnoff for Titus Canyon Road. Travel up this dirt road for 2.6 miles to the mouth of Titus Canyon where there is a parking area.

From the Titus Canyon parking area walk along the base of the mountains 0.9 mile north to a large wash that exits the mountains. Follow this wash upstream into Fall Canyon. The bottom section of the canyon is wide, but as you proceed upstream it becomes gradually narrower and narrower until a point some 2.6 miles upstream where the canyon is no more than 8 feet across! The walk along the lower canyon is easy, except for the rubbernecking you'll do as you gaze upward at the high canyon walls. At 3 miles there is an 18-foot waterfall (usually dry); most people turn around here and return to the starting point.

To negotiate this obstacle, look for a bypass "route" on the south side of the canyon marked by cairns about 300 feet before the falls. This route involves some climbing, so should only be attempted by those with rock-climbing skills. If you manage to get beyond the falls, the canyon narrows significantly for about a third of a mile, then opens up a bit while the canyon walls remain high. If you continue up the canyon there are additional side canyons to explore, a few more obstacles to surmount (all easier than the first falls), and eventually the canyon opens into a valley with pinyon pine and juniper as it reaches its headwaters beneath 6,701-foot Palmer Mountain. Bighorn sheep have been sighted in the upper canyon.

DAY HIKE: TITANOTHERE CANYON—GRAPEVINE MOUNTAINS

One-way length: 12 miles
Low and high elevations: 110 to 5,000 feet
Difficulty: moderately strenuous

This is a long hike at the southern end of the Grapevine Mountains with an elevation change of 4,700 feet. There are springs, fascinating geologic formations, and spectacular views of Death Valley. The canyon is named for a dinosaur—the Titanothere—whose fossil remains have been recovered from sediments in the Grapevine Mountains. The Titanothere looked something like a modern rhinoceros and became extinct some 40 million years ago.

Although the total hike is 12 miles, you can start at the top and hike downhill. You will, however, need to arrange for pickup in Death Valley or a car shuttle prior to beginning the hike.

The start of the hike is located 11 miles down Titus Canyon Road. The start of the "hiking route" can be reached by taking the one-way graded road 6.1 miles west of Beatty, Nevada, off Nevada Hwy 374. Make sure you don't drive too far down Titus Canyon Road—it's one way, so you can't drive back. The route begins just after the Titus Canyon Road crosses its first pass and drops down into the upper reaches of Titanothere Canyon. Go no more than a half mile or so beyond the pass and drop into the upper part of the canyon before you park. Begin hiking and head southwest down the main opening of the canyon.

You encounter an 80-foot waterfall shortly after starting down the canyon, but you can bypass it by climbing down a talus slope to the side of the drop. At one point the canyon narrows to less than 50 feet wide. Just beyond this point is Lost Man Spring—which is usually dry, but is marked by a few cottonwood trees. The final few miles of the hike are across Kit Fox Hills to Scotty's Castle Road.

DAY HIKE: TITUS CANYON—GRAPEVINE MOUNTAINS

One-way length: 2.1 miles
Low and high elevations: 900 to 1,200 feet
Difficulty: easy

Titus Canyon reminds one of the slot canyons of the Colorado Plateau. Water created this narrow canyon, cutting down along the Titus Fault through the limestone and dolomite that make up the canyon walls. A one-way road follows the fault down through the canyon, and most people drive through it. However, the lower narrows of the canyon are best enjoyed on foot. Rubbernecking is permitted. At one point the canyon narrows to 15 feet, while the canyon walls soar hundreds of feet above you. After 2.1 miles the canyon opens into a broader valley, although still enclosed by high walls. Most people turn around at this point, but for a longer hike you can continue up the road through the second narrows, which begins another 0.3 mile up the road. This hike is about 1.8 miles long.

To find the trailhead, drive 11.9 miles north on Hwy 374 toward Scotty's Castle from its junction with Hwy 190. There is a signed dirt road heading east toward the mountains. Follow this road 2.7 miles up an alluvial fan to the parking area at the mouth of Titus Canyon. Beyond this point the road is one way—coming down Titus Canyon.

DAY HIKE: COTTONWOOD CANYON—
COTTONWOOD MOUNTAINS

One-way length: 1.1 miles
Low and high elevations: 2,800 to 3,000 feet
Difficulty: easy

Cottonwood Canyon harbors three lovely springs and cottonwood-lined oases—hence its name. The canyon is also one of the longest in the Cottonwood Mountains and can be hiked for nearly 20 miles for those with the willpower and skill to scramble up a trailless canyon.

You can drive much of the way up Cottonwood Canyon. The road from Stovepipe Wells to the beginning of the roadless section of the canyon is 19.2 miles. To find your way to the trailhead, look for Cottonwood Road, which begins at the northwestern corner of Stovepipe Wells Campground. The first 8.6 miles of this road are passable to most 2wd vehicles. Once you reach Cottonwood Wash, a high-clearance 4wd vehicle is recommended. You can always park and hike from this point or try using a mountain bike (although the sandy sections are difficult to negotiate on a bike). Almost immediately on entering the canyon you pass through a narrows, then 10.8 miles from Stovepipe Wells you come to the junction with Marble Canyon. Continue up Cottonwood Canyon, passing through a second narrows to the end of the road. If you park at the mouth of the canyon, just hiking to the second narrows makes for a long day hike. From the end of the road to the first spring is 1.1 miles up the canyon. There is usually flowing water here. Camping is permitted, but you must be more than 200 feet from the springs. If you are inclined, there are two more springs—Middle and Cottonwood. Cottonwood Spring is 4 miles from the end of the road.

For those with more energy, an overnight backpack loop is possible by ascending Cottonwood Canyon from the junction of Marble and Cottonwood Canyons. It is 9.5 miles to the lower spring from the junction of the canyons—most of it hiking up the "road." From the lower spring you travel upcanyon to Cottonwood Spring (usually reliable water) and then to Deadhorse Canyon. You follow Deadhorse Canyon to Marble Canyon and then travel 8.4 miles down Marble Canyon to the starting point. There are beautiful, narrow canyons and the potential of seeing bighorn sheep along this route.

> **DAY HIKE: MARBLE CANYON—COTTONWOOD MOUNTAINS**
> One-way length: 4.8 miles
> Low and high elevations: 1,790 to 3,110 feet
> Difficulty: moderate

Colorful Marble Canyon with its deep narrows and more petroglyphs than any other part of the park makes for a wonderful day hike into the heart of the Cottonwood Mountains. To reach the trailhead from Stovepipe Wells, head west on Cottonwood Creek Road (just west of the campground). It is drivable for 8.4 miles by 2wd vehicle to the edge of Cottonwood Wash. Beyond this point it is best to have a 4wd high-clearance vehicle. Another 2.3 miles up the canyon brings you to the junction of Cottonwood and Marble Canyons. It is easy to miss Marble Canyon. At this point Marble Canyon Road takes off to the northwest (right) and can be driven another 2.6 miles to a road closure.

Marble Canyon is only 6 feet wide at the road closure and resembles, in some ways, the narrows of Titus Canyon. The canyon remains narrow for about 1 mile. At the end is a huge granite boulder—brought down by repeated flash floods from Hunter Mountain. After the first narrows there is a second narrows where over the centuries flash floods have worn a smooth-walled cavity into the dolomite. Beyond the second narrows the canyon opens up into a wash, although there are occasional constrictions so that every turn of the canyon brings new vistas.

At the 3.5-mile point, the canyon narrows and black-and-white sedimentary rocks line the canyon. At 4.8 miles from the starting point you come to Deadhorse Canyon, which enters from the left (or the southwest). This junction has a number of good campsite possibilities for those willing to haul water in for an overnight stay.

> **DAY HIKE: GROTTO CANYON—PANAMINT RANGE**
> One-way length: 2 miles
> Low and high elevations: 260 to 800 feet
> Difficulty: easy

Grotto Canyon, as its name implies, contains a number of alcoves that were carved by the erosive power of water. Grotto Canyon is just north of Mosaic Canyon on Tucki Mountain south of Stovepipe Wells. To find the trailhead, drive south from Stovepipe Wells on Hwy 190. In about 2.4 miles there is a signed road on your right. The road is best left to those in 4wd vehicles, although some 2wd vehicles manage to get about 1 mile up the road before stopping. If you choose to park on the highway, it's about a 1.1-mile walk to the canyon mouth.

The walk from the highway up the road leads up an alluvial fan. The first grotto is reached at 1.8 miles. After the more open canyon, the grotto provides some welcome shade. The passage narrows and ends at a pair of dry waterfalls. You can climb beyond the falls on a cairn-lined path that begins just before the falls, and continue up the canyon a short distance to another set of dry falls, which is usually the end of the line for most people.

Sunset on Telegraph Peak from Wildrose Peak, Panamint Range, Death Valley National Park.

DAY HIKE: HANAUPAH CANYON—PANAMINT RANGE
One-way length: 1.2 miles
Low and high elevations: 3,680 to 4,320 feet
Difficulty: moderate

Hanaupah Canyon drains into the eastern face of the Panamint Range just below Telescope Peak. It is possible to use this route to hike from Death Valley to the top of Telescope Peak, passing lush perennial streamside vegetation, waterfalls, and granite outcrops.

To find the trailhead from Furnace Creek Inn, drive south on Badwater Road 7.1 miles. Turn onto the dirt West Side Road. Go south for 10.7 miles to the second dirt road heading west to the mountains. This is Hanaupah Canyon Road. Go 5 miles up the alluvial fan to the mouth of the canyon and park before the road drops into the wash. From here the road requires a 4wd high-clearance vehicle to negotiate it and continues another 4.5 miles up the south fork. Walk or drive up the road 1.5 miles to where the canyon splits. From here one can hike at least 3 miles up the middle fork or continue up the south fork another 3 miles to road's end.

Along the banks of the south fork of Hanaupah Creek are wild grape, willows, coyote melon, and cliff rose. You reach Hanaupah Spring in 0.7 mile. It flows from a fault in the side of the canyon, and water drips down the cliff face covered with a luxuriant growth of ferns and mosses. Just 0.2 mile beyond the spring, the canyon narrows. There are several more small springs that flow from the side of the canyon and cascade down into the wash. The vegetation can be quite thick, and bushwhacking is required to get through this section of the canyon. Then at 1.2 miles you reach a 25-foot falls nestled in a deep grotto. This is usually as far as most people hike. Really dedicated hikers have continued up the canyon, passing several more narrows and more waterfalls, and ascended the steep face of Telescope Ridge. This is a grueling climb.

> ### DAY HIKE: HUNGRY BILL'S RANCH, JOHNSON CANYON—PANAMINT RANGE
> One-way length: 1.8 miles
> Low and high elevations: 3,960 to 8,070 feet
> Difficulty: moderately strenuous

This hike offers a little of everything, and depending on your mood can either be a short jaunt, a more strenuous day hike, or a multiday overnight backpack trip into the heart of the Panamint Range. En route you pass old ranch ruins and springs, and are treated to wonderful views.

To find the trailhead from Furnace Creek Ranch, go 7.1 miles south on Badwater Road to West Side Road. Go southwest on this dirt road for 21.7 miles to Johnson Canyon Road. Turn west and go 10.5 miles up Johnson Canyon to the road's end at Wilson Spring. A high-clearance vehicle is recommended, particularly for the last 3.5 miles.

William Johnson established a homestead on Johnson Creek, after the discovery in 1873 of a rich silver deposit in Surprise Canyon that drew more than 1,000 residents to the remote upper Surprise Canyon basin—where Panamint City was founded. In response to the growing market on the other side of the mountains, Johnson developed some irrigated, terraced gardens where he grew corn, beans, melons, squash, and planted a nut and fruit orchard. A devastating flood in Surprise Canyon and declining ore quality led to the abandonment of Panamint City before the farm could begin to reap a profit. Later, a Shoshone named Hungry Bill took over the ranch and fruit trees, lending his name to the canyon as well.

The road at the end of Johnson Canyon ends at Wilson Spring, a lovely spot with cottonwood and willow. From the spring you work your way up the wash, following "use" trails and crossing back and forth across the canyon. At 0.5 mile you have to climb around some rock spires on the left. Continue upstream to the lower ranch site at 4,600 feet, which is reached after hiking 1.5 miles. Here you find rock ruins, fruit trees, and water. Don't turn around yet. Continue upstream another 0.3 mile to the main ranch area, where there are more fruit trees, more rock ruins, and a large open area with great views of the Panamint Range.

Most people turn back at the ranch; however, if you're really motivated and have the time you can continue up to Panamint Pass. From the ranch, the pass is another 3.2 miles and climbs more than 3,000 feet. You will be bushwhacking all the way. For the last mile or so there is an old route with switchbacks that takes you to the pass. If a pickup can be arranged in advance, a longer two- to three-night stay is possible by continuing over Panamint Pass and hiking down Surprise Canyon to Chris Wicht Camp. There is water here and there along this entire route, making it an attractive longer trek.

12 El Paso Mountains Wilderness

Evening light on Freeman Wash, El Paso Mountains Wilderness. The southern end of the Sierra Nevada is visible in the distance.

LOCATION: Kern County; 6 miles southwest of Ridgecrest, California

SIZE: 23,780 acres

ELEVATION RANGE: 2,800 to 5,259 feet

ADMINISTRATION: BLM Ridgecrest Resource Area Office

MAPS: Desert Access Guide Ridgecrest #4, Red Mountain #7; AAA Kern County

The El Paso Mountains mark a major geologic transition zone. The southern edge of the mountains are bounded by the Garlock Fault, one of the major faults that defines southern California's geology. The Garlock Fault runs 150 miles from Death Valley to the town of Gorman, defining the El Paso Mountains, the southern Sierra Nevada, and Tehachapi Mountains along the way. The south side of the fault has been displaced eastward 30 miles. Labyrinthlike badlands, rugged mesas, and rolling hills characterize this wildland. Black Mountain (elevation 5,259 feet) at the southern edge of the wilderness is the highest point. Red Rock Canyon State Park borders the area on the southwest.

The El Paso Mountains contain some of the oldest nonmarine fossils in the West. These 58-million-year old stream and lake deposits contain fossils of early camels and other horselike animals.

In addition, the El Paso Mountains contain one of the most significant concentrations of archeological sites in

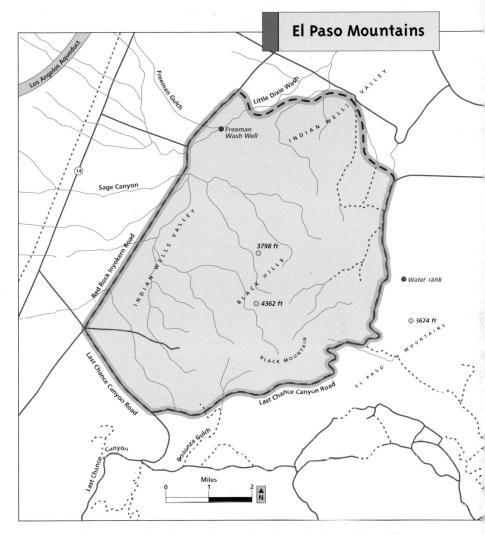

El Paso Mountains

the region. These sites are listed on the National Register of Historic Places. There are extensive village sites with house rings, rock shelters, processing sites, quarries, and numerous petroglyphs and rock alignments.

Another special feature of this wilderness is its abundance of raptors. The El Paso Mountains support one of the densest known breeding concentrations of golden eagles, prairie falcons, and other raptors in the California desert.

Most of the wilderness is dominated by creosote bush, although there are some concentrations of Joshua tree on the western side of the area.

ACCESS

The Red Rock Inyokern Road, a washboard dirt road, is the western boundary of this wilderness area. The road is easily accessed from Hwy 14 north of Red Rock Canyon State Park. The road crosses Freeman Wash, which heads west into the wilderness. The wash makes a good hiking route to follow into the hills.

13 Fish Slough – Volcanic Tablelands Proposed Wilderness

Pictographs along Volcanic Tablelands near Bishop.

LOCATION: Inyo County; 5 miles north of Bishop, California

SIZE: 25,000 acres

ELEVATION RANGE: 4,382 to 5,800 feet

ADMINISTRATION: BLM Bishop Resource Area Office

MAP: AAA Eastern Sierra Nevada

The Fish Slough-Volcanic Tablelands proposed wilderness takes in two wilderness study areas north of Bishop, California. The Diablo Mine Road separates these roadless units.

The proposed wilderness lies on the western margin of the Basin and Range Province and at the southern edge of the Volcanic Tablelands. The Volcanic Tablelands extend northward from Bishop to the Lake Crowley region and include lands administered by both the BLM and the Inyo National Forest Service.

The Volcanic Tablelands were created 700,000 years ago by the eruption of the huge Long Valley volcano. Cinders and hot gas combined with rhyolitic ash (now known as Bishop tuff) to create a broad, slightly sloping landscape that subsequently has been carved by erosion. Topography is rolling, with occasional deep canyons like Owens River Gorge to the west of the proposed wilderness. The views of both the Sierra Nevada and the White Mountains from within the wilderness are outstanding. There are a number of parallel cliffs created by faulting. In addition to the scenic variety there are fumarolic mounds. The overall pink-reddish color of the rock is quite striking.

Vegetation consists primarily of sagebrush plus shadscale, spiny hopsage, and even a few cholla cactus. Wildlife include a substantial mule deer herd and sage grouse population.

On the eastern edge of the proposed wilderness lies Fish Slough. Although not within the proposed wilderness boundaries, it is a significant natural attraction. This natural desert oasis is the last, intact natural spring in Owens Valley. Rain and snow soak the porous Bishop tuff, which acts as a natural reservoir for water. This water eventually surfaces at Fish Slough. The water attracts a wide variety of wildlife, including great blue heron, American bittern, and cinnamon teal. The Fish Slough region also boasts the highest raptor population in Owens Valley, including golden eagle, prairie falcon, and northern harrier.

The waters of Fish Slough are home to several endangered species, including the Owens Valley pupfish, Owens tui chub, and Fish Slough snail. The Fish Slough milk vetch, a rare plant, also occurs here. The Fish Slough and adjacent portions of the Volcanic Tablelands are now managed by the BLM as an Area of Critical Environmental Concern (ACEC).

There are also a number of sites of archeological interest, including some outstanding petroglyphs. Numerous rings of stone, obsidian chips, and other cultural features abound.

ACCESS

From Bishop drive north on Hwy 6 for 1.5 miles. Bear left on Five Bridges Road. Go 2.5 miles to a three-way junction. The right fork leads to Fish Slough and the eastern border of the proposed wilderness. The middle fork leads to Casa Diablo and splits the two roadless lands in half. Either road provides easy access to the proposed wilderness.

Fish Slough-Volcanic Tablelands

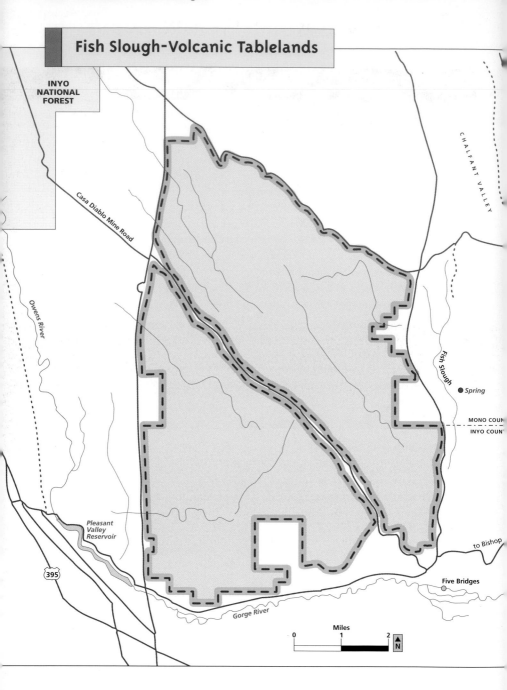

INYO
NATIONAL
FOREST

Casa Diablo Mine Road

CHALFANT VALLEY

Owens River

Fish Slough

● Spring

MONO COUN
INYO COUN

Pleasant
Valley
Reservoir

395

Gorge River

to Bishop

Five Bridges

Miles

0   1   2

N

Funeral Mountains Wilderness `14`

Funeral Mountains Wilderness.

The Funeral Mountains are largely located within Death Valley National Park, but the most southeasterly portion of the range is managed by the BLM. The range runs from Furnace Creek on the south to Boundary Canyon, which marks the northern break from the Grapevine Mountains. The Funeral Mountains are the lowest mountains bordering Death Valley; 6,703-foot Pyramid Peak (outside of Funeral Mountains Wilderness) is the highest summit in the range. In the rain shadow of the much higher Panamint Range to the west, the Funeral Mountains are among the driest mountains within Death Valley National Park. Yet despite the overall dryness of the range, the largest springs in Death Valley are located in the Funeral Mountains, including Travertine Springs, which produces 2,000 gallons a minute. Most of the flow from the larger springs is appropriated for the Furnace Creek Resort and other development in the valley.

LOCATION: Inyo County; 3 miles northwest of Death Valley Junction

SIZE: 28,110 acres

ELEVATION RANGE: 2,200 to 4,950 feet

ADMINISTRATION: BLM Barstow Resource Area Office

MAPS: Desert Access Guide Amargosa #3; AAA Death Valley National Park

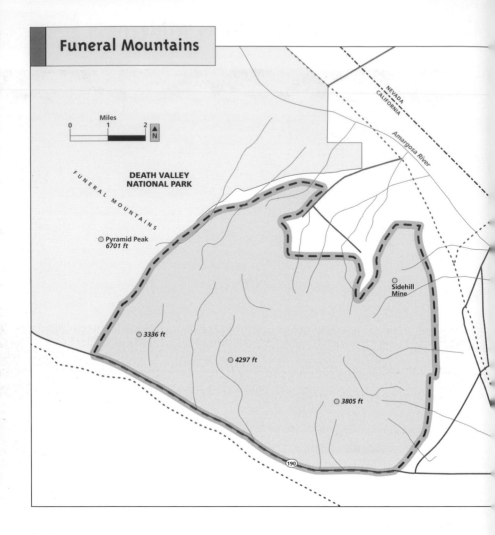

Funeral Mountains

Miles
0   1   2

DEATH VALLEY
NATIONAL PARK

FUNERAL MOUNTAINS

Pyramid Peak
6701 ft

Sidehill
Mine

3336 ft

4297 ft

3805 ft

NEVADA
CALIFORNIA

Amargosa River

190

This lonely, little used wilderness lies immediately north of Hwy 190, which forms the southern boundary. Considering the easy access and the abundance of limestone peaks and numerous cleft canyons, one would expect more visitation. The highest peak, Bat Mountain, rises to just under 1 mile in height. The colorful Red Amphitheater Valley in the northwest corner of the wilderness is a geologically enclosed valley.

Vegetation consists of creosote bush, burrobush, spiny hopsage, and Mormon tea. Bighorn sheep are known to roam the area.

ACCESS

The best access is from Hwy 190. Just park off the road and walk north.

Golden Valley Wilderness

15

View of Golden Valley Wilderness from Klinker Mountain.

Golden Valley Wilderness consists of two mountain ranges with a valley—Golden Valley—in between. Dome Mountain, at 4,974 feet, is the highest summit. The higher Lava Mountains are to the west. Cut by several steep-walled canyons, these mountains consist of multicolored rock formations. The Almond Mountains lie along the southeastern corner. Under the right conditions of winter rain and warmth, wildflower displays in Golden Valley can be spectacular and are among the best in the entire California desert. Most of the year, however, you have to settle for the less striking vegetative cover, which consists mostly of creosote bush and Joshua tree. The entire area is inhabited by the Mojave ground squirrel, a species considered rare in the state of California.

The area was used by prehistoric native American cultures. Some archeological remains are associated with Bedrock Spring on the northern corner of the wilderness,

LOCATION: San Bernardino County; 10 miles southeast of Ridgecrest, California

SIZE: 37,700 acres

ELEVATION RANGE: 3,000 to 5,000 feet

ADMINISTRATION: BLM Ridgecrest Resource Area Office

MAPS: Desert Access Guide Red Mountain #7; AAA San Bernardino County

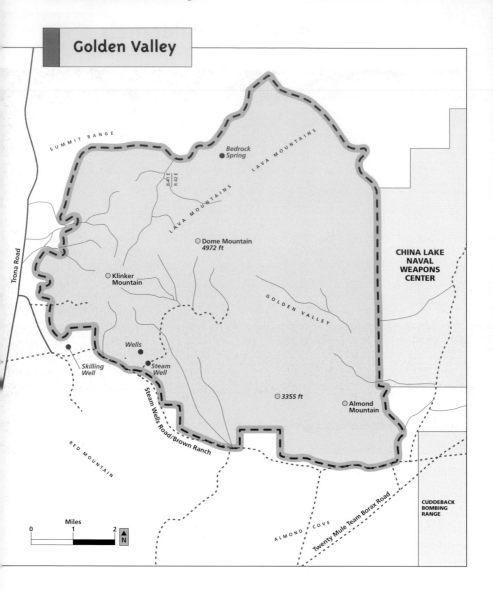

Golden Valley

and an ancient quarry for chalcedony, a rock used in the manufacture of stone weapons, is also evident.

ACCESS

From Ridgecrest head south on Hwy 395 for 17 miles. One mile north of Red Mountain, turn on to Trona Road. Head east to Steam Wells Road. The wilderness lies to the north of the road.

Grass Valley Wilderness 16

*View of Grass Valley Wilderness and peaks
in adjacent Golden Valley Wilderness.*

There are other values to wilderness besides scenery, and Grass Valley is one that definitely isn't set aside for its breathtaking landscape. The name Grass Valley may conjure up images of waving fields of golden prairie, but don't be misled. Most of this area is relatively flat and covered with creosote bush with an occasional Joshua tree to break up the monotony. Grass Valley covers three-quarters of the area, with only a few hills on the fringes of the wilderness. In the rare wet years there is indeed grass, and even an abundance of flowers.

The old Barstow-Red Mountain Road bisects the wilderness, making access easy but reducing any sense of solitude. Given the low, open vegetation and nearly featureless surface of the valley, getting beyond the sight of the road and any intrusions is not easy. But, on the other hand, this place is not overrun with visitors, so it's unlikely you will encounter others.

LOCATION:
San Bernardino County; 20 miles southeast of Ridgecrest, California

SIZE: 31,695 acres

ELEVATION RANGE:
3,000 to 3,847 feet

ADMINISTRATION:
BLM Ridgecrest Resource Area Office

MAPS: Desert Access Guide Red Mountain #7; AAA San Bernardino County

Other "unnatural" features include some fencing and stock watering troughs. (You wouldn't think that a place called Grass Valley would be ungrazed by cows, would you?) Other cultural features of an older nature are found in the area, including evidence of an aboriginal settlement more than 3,000 years old.

The area also is home to the Mojave ground squirrel and desert tortoise—two relatively rare species.

The flat terrain makes this a good wilderness area to take children for a desert walk. Don't let the lack of soaring peaks keep you from enjoying this place. Look down and enjoy the patterns of rock and sand, and scan the spacious bowl of sky.

The wilderness is immediately west of the China Lake Naval Weapons Center, so beware of wandering too far eastward.

ACCESS

To reach the wilderness, follow Hwy 395 south from Ridgecrest for 17 miles. Just north of Red Mountain turn on to Trona Road and follow it eastward to Steam Wells Road to Granite Wells Road. In about 16 miles it intersects Twenty Mule Team Road. The wilderness lies just south of this intersection.

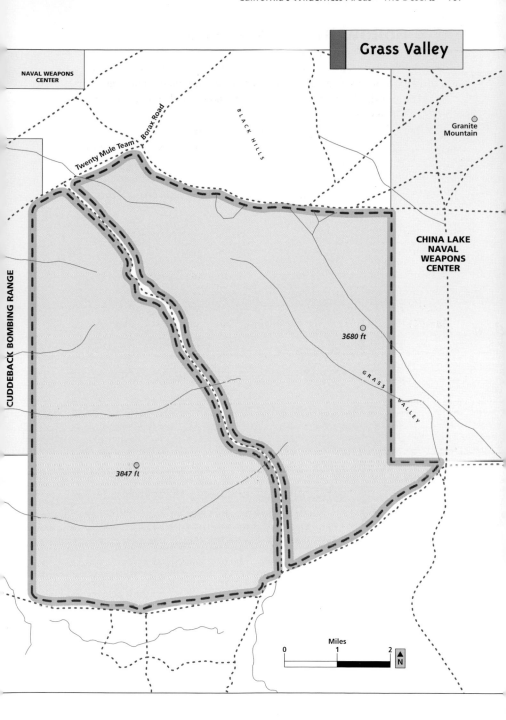

Grass Valley

NAVAL WEAPONS
CENTER

Borax Road

Twenty Mule Team

BLACK HILLS

Granite
Mountain

CHINA LAKE
NAVAL
WEAPONS
CENTER

3680 ft

GRASS VALLEY

CUDDEBACK BOMBING RANGE

3847 ft

Miles

0   1   2

N

17 Hollow Hills Wilderness

Hollow Hills Wilderness.

LOCATION:
San Bernardino County;
4 miles north of Baker,
California

SIZE: 22,240 acres

ELEVATION RANGE:
300 to 3,792 feet

ADMINISTRATION:
BLM Barstow Resource
Area Office

MAPS: Desert Access
Guide Irwin #8, New
York Mountains #9;
AAA San Bernardino
County

Located just off the interstate, this is a wilderness one can visit for even a brief stretch of the legs while cruising between Los Angeles and Las Vegas. Hollow Hills Wilderness consists of gently-sloping bajadas and low hills that angle toward Silver Dry Lake. The old, abandoned Tonopah and Tidewater Railroad lies just inside the wilderness. The slopes are mostly covered with creosote bush. With no trails and no visible barriers to overcome, this is a place that challenges or poses limitations on recreation, depending on your perspective.

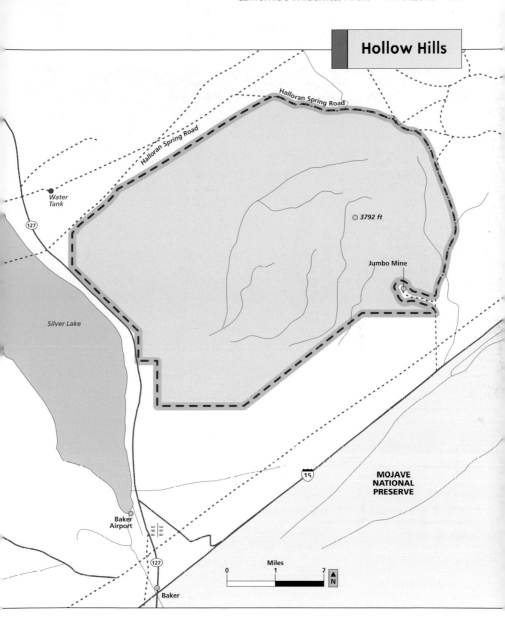

ACCESS

Travel 4 miles north from Baker on Hwy 127, which becomes the western border of the area. Take off from the highway and head east. There is also a power line access road some 6 miles north of Baker that heads east along the entire northern border of the wilderness. This route provides greater access to the higher elevations, which are generally on the eastern edge of the wilderness.

18 Ibex Hills Wilderness

Looking toward Sheephead Mountain in the northern end of Ibex Hills Wilderness.

LOCATION: Inyo County; 3 miles southwest of Shoshone, California

SIZE: 26,460 acres

ELEVATION RANGE: 3,000 to 4,752 feet

ADMINISTRATION: BLM Barstow Resource Area Office

MAPS: Desert Access Guide Dumont/Clark Mountain #6; AAA Death Valley National Park

This wilderness borders the southeastern corner of Death Valley National Park, just southeast of the small settlement of Shoshone. Saddle Peak Hills Wilderness lies just to the south.

The Ibex Hills form the north-south divide between the Black Mountains on the west and Greenwater Valley to the east. The "hills" should more appropriately be called mountains due to their ruggedness. These mountains are made up of colorful volcanic and metamorphic rock aligned in horizontal bands. The highest peaks, such as Sheephead Mountain on the north and 4,752-foot Ibex Peak to the south, lie along the divide. The terrain is open and covered with typical desert vegetation, including creosote bush and assorted cactus. The area is a historic desert bighorn sheep habitat, although it is unclear if any exist today.

Much of the area is part of a historic mining district. Evidence of past mining activity abounds at all the major access sites. Native Americans used to collect talc in this area. Later mining efforts produced gold, copper, lead, zinc, and silver. There is one patented mining claim on the border of the wilderness. Some of the old mining roads provide access to the wilderness today.

There are no formal trails in the wilderness, although several now-closed, old mining roads and tracks offer potential as "trails." Due to the open terrain, cross-country hiking is easy. When combined with the designated wilderness in the adjacent Death Valley National Park, which forms the western border of Ibex Hills Wilderness, long multiday hikes are possible.

ACCESS

The wilderness can be accessed in several places from Hwy 127 south of Shoshone. The southern edge is about 44 miles north of Baker and I-15. Starting at Shoshone go south 3 miles on Hwy 127 until you come to the right turn (west) for Greenwater Valley Road. This gravel road, which heads northwest, eventually connects to Hwy 178. Go approximately 1 mile. For the next 7 miles the road forms the eastern border of the wilderness. Simply take off hiking west from the road across the bajada to the base of the hills. An old, now-closed mining road heads west from Greenwater Valley Road to Sheephead Pass on the Ibex Hills divide. You can gain access to this road by driving some 4 miles or so up Greenwater Valley Road. When the road crosses Greenwater Valley Wash, go another half mile or so and watch for a closed dirt road. Take that road and head southwest 1.5 miles before turning west. This leads to the Sheephead Pass "trail." It is possible to continue on across Ibex Hills by way of Sheephead Pass and Bradbury Wash west of the divide to Hwy 78 in Death Valley National Park. Such a hike would require a pickup or shuttle.

Another access point further south is the 4.8-mile dirt road heading west from Hwy 127 to Paddy's Pride Mine, which penetrates deeper into the wilderness. The turnoff lies 1 mile south of the intersection of Hwy 17 and Old Spanish Highway and the turn for Tecopa. The road dead ends 4.8 miles from the highway. The wilderness lies along both sides of this road.

A third access, on the southern border of the wilderness, takes off to the west from Hwy 127 a half-mile north of Ibex Pass. This 3.6-mile dirt road leads to Giant Mine and the wilderness border.

Ibex Hills

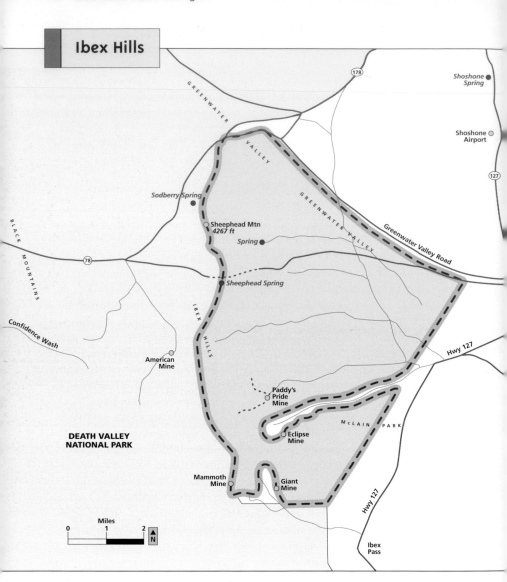

Shoshone Spring

Shoshone Airport

178

127

GREENWATER VALLEY

Sodberry Spring

Sheephead Mtn 4267 ft

Spring

GREENWATER VALLEY

Greenwater Valley Road

BLACK MOUNTAINS

78

Sheephead Spring

IBEX HILLS

Confidence Wash

American Mine

Paddy's Pride Mine

Hwy 127

DEATH VALLEY NATIONAL PARK

Eclipse Mine

McLAIN PARK

Mammoth Mine

Giant Mine

Hwy 127

Miles
0   1   2
N

Ibex Pass

Inyo Mountains Wilderness 19

Looking north along the crest of the Inyo Mountains.

Inyo Mountains Wilderness is sandwiched between Death Valley National Park, which lies to the east, and Owens Valley and the Sierra Nevada, which lie to the west. Views of the Sierra Nevada from the wilderness, particularly at sunrise, are impressive. The northern third of the range is administered by the Inyo National Forest, whereas the southern two thirds is under BLM administration.

Inyo Mountains Wilderness, at 205,000 acres, is one of the largest wilderness areas designated in the California Desert Bill. Although, with a few minor road closures, a wilderness of more than 300,000 acres could be established. An even more ambitious goal is the closure of Saline Valley Road, and the creation of a million-acre-plus desert wilderness stretching from the Inyos to the Last Chance Range in the northern portion of Death Valley National Park.

This wilderness is one of the most dramatic in the California desert. Rising from 1,000 feet in the dry, hot

LOCATION: Inyo County; 5 miles east of Lone Pine, California, and east of Death Valley National Park

SIZE: 205,020 acres

ELEVATION RANGE: 1,000 to 11,125 feet

ADMINISTRATION: BLM Bishop Area Resource Area Office, Inyo National Forest

MAPS: Desert Access Guide Eureka/Saline #1; AAA East Side of Sierra Nevada, Inyo National Forest

Saline Valley on the east, the fault-block Inyo Mountains soar to more than 11,000 feet in less than 6.5 miles, creating one of the most spectacular desert ranges in the state. Waucoba Mountain, at 11,125 feet, is the highest point in the wilderness. Several other mountains reach above 11,000 feet, including Keynot Peak and Mount Inyo. Most of the mountains consist of sedimentary rock like limestone, with occasional granitic outcrops. These mountains are steep, with spectacular cliffs and rock exposures, and deep, nearly inaccessible canyons. However, once you gain the crest of the range, the terrain is relatively gentle and rolling.

Lower elevations are cloaked in creosote bush, shadscale, and big sagebrush, whereas the higher elevations have limited forest cover of juniper, pinyon pine, and limber pine. Some of the densest and most extensive forests of the rare bristlecone pine in California grow along the mountain crest.

Outcrops of limestone support a number of rare plant assemblages. Rare plants noted for the Inyos include *Caulostraminia jageri, Eriogonum microtecum* var. *panamintense, Erigonum eremicola, Perityle inyoensis,* and *Phacelia amabilis.*

Due to their height, winter snows provide a source of water for a number of perennial streams that cascade down narrow, steep canyons to the valleys on either side of the range. Some of these streams have a limited amount of riparian vegetation, including cottonwood trees and willows, particularly on the eastside canyons. Ironically, the water often poses a problem for canyon explorers, creating insurmountable waterfalls that form barriers to upstream travel.

The Inyos harbor herds of bighorn sheep and mule deer, plus coyote and mountain lion. An unexpected species found here is the Inyo Mountain salamander, a rare species associated with the riparian zones of some of the canyons including Willow, McElvoy, Hunter, Beverage, Keynot, and Craig.

Evidence of old mining efforts are visible throughout the wilderness. Deposits of gold, silver, lead, zinc, copper, tungsten, molybdenum, and talc are all known to occur in the range. Many of the dirt roads that penetrate the range lead to abandoned mining sites. One of the most spectacular remnants of this era is a tram in the southern part of the wilderness that was built in 1913 to haul salt from the Saline Valley over the Inyo Mountains to Owens Valley. Considered the steepest in the world, the tram went up Daisy Canyon near Salt Lake in the Saline Valley, and over to Swansea near Owens Lake. The salt was harvested from Salt Lake and was so pure that it required no further refining before sale.

Due to its ruggedness, access is extremely limited. Solitude is easily obtained. Although the lower elevations are accessible year round, travel at higher elevations is restricted in the winter due to snow. The snow, however, does open up many overnight camping possibilities, particularly later in the spring. By melting snow as a water source, unlimited possibilities exist for longer trips among the higher elevation basins or rolling crest of the range.

ACCESS

You can reach the wilderness from both sides of the range. Saline Valley Road in Death Valley National Park is easily traversed in a 2wd vehicle and provides access to eastside canyons. However, you do need to cross high passes (up to 7,000 feet) at either end of the road to enter Saline Valley. In winter the road may be blocked temporarily by snow, particularly the shaded portions of Grapevine Canyon at the south end of the valley. Keep in mind that winter storms can trap you in Saline Valley for days until the roads are opened by vehicular traffic tramping down the snow and melting—so, plan accordingly. From Saline Valley Road one can follow most of the canyon bottoms at least a short way into the mountains, although most (including Hunter Canyon, Beveridge Canyon, Craig Canyon, and McElvoy Canyon) have waterfalls or steep pitches that require scrambling skills and discourage all but the most determined hiker/climber from continuing.

Hunter Canyon is a good one to explore. Its abundance of water makes this canyon seem almost tropical—at least for the desert—with ferns, mosses, and lots of willows. Almost immediately on entering the canyon, however, you encounter two back-to-back waterfalls that are difficult but not impossible to traverse. A short distance beyond these two waterfalls there is a third one that stops most people from further exploration.

An old, historic mining trail, sometimes called the Bighorn Mine Trail, goes up the slopes of Little Hunter Canyon immediately south of Hunter Canyon. It is steep, difficult to follow, but for hikers with good map-reading skills and plenty of water, the trail offers access to the upper part of Hunter Canyon at Bighorn Spring and can even be followed to the crest of the range. Numerous burro trails complicate route finding, but the BLM has marked the path with occasional cairns. The views are terrific.

The trail begins at the end of Hunter Canyon Road, beyond the mining ruins. It crosses the wash and continues up the south side of Little Hunter Canyon to its headwaters at around 5,000 feet. It continues to a ridge and drops down into Hunter Canyon at Bighorn Spring. Bighorn Mine is to the north above the spring. This is remote country.

For the really adventurous it is possible to make a loop trip out of Little Hunter and Hunter Canyons. Go up the Bighorn Mine Trail via Little Hunter Canyon and drop into Bighorn Spring at 5,040 feet in Hunter Canyon. From there, descend Hunter Canyon back to Saline Valley. This requires a number of rappels around waterfalls. Reportedly, the first obstacle is encountered at 3,200 feet and requires a rappel of 125 feet followed by four other shorter rappels.

Mazourka Canyon Road is the best access point to the high country on the west side. High clearance, but non-4wd vehicles can usually make it the first 18 miles to Badger Flat, which at 9,000 feet makes for a good base camp for day hikes up to the crest. Just head across country in the direction of the crest. As you gain elevation you soon leave behind the pinyon and juniper forest, and eventually break out into bristlecone pine woodland. The open forest is conducive to off-trail hiking.

Although outside of the wilderness, the views of the eastern face of the Sierra Nevada from the electronics site on Mazourka Peak make for a worthwhile side trip. The road beyond Badger Flat is steep in places, but still passable in a high-clearance 2wd vehicle if the road is dry. Those with 4wd can continue on toward Blue Bell Mine, which provides a good jumping-off point for the hike

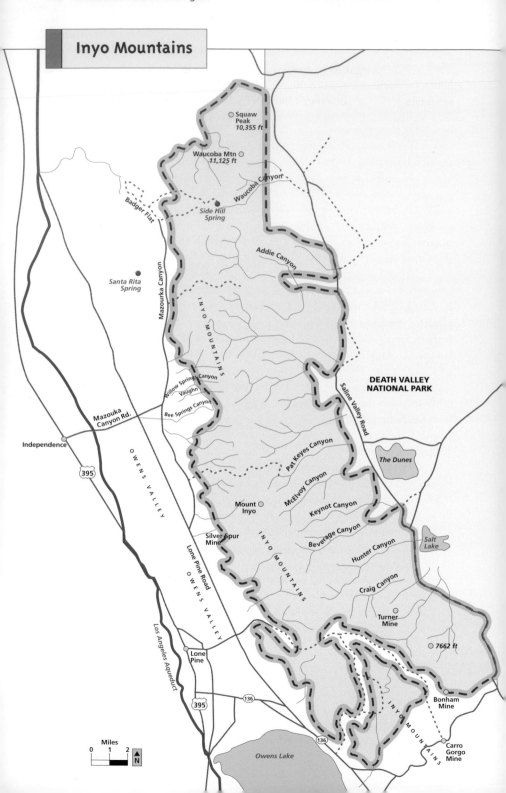

Inyo Mountains

Squaw Peak
10,355 ft

Waucoba Mtn
11,125 ft

Waucoba Canyon

Badger Flat

Side Hill Spring

Addie Canyon

Santa Rita Spring

Mazourka Canyon

INYO MOUNTAINS

DEATH VALLEY NATIONAL PARK

Willow Springs Canyon

Vaughn

Saline Valley Road

Mazouka Canyon Rd.

Bee Springs Canyon

Independence

395

OWENS VALLEY

Pat Keyes Canyon

The Dunes

McElvoy Canyon

Mount Inyo

Keynot Canyon

Silver Spur Mine

INYO MOUNTAINS

Beverage Canyon

Hunter Canyon

Salt Lake

Lone Pine Road

OWENS VALLEY

Craig Canyon

Turner Mine

7662 ft

Los Angeles Aqueduct

Lone Pine

INYO MOUNTAINS

Bonham Mine

395

136

Carro Gorgo Mine

Miles
0   1   2

N

136

Owens Lake

up 11,125-foot Waucoba Mountain. Old jeep roads (now closed) make for excellent hiking trails that take one nearly to the summit.

Old mining roads and pack trails provide the majority of unmaintained hike access, although cross-country travel is possible in many areas—if you're half mountain goat. The Lonesome Miner Trail is a 40-mile route that crosses the range from Reward in Owens Valley to Hunter Canyon on the Saline Valley side of the mountains.

Mount Inyo is also a "popular" destination, keeping in mind that popular in the Inyos is a relative term. The best approach is out of Lone Pine. Go north from Lone Pine less than 1 mile and turn east on the paved Lone Pine Road. After approximately 3 miles the road turns north and parallels an old railroad right-of-way. Continue north on this road for 5 miles until you come to a good dirt road heading east up the mountain slope toward the Silver Spur Mines (marked on the AAA Death Valley National Park Map). Drive as far as practical, then hike. It is about 6,000 to 7,000 feet up and 5 miles or less in distance (depending on where you park) to Inyo Peak. Overnight campers can stay at Bedsprings Camp (no water—bring your own) at 9,500 feet in the saddle between Mount Inyo and Keynot Peak. Once on the ridgeline you can scramble along the crest to the summit of either Mount Inyo or nearby Keynot Peak—both are higher than 11,000 feet.

20 Kingston Range Wilderness

Joshua tree frames the high ridgeline of the Kingston Range Wilderness. Some 17 miles of the crest is above 6,000 feet.

LOCATION:
San Bernardino County;
50 miles northeast of
Baker, California

SIZE: 209,608 acres

ELEVATION RANGE:
1,500 to 7,323 feet

ADMINISTRATION:
BLM Barstow Resource
Area Office

MAPS: BLM Desert
Access Guide Dumont/
Clark Mountain #6,
Irwin #8, New York
Mountains #9; AAA San
Bernardino County

The dramatic turrets and towers of Kingston Range Wilderness float like an island above the desert, rising nearly a mile above the surrounding desert lowlands. Some 17 miles of the ridgeline on both sides of 7,323-foot Kingston Peak is continuously above 6,000 feet. South of Kingston Wash lies the Shadow Mountains unit of the wilderness. This area has lower, rounded peaks with interior canyons. The Amargosa River, one of only three perennial rivers in the California desert, flows across the northwestern corner of the wilderness in a canyon with permanent flowing water.

The wilderness lies just west of the Nevada-California state line and only 50 miles from Las Vegas. It consists of three separate units, and Valjean Valley Road separates the two largest tracts into two nearly equal parts. The highest and most rugged peaks are in the northern half.

The northern portion of the Kingston Range consists of an exposed, central granitic pluton surrounded by dolomite.

Minerals known to exist in these mountains include gold, silver, copper, and lead, as well as talc and gypsum. Old mining ruins and several abandoned ghost towns surround the wilderness.

The vertical relief and presence of year-round water at several perennial springs provide a wide variety of habitats. More than 500 plant species, including pinyon and juniper woodlands and an isolated stand of white fir (one of three locations for this species in the California desert) make this one of the most botanically diverse wildernesses in the California desert. Another unusual plant occurrence is the presence of Giant Nolina (*Nolina wolfii*), some as tall as 15 feet, near Tecopa Pass. The only other location for this species in California is Joshua Tree National Park. One of the densest stands of Joshua tree in California is found along Excelsor Mine Road on the eastern border of the wilderness. Other rare plants known to occur in the wilderness include pygmy agave, willow bricklebrush, Kingston bedstraw, Death Valley beard-tongue, and Kingston rock cinquefoil.

A herd of bighorn sheep inhabits the wilderness, relying upon tinajas (water-carved basins) in Sheep Tank Canyon. Ringtail, coyote, kit fox, and the Panamint chipmunk are found here. Several unusual wildlife sightings are also known in this wilderness, including Virginia's warbler and the hepatic tanager. The Kingston Range is also one of four California locations where the banded Gila monster has been sighted. The Amargosa vole, yellow-billed cuckoo, and least Bell's vireo—all threatened or endangered species—are recorded in the Amargosa River Canyon. The river itself supports the Amargosa pupfish, speckled dace, and Amargosa toad.

The water in the Amargosa River has attracted humans for at least 8,000 years. Archeological remains include metates, mortars, pottery, scrapers, and projectile points. More recently the Old Spanish Trail, a major route linking missions in California with those in New Mexico during the Spanish/Mexican occupation of the region, traversed the northern flank of Kingston Range and was traveled by traders, immigrants, and miners. A portion of the Tonopah and Tidewater Railroad, which was constructed in 1906 to transport borax from Death Valley, passes by the northern portion of the wilderness. Although the railroad ceased operation in 1940, the old railroad bed is still visible.

ACCESS

From Baker head east on I-15 for 26 miles to the exit for Kingston Road. Go north 14 miles to Excelsor Mine Road, which forms the eastern border of the wilderness and provides numerous access points to the wilderness.

As with most desert wildernesses, there are no formal trails. Hikers just pick a route—usually along a ridge or up a wash—and head toward some distant visible goal. The Excelsor Mine Road is paved for the first few miles then is comprised of good gravel most of the way to Tecopa Pass, but degenerates into a steep dirt track north of the pass that may not be passable to 2wd vehicles, particularly if the road is wet.

The wilderness can also be reached from the west off Hwy 127 by turning on Valjean Valley Road approximately 19 miles north of Baker. The Valjean Valley Road turnoff is just north of Silurian Dry Lake. It is 9 miles from the highway to the border of the wilderness.

Kingston Range

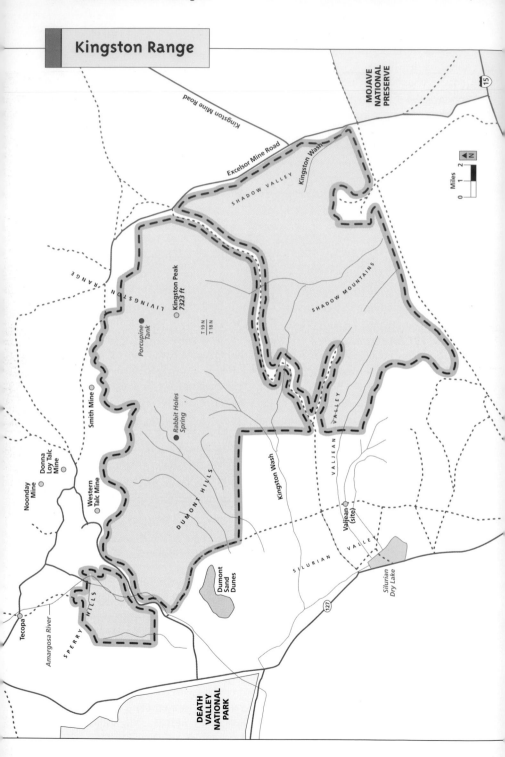

Malpais Mesa Wilderness

Basalt from the Malpais Mesa basalt flow.

Malpais is Spanish for bad country, and the name is accurate to a degree. This is rugged, hot country. Malpais Mesa is named for a recent volcanic flow that covered the southern end of the Inyo Mountains. The hard, volcanic rock resists erosion and has formed a flat-topped, steep-sided plateau.

Malpais Mesa Wilderness takes in the southern end of the Cerro Gordo Peak roadless area just west of the expanded Death Valley National Park. California Hwy 190 forms the western border of the wilderness, whereas Saline Valley Road forms its southeastern border and the White Mountain Talc Mine Road makes up the eastern border. A 4-mile cherry stem road penetrates the wilderness on the east, terminating at the Santa Rosa Mines.

Vegetation consists of the ever-present creosote bush, with pinyon pine and juniper to the north. One of the most outstanding Joshua tree woodlands lies along the eastern edge of the wilderness at Santa Rosa Flat. Mule deer occur in the area.

LOCATION: Inyo County; 15 miles northeast of Olancha, California

SIZE: 32,360 acres

ELEVATION RANGE: 4,200 to 7,728 feet

ADMINISTRATION: BLM Ridgecrest Resource Area Office

MAPS: Desert Access Guide Panamint #2; AAA Death Valley National Park

The area surrounding the wilderness has been a popular mining district since the late 1800s when gold, silver, lead, zinc, copper, and talc were mined within the Cerro Gordo mining district. Silver deposits were first discovered on the slope of Buena Vista Peak (now known as Cerro Gordo Peak) in 1865. By 1871 some 2,000 people were living in Cerro Gordo (the town) and working the mines.

Getting water for the town and lumber for charcoal production to run the smelters was a major obstacle to mining operations. By 1878 lumber was being cut in the Sierra Nevada at the headwaters of Cottonwood Creek, then was transported down a flume to Cottonwood Landing on Owens Lake, where it was placed in kilns and transformed into charcoal. Finally it was loaded on a boat for shipment across the lake and eventually transported up to the smelters near the mines. Water was pumped up 1,800 feet to the town from the eastern slope of the Inyo Mountains.

Despite these efforts, by 1879 the silver veins began to play out and the mines nearly died out. Fortunately enough zinc was discovered to keep the mines operating for another four years. The mines were then nearly abandoned. However, another run on zinc between 1906 and 1936 pumped new life back into the town. Today the town is largely abandoned. Among the major mining areas surrounding the wilderness were the Morning Star, Santa Rosa, Old Timer, Perry Smith, and Keeler Mines.

ACCESS

Entry to the wilderness from any of the surrounding roads is relatively easy. All travel is off trail and cross country. The easiest access is from Olancha on Hwy 395. Starting at Olancha go east 25 miles on Hwy 190. Turn north onto Saline Valley Road. Go 6 miles to the fork and turn northwest (left) onto Santa Rosa Mines Road. The wilderness lies on either side of the last 3 miles of the road.

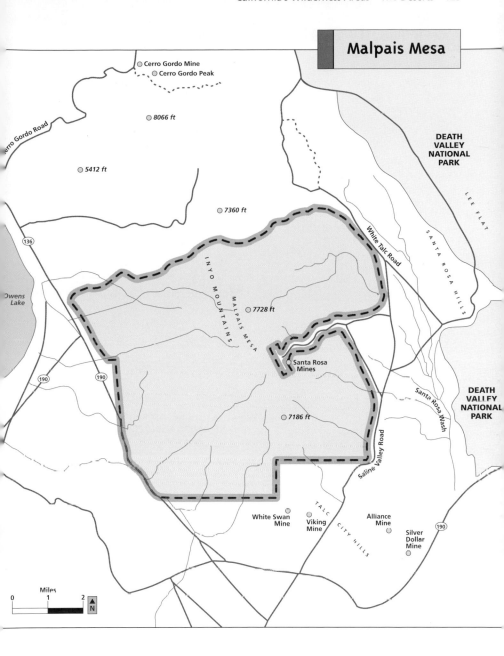

Malpais Mesa

- Cerro Gordo Mine
- Cerro Gordo Peak

Cerro Gordo Road

8066 ft

DEATH VALLEY NATIONAL PARK

LEE FLAT

5412 ft

7360 ft

136

White Talc Road

SANTA ROSA HILLS

Owens Lake

INYO MOUNTAINS

MALPAIS MESA

7728 ft

190   190

Santa Rosa Mines

Santa Rosa Wash

DEATH VALLEY NATIONAL PARK

7186 ft

Saline Valley Road

White Swan Mine

Viking Mine

TALC CITY HILLS

Alliance Mine

190

Silver Dollar Mine

Miles
0   1   2
N

22 Manly Peak Wilderness

Manly Peak from Panamint Valley, Manly Peak Wilderness.

LOCATION:
Inyo County; 30 miles
northeast of Ridgecrest,
California, and border-
ing Death Valley
National Park

SIZE: 16,105 acres

ELEVATION RANGE:
1,100 to 7,196 feet

ADMINISTRATION:
BLM Ridgecrest
Resource Area Office

MAPS: Desert Access
Guide Ridgecrest #4;
AAA Death Valley
National Park

The Panamint Range is one of the most spectacular desert ranges in California, rising from near sea level to more than 11,000 feet. Manly Peak, the most southerly peak, reflects the overall rugged nature of the range, rising abruptly from the Panamint Valley floor to 7,196 feet. Alluvial fans cloak the flanks of the range, whereas deep canyons penetrate the slopes. Manly Peak Wilderness lies east of Wingate Road, taking in the western flank of Panamint Range from South Park Canyon to Goler Wash immediately west of Death Valley National Park. The lower slopes are primarily volcanic rock, but Manly Peak consists of an outcrop of granitic rock.

A number of the canyons harbor intermittent streams and springs that support cottonwood and desert willow riparian vegetation. Outside of the canyons, creosote bush dominates the lower elevations, while pinyon and juniper woodlands grow on the higher ridges. Bighorn sheep roam the area.

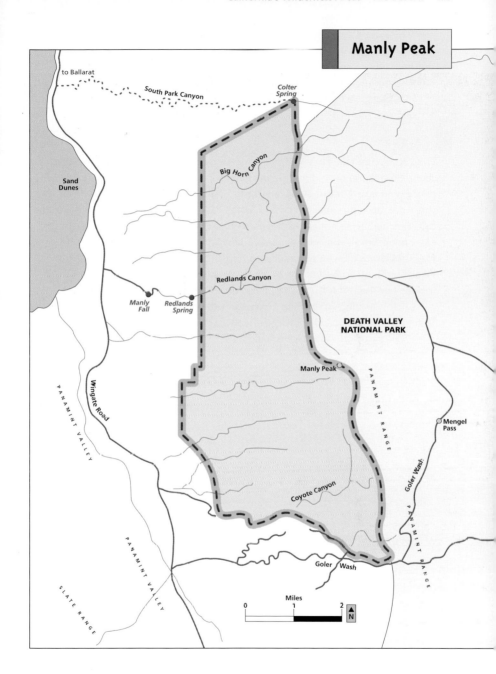

Manly Peak

to Ballarat

South Park Canyon

Colter Spring

Sand Dunes

Big Horn Canyon

Redlands Canyon

Manly Fall

Redlands Spring

DEATH VALLEY NATIONAL PARK

Manly Peak

PANAMINT RANGE

Mengel Pass

PANAMINT VALLEY

Wingate Road

Coyote Canyon

Goler Wash

PANAMINT VALLEY

SLATE RANGE

PANAMINT RANGE

Goler Wash

Miles

0   1   2

N

The entire Panamint Range has been actively explored and mined in the past. Evidence of old mining efforts are found in Coyote Canyon, in South Park Canyon on the northern border, and at Manly Falls just outside the wilderness. Active mining operations continue today, and you should be mindful of ore trucks on Wingate Road when you access the wilderness.

ACCESS

From Ridgecrest take Hwy 178 north for 45 miles to Panamint Valley. Go east about 4.5 miles to the old mining town of Ballarat (where there is a store, but no phone) and take Wingate Road south for 5 miles on a good oiled road, which leads past a new open pit mine. Once past South Park Canyon, the wilderness lies to the east. Park and begin hiking. Although there are no formal trails in the wilderness, old mining "tracks" can sometimes be followed in lieu of trails. The old mining road up Coyote Canyon makes a good "trail" into the heart of the range. Most hikers simply go cross-country. Manly Peak makes a good day hike/scramble destination. The summit is less than 4 miles from Wingate Road.

It is possible to drive up Goler Canyon (with a 4wd vehicle) to access Butte Valley and the eastern side of the wilderness. One can continue on this road from Butte Valley eastward into Death Valley.

Mesquite Mountains Wilderness 23

Joshua tree frames the Mesquite Mountains Wilderness.

The triangularly-shaped Mesquite Mountains Wilderness lies just west of the Nevada-California border. The wilderness is actually part of a much larger wilderness complex. Just south of the wilderness lies the Mojave National Preserve, and the narrow thread of Kingston Road is the only human artifact that separates this wilderness from North Mesquite Mountains Wilderness to the north. The namesake Mesquite Mountains are lower and less abrupt than Clark Mountains just to the south. The central portion of these mountains are composed of limestone. The bajadas that spread out from the mountains are cloaked in creosote bush, blackbrush, and some dense stands of Joshua tree. A species of concern within the wilderness is Rusby's desert mallow.

These mountains are not spectacular. Indeed, in its evaluation of the wilderness, the BLM noted that the area received almost no visitor use "presumably because there is nothing to attract visitors." Based on my own explorations of this wilderness, this is an accurate assessment. If you want to

LOCATION:
San Bernardino County; 50 miles northeast of Baker, California

SIZE: 47,330 acres

ELEVATION RANGE:
3,000 to 4,600 feet

ADMINISTRATION:
BLM Needles Resource Area Office

MAPS: Desert Access Guide Dumont/Clark Mountain #6; AAA San Bernardino County

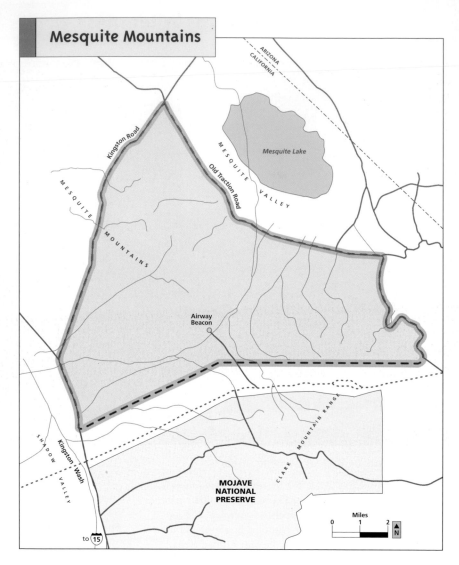

hike someplace where you don't have to compete with others for a camp spot, try these mountains. With no special destinations, it's a good place just to stretch your legs and see what you discover.

If you do decide to camp in this area, you will be following in the footsteps of various native Americans who have left middens, flaked tools, pottery, and other reminders of their past use of the area.

ACCESS

The easiest access is from I-15. Take the Cima/Kingston Road exit. Turn north on Kingston Road and travel for 7 miles. For the next 3 miles the wilderness lies just east of the road.

Nopah Range Wilderness 24

Barrel cactus on the slope of the Nopah Range,
Nopah Range Wilderness

The rugged 18-mile crest of the Nopah Range rises thousands of feet from the Chicago Valley, a large wash that drains the mountains. The western border of this wilderness lies less than a mile from the community of Shoshone, whereas the eastern border lies on the Nevada-California border. The Old Spanish Trail forms the border of the area to the south. The Precambrian and Cambrian limestone and sedimentary rock that dominate these mountains contain yellow, red, and brown striations. Barrel cactus is abundant on the mountain slopes. Bighorn sheep are reported from the area. Two historic eagle nest sites and one prairie falcon nest site are reported for the wilderness. Desert tortoise are reported to be numerous in certain parts of the area.

LOCATION: Inyo County; 1 mile east of Shoshone, California

SIZE: 110,860 acres

ELEVATION RANGE: 1,800 to 6,395 feet

ADMINISTRATION: BLM Barstow Resource Area Office

MAPS: Desert Access Guide Amargosa #3, Dumont/Clark Mountain #6; AAA Death Valley National Park

Nopah Range

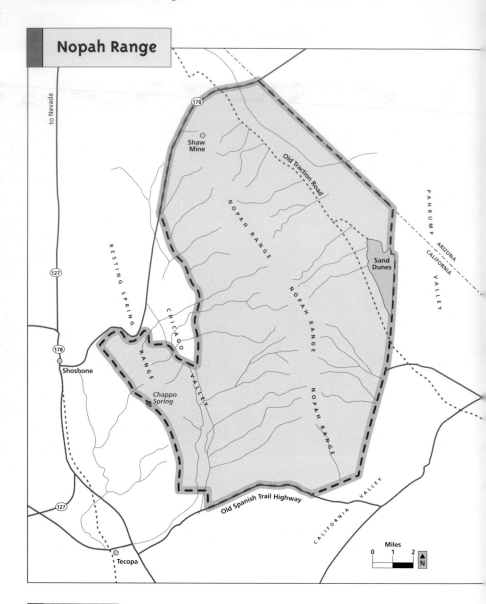

ACCESS

The easiest access to Nopah Range Wilderness is from the Old Spanish Trail. Just park and begin hiking. Nopah Peak is sometimes climbed. From the summit you can see into Death Valley National Park and east to Mount Charleston in the Spring Mountains. More dedicated hikers may choose to make the challenging 18-mile trek of the crest of Nopah Range.

North Mesquite Mountains 25
Wilderness

Joshua tree frames North Mesquite Mountains Wilderness. The Clark Mountains in the Mojave National Preserve are visible in the background.

The North Mesquite Mountains lie just east of Kingston Range Wilderness and north of Mesquite Mountains Wilderness. The "mountains" are more like rolling hills. Limestone and dolomite dominate the eastern section, and small outcrops of gneiss occur in the western section. Gold and other minerals have been associated with the metamorphic rock, and evidence of past mining activity is found along the edge of the wilderness. The main attraction of North Mesquite Mountains Wilderness is the role it plays in creating a larger wildland complex. This triangularly-shaped wilderness has a number of cherry stem roads that nearly cut it into pieces. At one point, less than a mile separates one road from another. Outstanding examples of Joshua tree forests cloak the slopes of the North Mesquite Mountains.

Recreationally this wilderness is not likely to attract a lot of attention. The nearby Kingston Range is more spectacular

LOCATION: San Bernardino County; 60 miles northeast of Baker, California

SIZE: 25,540 acres

ELEVATION RANGE: 500 to 4,200 feet

ADMINISTRATION: BLM Needles Resource Area Office

MAPS: Desert Access Guide Dumont/Clark #6; AAA San Bernardino County

North Mesquite Mountains

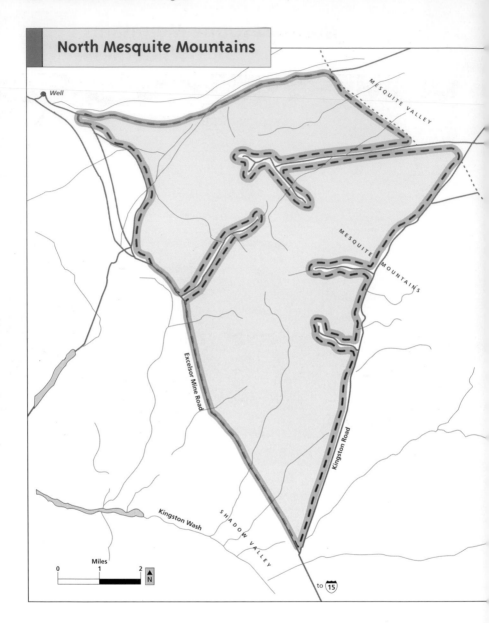

and varied. Nevertheless, if you enjoy exploring little-traveled wildlands, the North Mesquite Mountains may be for you. The eastern portion contains more canyons than the flatter, less spectacular western section.

ACCESS

Take the Cima/Kingston Road exit off I-15. Travel north approximately 8 miles to the intersection of Excelsor Mine Road and Kingston Road. The wilderness lies between these two roads.

Pahrump Valley Wilderness

26

Yucca in bloom near Nopah Range Pass frames the creosote bush covered expanse of Pahrump Valley Wilderness.

Pahrump Valley Wilderness is a seldom-visited area located on the Nevada border just south of Old Spanish Trail. It is, as its name implies, a sweeping valley. Actually, it is three valleys: the California, Mesquite, and Pahrump. The southern edge of the wilderness encompasses a portion of the Kingston Range. Here's a wilderness one can visit if solitude is your goal.

Most of the wilderness is cloaked with creosote bush, but yuccas dominate some slopes, bringing a flash of color when their large blossoms bloom in early summer. Since most of the wilderness is just gentle, sloping bajada, it is relatively easy to cross. The abandoned Old Traction Road traverses the northeastern-eastern portion of the wilderness. The road was originally built to haul borax from Death Valley, and it provides a "trail" of sorts that crosses the entire wilderness.

LOCATION: San Bernardino and Inyo Counties; 25 miles east of Tecopa, California

SIZE: 74,800 acres

ELEVATION RANGE: 2,720 to 4,569 feet

ADMINISTRATION: BLM Barstow Resource Area Office

MAPS: Desert Access Guide Dumont/Clark Mountains #6; AAA San Bernardino County

Pahrump Valley

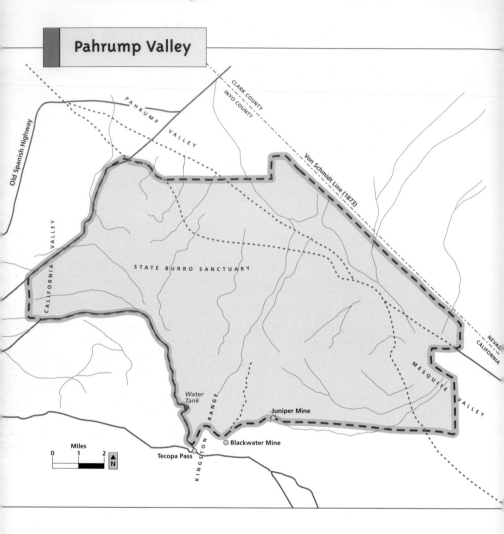

ACCESS

The easiest access to Pahrump Valley Wilderness is 25 miles east of Tecopa.
Take Old Spanish Highway out of Tecopa. Once you cross Nopah Range Pass,
the wilderness lies just south of the road.

Piper Mountain Wilderness

27

Piper Peak in Piper Mountain Wilderness rises above Deep Springs Valley.

Piper Mountain Wilderness takes in the easternmost out-lying ridges of the Inyo Mountains and the Piper Mountains just north of Death Valley National Park in one of the more remote sections of the California desert. The wilderness lies near the California Nevada border. A fault-block mountain range, the Inyo Mountains rise steeply from the surrounding valleys, with 7,703-foot Piper Mountain the highest named peak in the wilderness. Deep canyons penetrate the range and large alluvial fans radiate from the mountain bases. The views from the crest of the mountains are superb, with stunning vistas of the Saline Range, Last Chance Range, and Fish Lake and Eureka Valleys.

    Vegetation consists primarily of sagebrush, with juniper and pinyon woodlands at the highest elevations. One of the northernmost stands of Joshua tree is found at Joshua Flats near the base of the Inyo Mountains. Bighorn sheep, mule deer, chukar partridge, quail, and coyote are all known to frequent the area.

LOCATION: Inyo County; 30 miles east of Big Pine, California

SIZE: 72,575 acres

ELEVATION RANGE: 1,000 to 7,703 feet

ADMINISTRATION: BLM Ridgecrest Resource Area Office

MAPS: Desert Access Guide Eureka/Saline #1; AAA Death Valley National Park

Piper Mountain

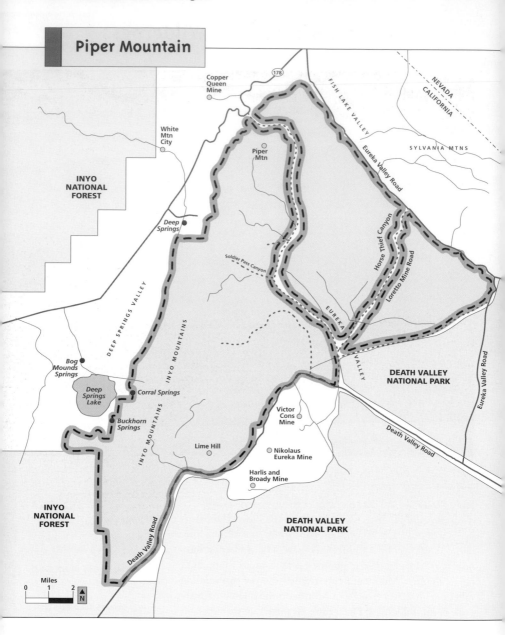

ACCESS

The wilderness is divided into three segments by Loretto Mine Road and Eureka Valley Road. These dirt roads also offer easy access to the Piper Mountain Wilderness. Hwy 168 through Deep Springs Valley provides paved-road access to the northern parts of the range. For those who want to scale Piper Mountain, a dirt road that leaves Hwy 168 at Gilbert Pass provides access to the base of the peak. Old mining roads, now closed, provide additional "trail" routes into these mountains.

Resting Spring Range Wilderness

28

Eagle Mountain from Amargosa Valley, Resting Spring Range Wilderness.

Resting Spring Range is a fault-block mountain area lying near the Nevada-California border just east of Death Valley National Park. Colorful bands of volcanic rock, including pinks, reds, greens, and tans, set among rugged peaks and deep canyons contribute to the scenic beauty of this mountain range. One of the more scenic features of the wilderness is the craggy eminence of 3,806-foot Eagle Mountain, which rises dramatically from the Amargosa River Valley.

The Amargosa River Valley is gently sloping and covered primarily with the ubiquitous creosote bush. Barrel cactus and yucca are more common on the mountain slopes. Wildlife include several raptors, such as the golden eagle and the prairie falcon, as well as bighorn sheep.

The remains of the now-abandoned Tonopah and Tidewater Railroad grade lies along the western border of the wilderness. The railroad operated from 1906 to 1940 and

LOCATION: Inyo County; 5 miles southeast of Death Valley Junction and 4 miles north of Shoshone, California

SIZE: 78,868 acres

ELEVATION RANGE: 2,000 to 5,264 feet

ADMINISTRATION: BLM Barstow Resource Area Office

MAPS: Desert Access Guide Amargosa #3; AAA Death Valley National Park

Resting Spring Range

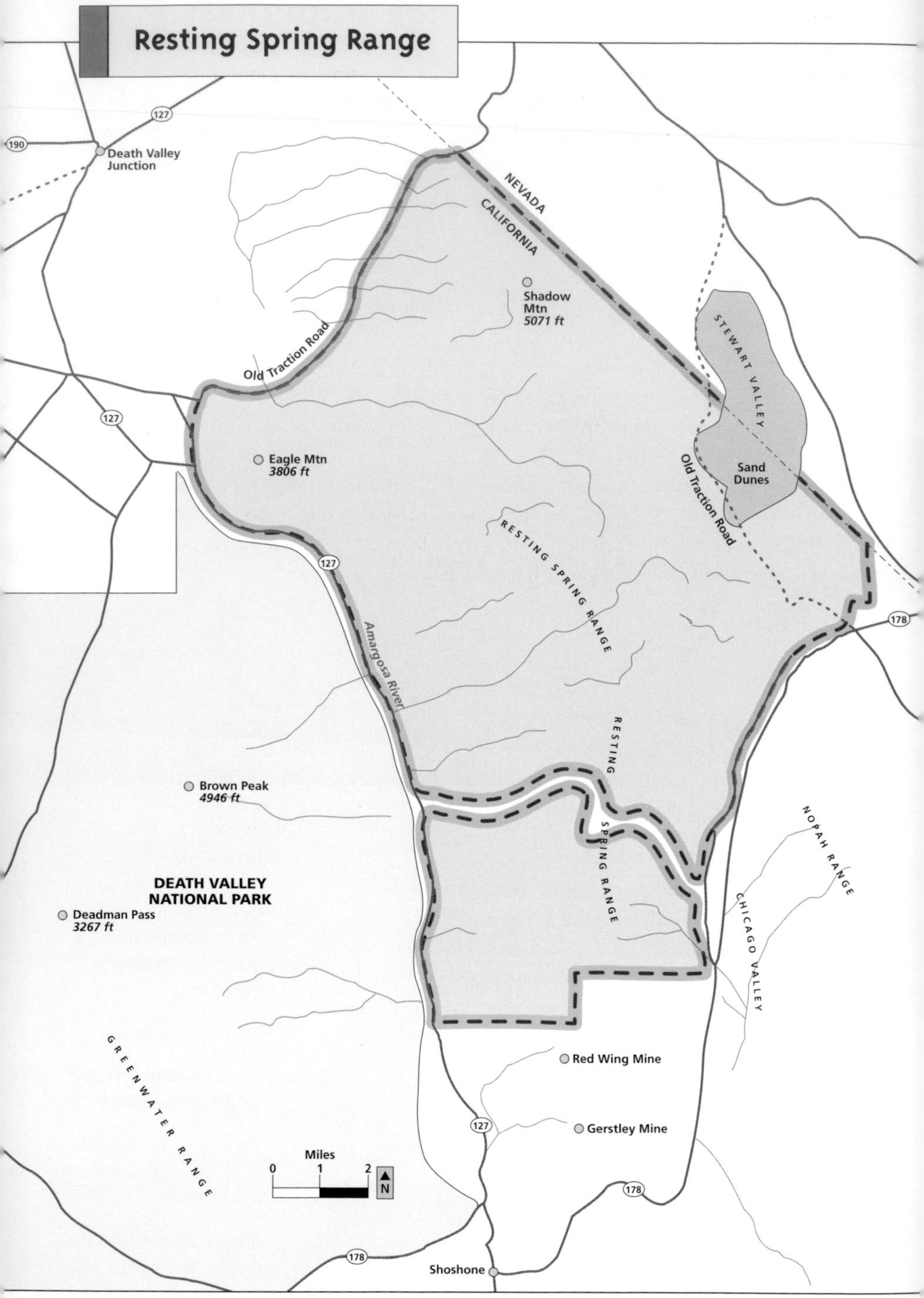

127

190
○ Death Valley
   Junction

127

Old Traction Road

NEVADA
CALIFORNIA

○ Shadow
   Mtn
   5071 ft

STEWART VALLEY

○ Eagle Mtn
   3806 ft

RESTING SPRING RANGE

Old Traction Road

Sand
Dunes

127

178

Amargosa River

○ Brown Peak
   4946 ft

RESTING

SPRING RANGE

**DEATH VALLEY
NATIONAL PARK**

○ Deadman Pass
   3267 ft

NOPAH RANGE

CHICAGO VALLEY

G R E E N W A T E R   R A N G E

○ Red Wing Mine

Miles
0   1   2

▲
N

127

○ Gerstley Mine

127

178

178

Shoshone ○

originally hauled silver ore from the mines at Goldfield, Nevada, to the railhead for the Southern Pacific at Ludlow, California. Eventually borax became the major commodity transported, with the railroad replacing the 20-mule-team wagon trains.

Mining efforts in the Resting Spring Range have uncovered deposits of gold, silver, zinc, lead, and borate. Despite this mineral potential, the area never supported significant mineral development and is now closed to mining.

ACCESS

Hwy 127 is essentially the western border of the wilderness and it provides easy access to these mountains. In most instances the usually dry Amargosa River provides no obstacle to the wilderness; however, after a wet winter, wading the river may be necessary. One of the most popular hikes is the ascent of Eagle Mountain. It is a 4-mile round-trip climb to the top, however, the last scramble to the summit is steep and rocky. Nonclimbers may feel more comfortable if they have a rope for protection.

Just 9 miles north of Shoshone, a nonwilderness 4wd corridor to Baxter Mine splits off the southern fourth of the wilderness, but also provides access into the heart of the range. You might want to walk or ride a mountain bike on this road if you don't have a high-clearance vehicle.

Saddle Peak Hills Wilderness

The uninspiring plateau of Saddle Peak Hills Wilderness.

LOCATION:
San Bernardino County;
38 miles north of Baker,
California

SIZE: 1,440 acres

ELEVATION RANGE:
500 to 2,500 feet

ADMINISTRATION:
BLM Barstow Resource
Area Office

MAPS: Desert Access
Guide Dumont/Clark
Mountains #6; AAA San
Bernardino County

Saddle Peak Hills Wilderness is tiny—about 1 mile wide and 4 miles long. The only reason it exists is that it is immediately adjacent to the 3.4-million-acre Death Valley National Park, which surrounds it on two sides.

Saddle Peak Hills themselves, most of which are in Death Valley, are actually quite dramatic—almost more than hills. But the area in this wilderness is more like a dissected, rolling plateau than mountains. Creosote bush covers the terrain. Chances are, if you visit this wilderness you won't find it crowded.

ACCESS

Access to this wilderness is directly west of Hwy 127, which forms the eastern border of the wilderness. As you head north from Baker, note the microwave station on your left just before you reach Ibex Springs Road, which

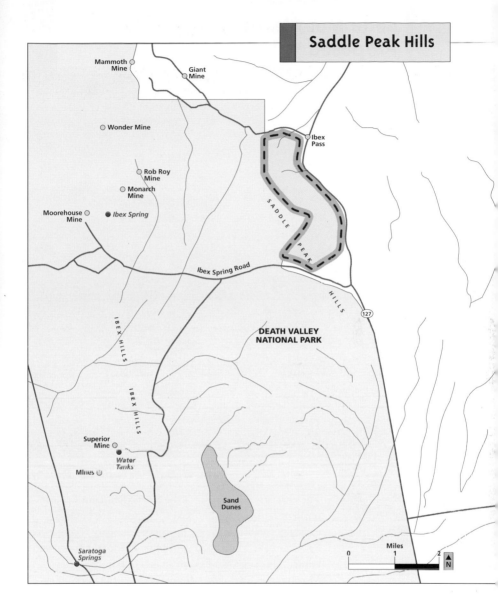

Saddle Peak Hills

Mammoth Mine

Giant Mine

Wonder Mine

Ibex Pass

Rob Roy Mine

Monarch Mine

Moorehouse Mine

Ibex Spring

SADDLE PEAK HILLS

Ibex Spring Road

IBEX HILLS

127

DEATH VALLEY NATIONAL PARK

IBEX HILLS

Superior Mine

Water Tanks

Mines

Sand Dunes

Saratoga Springs

Miles
0   1   2

N

marks the southern boundary of the wilderness. The wilderness lies east of Hwy 127 for the next 4 miles. You can also gain entry to the wilderness off Giant Mine Road. This road, located just north of Ibex Pass, provides access to the southern border of the adjacent Ibex Hills Wilderness. Saddle Peak Hills Wilderness is just south of this road.

30 Soda Mountains Proposed Wilderness

The proposed Soda Mountains Wilderness.

LOCATION: San Bernardino County; 2 miles northeast of Baker, California

SIZE: 132,000 acres

ELEVATION RANGE: 880 to 3,663 feet

ADMINISTRATION: BLM Barstow Resource Area Office

MAP: AAA San Bernardino County

The dramatic escarpment of the Soda Mountains lies just north of I-15 and west of Baker. The southern boundary generally parallels I-15, the northern boundary is delineated by Silver Lake Mine Road, and Hwy 127 marks the eastern border. This large, roadless area takes in both the Soda Mountains and Cronese Mountains, plus the intervening valleys. The rugged Soda Mountains are dissected by colorful canyons with steep walls that vary from red to gold. Some 10 percent of the wilderness consists of playas; the three largest are the West Cronese, East Cronese, and Silver Dry Lakes. Some 80,000 acres of this area were designated a wilderness study area by the California Desert Protection Act.

Vegetation is largely creosote bush and saltbush. Two sensitive species—*Androstephium brevifolium* and *Linathus arenicola*—occur in the area. A stand of crucifixion thorn is reported for the area.

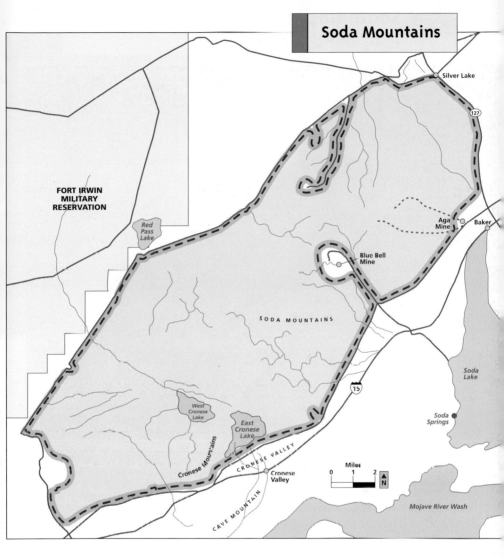

Mining activity has occurred sporadically, with gold, silver, copper, lead, zinc, and other minerals recorded for the area. A grazing allotment covers a portion of the proposed wilderness.

ACCESS

Although the interior of this large wildland is remote, getting to the edge of it is not difficult. I-15 forms the southern boundary between the Baker and Afton exits. North of Baker, Highway 127 forms the eastern border. Just hike from either road.

Another access point that penetrates into the heart of the mountains is an old mining road to the Blue Bell Mine, which is accessible off I-15. Take the ZZYZX Road exit 5.5 miles west of Baker and head north approximately 5 miles.

31 South Nopah Range Wilderness

Barrel cactus on limestone frames South Nopah Range Wilderness.

LOCATION: Inyo County; 3 miles east of Tecopa, California

SIZE: 16,780 acres

ELEVATION RANGE: 1,500 to 4,200 feet

ADMINISTRATION: BLM Barstow Resource Area Office

MAPS: Desert Access Guide Dumont/Clark Mountain #6; AAA Death Valley National Park

South Nopah Range Wilderness is part of a larger wildlands complex. Death Valley National Park is only 9 miles to the northwest, and the main body of the Nopah Range lies to the north of Old Spanish Trail Highway and is protected as part of the Nopah Range Wilderness. Mesquite Valley Road forms the southeastern border, separating the wilderness from Pahrump Valley Wilderness. Kingston Range Wilderness is only 5 miles south of the southern border of South Nopah Range Wilderness. The closure of a few dirt roads and unification of Kingston Range Wilderness, Pahrump Valley Wilderness, North Mesquite Mountains Wilderness, and South Nopah Wilderness into one large wildlands complex is an attractive possibility.

South Nopah Range is a rugged range composed of colorful Precambrian and Cambrian sedimentary rock. The area is adjacent to the Tecopa mining district, which produced $54 million in gold, silver, lead, copper, and zinc.

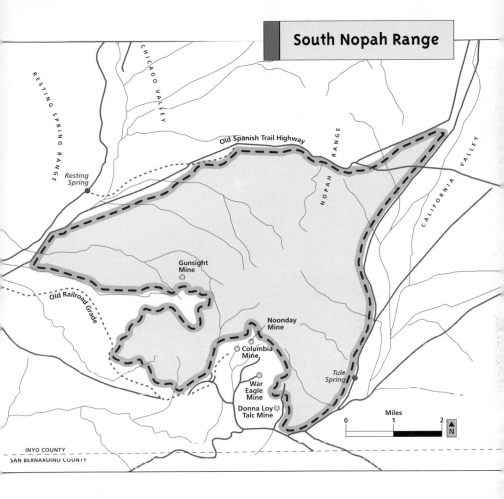

As the presence of Tecopa Hot Springs to the west indicates, the potential for geothermal resources is high in this wilderness, and this fact was used by opponents to argue against wilderness designation.

Creosote bush covers the bajadas, and barrel cactus is common on the rocky slopes. The area once supported bighorn sheep, and expansion of herds in Nopah Range Wilderness to the south may allow for recolonization of the area by wild sheep.

ACCESS

To reach the northern border of South Nopah Range Wilderness, drive east from Tecopa on the paved Old Spanish Trail Highway. The wilderness lies immediately to the south for the next 8 miles.

32 Stateline Wilderness

Clark Mountain seen from Stateline Wilderness.

LOCATION:
San Bernardino
County; 3 miles north
of Stateline, Nevada,
and I-15

SIZE: 7,050 acres

ELEVATION RANGE:
2,500 to 4,500 feet

ADMINISTRATION:
BLM Needles Resource
Area Office

MAPS: Desert Access
Guide Dumont/Clark
Mountains #6; AAA
San Bernardino County

This small wilderness lies on the Nevada-California border just north of I-15. It is surprising to be sitting on a ridge in this wilderness, seemingly alone in the world, only to look south and see thousands of vehicles racing along the interstate between Los Angeles and Las Vegas. The wilderness, although small, is actually part of a much larger wildlands complex. The Clark Mountain unit of the Mojave National Preserve lies just to the southwest, whereas Mesquite Mountains Wilderness is immediately west. Taken together, the area has a lot of room for exploration.

The mountains in Stateline Wilderness are the most easterly extension of the Clark Range. Most of the range lies in the Mojave National Preserve. They are composed of sedimentary rock, and, in particular, some limestone outcrops that have eroded into numerous caves. A wide, sloping bajada forms an apron to the peaks.

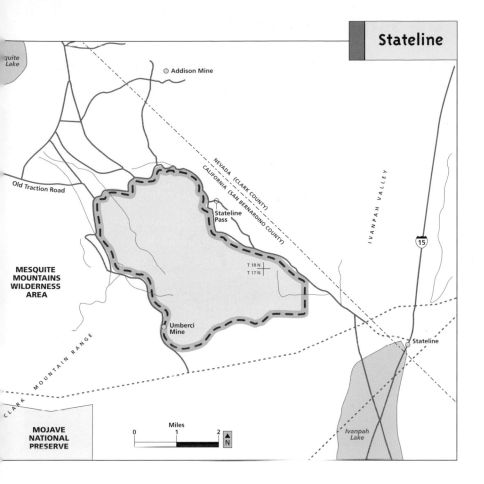

Vegetation consists of yucca, Joshua tree, fishhook cactus, cholla, hedgehog cactus, and the ubiquitous creosote bush. Higher elevations support some pinyon and juniper. The area is a migration route for bighorn sheep crossing from the Clark Mountains to the Spring Mountains in Nevada. Golden eagle, prairie falcon, and red-tailed hawk are thought to nest in the area.

ACCESS

This is a relatively easy wilderness to access. Take the Stateline exit on I-15. Go behind the parking garage at the Whiskey Pete Casino and look for a dirt road heading north. There is a cattle guard where you cross from the casino onto BLM land. Ignore side roads and stay on the main dirt pathway, which leads to some power lines about a mile or so north of the casino. Just beyond the power lines there is a white sign that indicates Stateline Pass Road. Follow this road north toward Stateline Pass. The wilderness is immediately west of the road for the next 7 miles. The road, although narrow and bumpy, is passable by a carefully driven 2wd vehicle, however high clearance is recommended.

33 Surprise Canyon Wilderness

Waterfall in Surprise Canyon, Panamint Range. The bottom of Surprise Canyon is not actually in the wilderness; it is a non-wilderness corridor that divides the designated wilderness in half.

LOCATION: Inyo County; 56 miles northeast of Ridgecrest, California, immediately west of Death Valley National Park

SIZE: 29,180 acres

ELEVATION RANGE: 1,000 to 7,000 feet

ADMINISTRATION: BLM Ridgecrest Resource Area Office

MAPS: Desert Access Guide Panamint #2; AAA Death Valley National Park

Surprise Canyon Wilderness takes in the western slope and bajada of the Panamint Range directly below Telescope Peak. The Panamint Range is one of the most dramatic mountain uplifts in the United States, rising more than 2 miles above Death Valley. The range contains the highest peaks in Death Valley National Park, with Telescope Peak topping out at 11,049 feet and several other peaks rising above 10,000 feet (outside the wilderness). Unlike most higher ranges in the West, there are no intervening foothills. The Panamints rise from the salt pan in Death Valley to the top of the range in just 12 miles, creating one of the steepest slopes of any mountain uplift in North America. Some of the western canyons, including Surprise Canyon, climb as much as 1,000 feet per mile.

This dramatic uplift is the result of a north-south fault along the western base of the range. While the adjacent valleys have been sinking, the mountains have been rising. Although a variety of rock types are exposed in the Panamints, including a granitic core, most of the Panamints are composed of marine deposits of Cambrian age.

Because they are so high, the Panamints capture more moisture than most nearby ranges. The higher peaks are often covered with snow, and as a consequence there are numerous springs and perennial streams. The higher moisture supports a diversity of plants, including forests of limber pine and bristlecone pine on the highest peaks, and pinyon and juniper forests at mid elevations.

Surprise Canyon is a reference to the perennial stream that flows down it. Coming from the dry Panamint Valley and finding a clear, cold stream bordered by riparian reeds, willows, cottonwood trees, and other vegetation is indeed a surprise. Water is abundant in the first 3.5 miles, occasionally cascading over ledges and small falls.

There are a number of hikeable canyons, including Jail, Surprise, and Happy Canyons. Most people choose to hike up Surprise Canyon, although some consider Happy Canyon with its mesquite-covered lower section to be the most scenic in the Panamint Range. Bear in mind that none of these canyons are actually in the wilderness, although the designated wildlands are found immediately adjacent to them.

ACCESS

To get to Surprise Canyon Trailhead, take Hwy 178 through the Panamint Valley to the old, nearly abandoned mining town of Ballarat. Ballarat was founded in 1897 as a mining supply center. At one time there were three general stores, 12 saloons, a two-story hotel, a school, and a post office. However, as area mining activity began to falter after the turn of the century, Ballarat's importance declined. It was declared a state historic site in 1949, but little was done to protect the area from vandals. Today one may see ruins, a few private dwellings, and a store where you can purchase some basic supplies, including cold drinks.

From Ballarat go north on Indian Ranch Road about 2 miles to the turn-off for Surprise Canyon. It is 4.1 miles up the bajada and into the canyon to Chris Wicht Camp, where there is parking opposite a private, active mining development. The road used to be passable for 2wd vehicles beyond this point, but a huge flood in 1984 swept the canyon, taking out much of the road. You quickly pass an old mill site as you wander up the canyon. Other occasional reminders of the mining era are encountered, including old vehicles and tractors.

Although the road was washed away more than a decade ago, Surprise Canyon is still used by 4wd enthusiasts. You may be surprised by the steep ledges apparently climbed by their vehicles. There are occasional narrow gorges with smooth, water-slick rocks. If you walk upstream 6 miles, you eventually reach Panamint City—an old silver mining town located at 6,300 feet in a broad pinyon- and juniper-covered basin. Panamint City got its start in 1873. During its heyday in the 1870s, more than 1,500 people lived in the community that included more than 200 stone houses. The town was abandoned after a severe flood in 1876 nearly washed the town away, killing 200 people. All that remains are some old

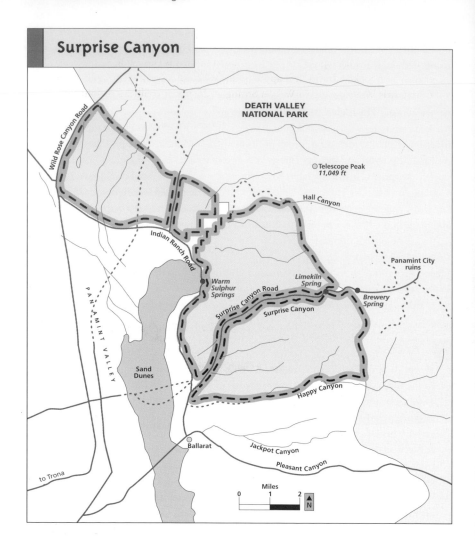

Surprise Canyon

DEATH VALLEY
NATIONAL PARK

Wild Rose Canyon Road

⊙ Telescope Peak
11,049 ft

Hall Canyon

Indian Ranch Road

Panamint City
ruins

P A N A M I N T   V A L L E Y

Warm
Sulphur
Springs

Limekiln
Spring

Brewery
Spring

Surprise Canyon Road

Surprise Canyon

Sand
Dunes

Happy Canyon

Ballarat

Jackpot Canyon

Pleasant Canyon

to Trona

Miles
0   1   2
N

ruins, including a 65-foot brick chimney that was part of the ore smelter. In 1982 there were attempts to revive the mines, which included bulldozing of much of the old town site.

As you walk, you repeatedly cross and recross the stream. It is hard to avoid getting your feet wet. Because there is water, you'll likely hear or see birds. (I heard a canyon wren trilling as I walked up the rocky gorge.) After you have hiked 3.4 miles up the canyon, the trail moves upslope—away from the water—for the remainder of the hike.

Most people turn around at Panamint City or before, but Surprise Canyon offers one of the better overnight hikes in the California desert. If you've made previous arrangements for a shuttle, it is possible to continue beyond Panamint City by ascending Frenchman Canyon to Panamint Pass. From the pass it is a relatively easy downhill hike to Willow Spring in Johnson Canyon in Death Valley National Park. This route has more water than just about any other in the Death Valley region. This cross-Panamint hike is best done as a two- to three-night backpack trip. It is approximately 12 miles (very steep, up and down) from Chris Wicht Camp to Wilson Spring at the upper trailhead in Johnson Canyon. Although you can hike this route either way, starting in Surprise Canyon presents a less steep grade. Surprise Canyon itself is a nonwilderness corridor that dissects the wilderness. Amazingly, 4wd vehicles sometimes climb up this corridor, going up waterfalls and smooth ledges that required the use of all four of my limbs to negotiate.

Narrow gorge of Surprise Canyon, Panamint Range, on the border of the Surprise Canyon Wilderness.

34 Sylvania Mountains Wilderness

Fresh snow in Sylvania Mountains Wilderness.

LOCATION: Inyo County; 30 miles east (as the crow flies) of Bishop, California

SIZE: 17,820 acres

ELEVATION RANGE: 5,000 to 8,000 feet

ADMINISTRATION: BLM Ridgecrest Resource Area Office

MAPS: Desert Access Guide Eureka/Saline #1; AAA Death Valley National Park

The rugged Sylvania Mountains, like other ranges in the Great Basin, are surprisingly steep and rise thousands of feet above the surrounding valleys. These mountains lie on the California-Nevada border and are part of a large wildlands complex that includes the adjacent Last Chance Range to the south in Death Valley National Park and Piper Mountains Wilderness to the west. Just a few dirt roads separate it from these other roadless lands. The western portion of Sylvania Mountains Wilderness consists of a sloping bajada that rises to craggy mountains along the eastern border of the wilderness. Steep cliffs in Willow Wash and Cucomunga Canyon add to the scenic diversity. From any of the higher parts of the wilderness you can look south to the Last Chance Range, east into the dry Fish Lake Valley, and west along the Inyo Range. It is big country.

Sagebrush dominates at lower elevations, and the highest peaks are cloaked in pinyon and juniper woodlands.

Sylvania Mountains

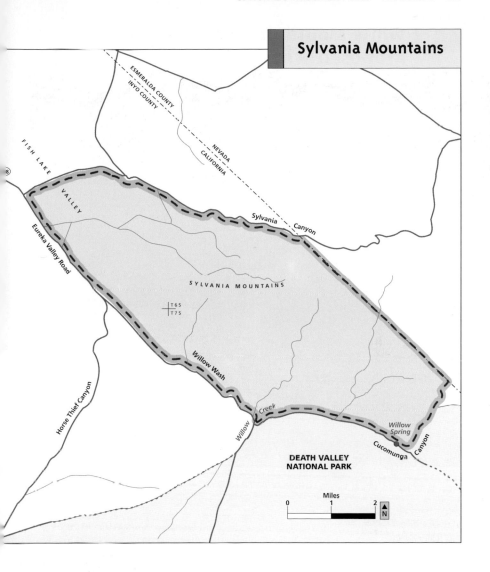

ACCESS

The easiest access is from Owens Valley via Hwy 168. From Big Pine drive north and then east on Hwy 168 for 32 miles. Just a mile or so before the junction with Hwy 266 there is a turn to the south on the gravel Eureka Valley Road, which leads to Death Valley National Park. After traveling 4 miles on this road, the road becomes the western edge of the wilderness for the next 8 miles.

35 White Mountains Proposed Wilderness

Bristlecone pine on the crest of the White Mountains proposed wilderness.

LOCATION: Inyo County; 15 miles east of Bishop, California

SIZE: 250,000+ (379,000 potential acres)

ELEVATION RANGE: 4,000 to 14,246 feet

ADMINISTRATION: Inyo National Forest

MAPS: Inyo National Forest; AAA Eastern Sierra

It is difficult to understand how the White Mountains have fallen through the cracks of wilderness protection. In total, with the closure of a few rough roads, more than 379,000 acres could be united to create a very large wilderness complex. The White Mountains contain the largest undesignated wildlands complex in California.

Not only is this a potentially large wilderness, but it contains some of California's most lofty terrain. White Mountain Peak, at 14,246 feet, is the third highest peak in California and the fifth highest peak in the lower 48 states—only 253 feet shorter than Mount Whitney in the Sierra Nevada. The drop from White Mountain Peak to Owens Valley is 9,700 feet over 7 miles! White Mountain Peak isn't the only high point in this range. Boundary Peak (elevation, 13,140 feet) just over the border in Nevada, is the highest peak in that state. The range is also the westernmost range in the Basin and Range Province.

As highest mountains in the Great Basin, there is probably no other mountain range quite as spectacular as the Whites in the entire California desert, and perhaps in the entire Great Basin. Indeed, at one time the White Mountains were studied as a potential Great Basin National Park, losing out in the end to the Snake Range on the other side of Nevada. Nevertheless, the entire range still has national significance and has been nominated for listing as a National Natural Landmark.

The steepest terrain is along the White Mountain Fault, which fronts Owens Valley. Steep slopes; narrow, deep canyons; and a rolling summit ridgeline characterize these mountains. In a few places the crest widens into a broad summit plateau.

The Whites have a granitic core like the Sierra Nevada. There are a number of different granitic plutons that have been embedded in the range, and they vary in age and chemical composition. Most of these granitic outcrops are overlain with some of the oldest sedimentary rock (primarily dolomite) in California. Fossils as old as 600 million years are found in these rocks, including the oldest trilobite fossils in North America. Some 10 million years ago, volcanic activity covered much of the range with lava flows, the remains of which can still be seen in the northern end of the range near Montgomery Pass. There is even evidence of past glaciation, which is unusual among California's desert ranges. Besides glacial activity, other frost-related features are evident. Pellisier Flat contains classic examples of active, polar-type features, including terraces formed by solifluction.

Yet despite their height, the White Mountains are definitely a "desert" range. It is a cold desert, with limited precipitation and occasional frigid temperatures. Temperatures as low as -26°F have been recorded. At the 12,000-foot-high Bancroft Laboratory, located on the crest of the range, an average of only 15 inches of precipitation is recorded annually. Yet due to the height of these mountains, sufficient snow is captured to feed 128 miles of perennial streams—a number of which contain trout populations, including the threatened Paiute trout.

What the Whites are famous for aren't high peaks or wilderness, but bristlecone pine. This is the longest lived plant known to science; some plants live more than 4,500 years. (Some claim that creosote bush clones are older.) These ancient, slow-growing, twisted trees typically grow on dolomite substrates near timberline. Several of the oldest trees and groves are protected and accessed by nature trails along White Mountain Road.

But bristlecone pine aren't the only species of tree found in the range. Due to the higher moisture and elevation of the Whites compared with other desert ranges, there is a great diversity of tree species (for a desert range). In addition to bristlecone pine there are water birch, aspen, lodgepole pine, limber pine, western juniper, ponderosa pine, Jeffrey pine, and narrowleaf cottonwood. Sagebrush dominates the non-forested terrain.

Wildlife include a wide variety of species such as yellow-bellied marmot, pika, white-tailed jackrabbit, black-tailed jackrabbit, ringtails, gray fox, marten, mule deer, bobcat, coyote, bighorn sheep, and even tule elk. The elk were introduced to Owens Valley and now range up to 8,000 feet in the White Mountains.

The native Americans who lived in the region no doubt utilized the meager resources of the mountains in numerous ways, from hunting bighorn sheep to collecting pinyon nuts. With the introduction of livestock in 1861, conflicts between ranchers and natives grew, with both settlers and native Americans losing many individuals to hostilities. The native Americans were eventually relocated to Fort Tejon south of Bakersfield, and the White Mountains were then open for unrestricted exploitation. Livestock were grazed from the valleys to the crest of the range. Eventually, the Forest Service asserted control over livestock use and numbers, but not sufficiently to remove all negative influences. Even today, livestock grazing continues on the fragile high-elevation vegetation.

In 1948, the US Navy sought out a location to test infrared sensors. They constructed a laboratory on Crooked Creek near the crest of the range. In 1978, this facility was turned over to the University of California at Berkeley as a research facility and is now known as the White Mountain Research Station. One laboratory site exists on the summit of White Mountain Peak and is the fourth highest high-altitude research facility in the world.

ACCESS

Most of the lower canyons are accessible by mining roads from adjacent valleys. The southern half of the area is bisected by White Mountain Road, which follows the crest of the range from Westgard Pass to White Mountain Peak. Most people coming to the White Mountains either attempt to climb White Mountain Peak or Boundary Peak. The hike to the summit of White Mountain Peak is 7.5 miles. The "trail" is a now-closed road. Most people accomplish this trek in a day, and it is strenuous, especially since most of the time you are hiking at elevations greater than 12,000 feet. Most people begin at the locked gate at the White Mountain Research Station, which is the limit for public access. The station is reached by driving White Mountain Road 22 miles from Hwy 168. The road as far as the Schulman Bristlecone Pine Grove is passable for regular 2wd vehicles, but beyond this point the road is rough and has some steep grades. Drive carefully.

Boundary Peak, the highest summit in Nevada, lies at the northern end of the White Mountains. Most people climbing this peak start on the eastern side of the range. Drive north from Bishop, California, on Hwy 6 over Montgomery Peak into Nevada. Some 5 miles beyond the junction with Hwy 360, take Hwy 264 to Fish Lake Valley. Watch for an unmarked, wide dirt road on the north side of Chiatovich Creek. Follow this toward the mountains for 12.2 miles, taking right forks at all junctions. From the parking area go up Trail Canyon to a saddle that is followed to the ridgeline of the range. The peak is to the south. It is a 4,400-foot-plus ascent to the peak.

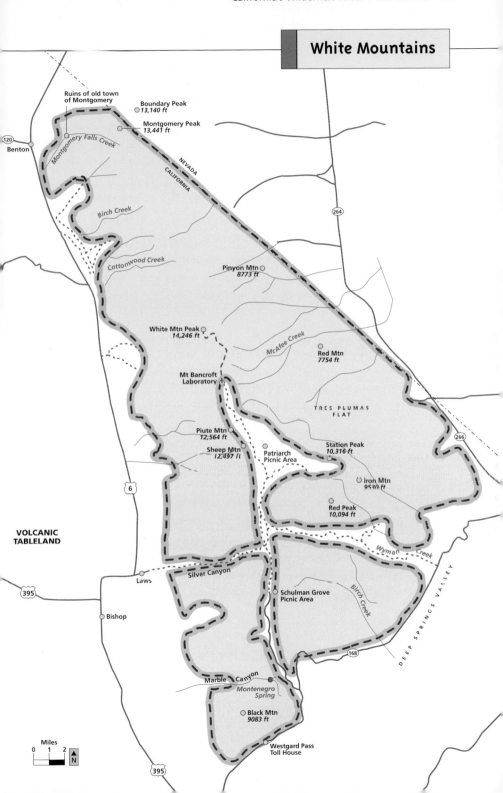

White Mountains

Ruins of old town
of Montgomery

Boundary Peak
13,140 ft

Montgomery Peak
13,441 ft

Montgomery Falls Creek

120

Benton

NEVADA

CALIFORNIA

264

Birch Creek

Cottonwood Creek

Pinyon Mtn
8773 ft

White Mtn Peak
14,246 ft

McAfee Creek

Red Mtn
7754 ft

Mt Bancroft
Laboratory

TRES PLUMAS
FLAT

266

Piute Mtn
12,564 ft

Sheep Mtn
12,497 ft

Station Peak
10,316 ft

Patriarch
Picnic Area

Iron Mtn
9530 ft

6

Red Peak
10,094 ft

VOLCANIC
TABLELAND

Wyman Creek

DEEP SPRINGS VALLEY

395

Laws

Silver Canyon

Schulman Grove
Picnic Area

Birch Creek

Bishop

168

Marble   Canyon

Montenegro
Spring

Black Mtn
9083 ft

Westgard Pass
Toll House

Miles
0   1   2

N

395

Mojave Desert Subregion

The Mojave Desert lies in a transition zone between the hot Colorado Desert (part of the Sonoran Desert) and the cooler and higher Great Basin Desert. This arid region of southeastern California and portions of Nevada, Arizona, and Utah occupies more than 25,000 square miles.

On the northwestern boundary, the Mojave extends from the Sierra Nevada Range to the Colorado Plateau in the east, and abuts the San Gabriel-San Bernardino Mountains in the southwest. For the purposes of this book, it encompasses the region lying south of I-15 and north of I-10, and includes Joshua Tree National Park and Mojave National Preserve.

The Mojave Desert can experience cold, freezing temperatures, and snow is not uncommon at higher elevations. Nevertheless, freezing periods are short term and unusual. Most of the annual precipitation of less than 5 inches comes in the winter.

Like the Great Basin Desert, the Mojave Desert is dominated by basin-and-range topography. Parallel ranges aligned in a generally north-south pattern are separated by huge basins and valleys. Many of these valleys were once covered by large Ice Age lakes, and are now dried to playas. Many of the playas are mined for borax, potash, and salt.

The Mojave Desert hosts about 200 endemic plant species found in neither of the adjacent deserts. Cactus are usually restricted to the coarse soils of bajadas. Dominant at higher elevations are "woodlands" of Joshua tree—the Mojave's trademark species. Other common plants include Mojave yucca, creosote bush, shadscale, and blackbrush. Unlike the Sonoran Desert, trees are few in distribution as well as species diversity.

The Province Mountains in Mojave National Preserve.

36 Bigelow Cholla Garden Wilderness

Bigelow cholla in the Sacramento Mountains, Bigelow Cholla Garden Wilderness.

LOCATION:
San Bernardino County;
18 miles west of Needles
just south of I-40

SIZE: 10,380 acres

ELEVATION RANGE:
500 to 1,000 feet

ADMINISTRATION:
BLM Needles Resource
Area Office

MAPS: Desert Access
Guide Needles #13;
AAA San Bernardino
County

Bigelow Cholla Garden Wilderness is located on the northern edge of the Sacramento Mountains—a dark, volcanic, highly eroded mountain area. Terrain is relatively unspectacular and consists of 60 percent hills, 20 percent dissected fans, 10 percent alluvial fans, and 10 percent pediments.

Named for the Bigelow cholla cactus, which is abundant on the slopes of these mountains, the wilderness reportedly contains the densest stands of this cactus in the state. Most of the washes host ironwood, acacia, and mesquite.

The desert tortoise habitat is abundant in the area, and bighorn sheep occasionally move into the region from the mountains further south.

The area was once crossed by a major native American trading route that ran from the Colorado River inland. It is still used by native Americans for ritual purposes.

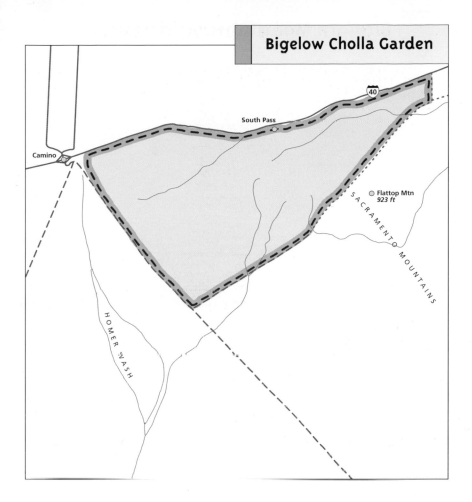

There are no trails in this wilderness. Hiking through the open slopes is easy, but beware of the cholla cactus, which seems to attach itself to shoes, clothes, and skin almost as if it were magnetically attracted.

ACCESS

A high-clearance vehicle is recommended if you leave pavement. A mountain bike might be useful. I-40 forms the northern boundary of the wilderness, and a pipeline road marks the southeastern border. Exit I-40 at Camino and turn south on a dirt road that forms the wilderness boundary. Hike from this road.

37 Bighorn Mountains Wilderness

The Bighorn Mountains in Bighorn Mountains Wilderness.

LOCATION:
San Bernardino County;
70 miles north of Palm
Springs and several
miles west of Landers
on the eastern slope of
the San Bernardino
Mountains

SIZE: 39,185 acres

ELEVATION RANGE:
2,000 to 7,500 feet

ADMINISTRATION:
BLM Barstow Resource
Area Office

MAPS: Desert Access
Guide Yucca Valley #14;
AAA San Bernardino
County

The Bighorn Mountains make up the eastern foothills of the San Bernardino Mountains. The western border is contiguous with the San Bernardino National Forest. The highest elevation is 7,500-foot Granite Peak located in the southwest corner. Most of the wilderness consists of flat plateaus and low hills.

The wilderness is divided by dirt roads into three units. Rattlesnake Canyon, a perennial stream, forms one corridor that provides access to the largest two subunits. The wilderness lies at the transition zone from high desert to conifer forest, with Joshua tree at lower elevations and forests of Jeffrey pine at the highest elevations. Mule deer, mountain lion, bobcat, and jackrabbit along with smaller mammals, birds, and rodents are found here. Bighorn sheep, for which the mountains are named, are now extirpated.

With a perennial stream, it is not surprising that archeological remains are numerous. Several semipermanent village sites are reported, as well as rock art, middens, roasting pits, and metates.

Bighorn Mountains

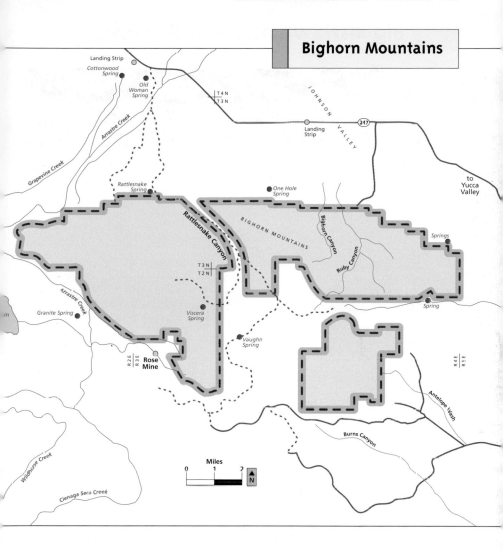

ACCESS

You'll need a good map, luck, and probably some time to find your way from the main highway to the mountains. There are far more "tracks" and "ways" on the ground than on the maps, and few named landmarks or route signs. You have to "follow your nose" and work toward the obvious base of the mountains. The best access is from Hwy 247 in Johnson Valley, 31 miles north of Yucca Valley. Turn left (southwest) onto a gravel-dirt road just before the main highway makes a definite turn from west to northwest. In 2.5 miles this road puts you at the mouth of Rattlesnake Canyon. It is also possible to find your way to the wilderness by following a number of subdivision roads west of Landers off Hwy 247. Go as far as you can proceed, then park and walk to the wilderness boundary.

38 Big Maria Mountains Wilderness

Dawn at Big Maria Mountains Wilderness.

LOCATION: Riverside County; 10 miles north of Blythe, California

SIZE: 47,570 acres

ELEVATION RANGE: 500 to 3,400 feet

ADMINISTRATION: BLM Palm Springs Resource Area Office

MAPS: Desert Access Guide Parker/Blythe #16; AAA Riverside County

The Big Maria Mountains are a rugged, sawtooth range just west of the Colorado River. Hwy 95 forms the southeastern boundary, whereas the northern boundary is just south of Big Wash. Big Wash separates Big Maria Mountains Wilderness from Riverside Mountains Wilderness to the north. Gentle bajadas form the lower slopes, but volcanic peaks dominate the main divide of the range, and numerous washes and canyons dissect it. Vegetation consists of creosote bush, burrobush, ocotillo, beavertail cactus, and cholla and barrel cactus. Palo verde and ironwood grow in the washes.

Although the wilderness itself is exceedingly dry, if camped near the boundaries when it is quiet and still, you can sometimes hear water birds and the sound of frogs coming from the riparian area by the Colorado River.

Centuries ago, native peoples living on the lower Colorado River Valley created gigantic human, animal, and geometric figures on the ground surface. These figures are

Big Maria Mountains

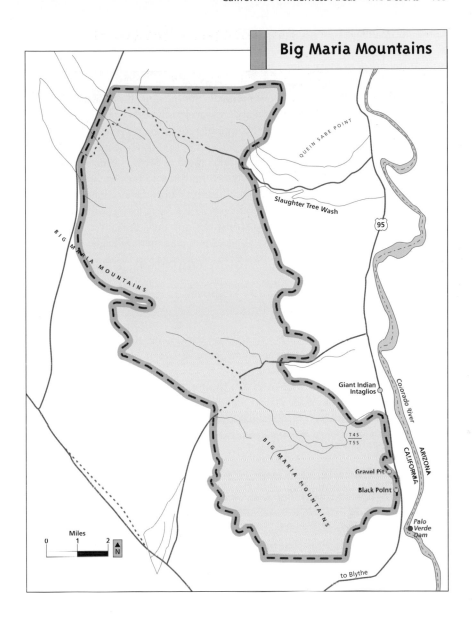

known to archeologists as intaglios (pronounced in-tal-yos), an Italian term that refers to an engraving process.

According to Mojave and Quechan tribes of the Lower Colorado River, the human figures represent Mastambo, the Creator of Earth and all life. The animal figures represent Hatakulya, one of two mountain lion-persons who helped in the Creation. In times past, sacred ceremonial dances were held in the area to honor the Creator of life. The figures continue to be important to the native peoples of the Lower Colorado River.

The Blythe Intaglios are located 15 miles north of Blythe, California, on two mesas. There are a total of six distinct figures in three locations, including a human figure at each location and an animal figure at two of the locations. The largest human figure measures 171 feet from head to toe. These intaglios are extremely rare globally, and only occur in Peru, England, Australia, and along the Lower Colorado River. The Blythe Intaglios, also known as geoglyphs, are extremely fragile ground figures. In recent years the geoglyphs have been subjected to vandalism and damage by people driving over them.

ACCESS

Access is from Hwy 95. There is a signed road that accesses the Giant Indian Intaglios off Hwy 95 that provides rough, generally 4wd or mountain bike access to the southern third of the wilderness.

The easiest access is from Blythe. Head north on Hwy 95 for approximately 11 miles to Palo Verde Dam. One mile beyond the dam you reach the border of the wilderness, which lies just west of Hwy 95 for the next 11 miles or so. Take any of several dirt roads heading west toward the mountains.

Bristol Mountains Wilderness 39

Basalt boulders on a ridge in Bristol Mountains Wilderness.

The trailless Bristol Mountains lie just west of the Mojave National Preserve and directly north of I-40. The terrain is rolling and consists of volcanic uplands. The lack of water means day hiking is probably the rule. Great sweeping views, particularly to the north, give a real sense of vastness. Creosote bush and desert grasslands are the dominant vegetative cover.

ACCESS

Take the Ludlow exit from I-40 and go north on a dirt road for 2 miles. Turn east on a pipeline road. The wilderness is to the south of this road. My vehicle nearly got stuck in soft sand, so beware. Park and walk if you encounter questionable road conditions.

LOCATION: San Bernardino County; 40 miles southeast of Baker, California

SIZE: 68,515 acres

ELEVATION RANGE: 2,200 to 4,500 feet

ADMINISTRATION: BLM Barstow Resource Area Office

MAPS: Desert Access Guide Johnson Valley #11, Providence Mountains #12; AAA San Bernardino County

Bristol Mountains

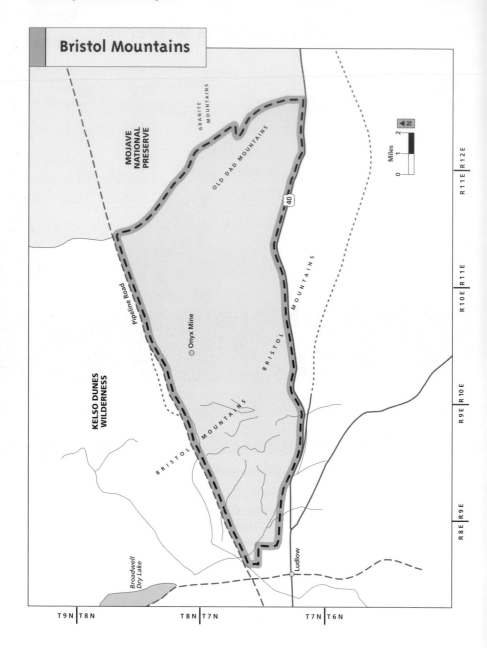

MOJAVE NATIONAL PRESERVE

GRANITE MOUNTAINS

OLD DAD MOUNTAINS

40

BRISTOL MOUNTAINS

Pipeline Road

○ Onyx Mine

KELSO DUNES WILDERNESS

BRISTOL MOUNTAINS

Broadwell Dry Lake

Ludlow

N

Miles

0   1   2

R11E | R12E
R10E | R11E
R9E | R10E
R8E | R9E

T9N | T8N   T8N | T7N   T7N | T6N

Cadiz Dunes Wilderness 40

Sand dunes in Cadiz Dunes Wilderness.

Cadiz Dunes Wilderness consists of some small dunes and wide open creosote flats in the middle of the broad Cadiz Valley. Vistas are expansive, with good views of Old Woman Mountains Wilderness, Ship Mountains proposed wilderness, and Sheephole Mountains Wilderness. The source of sand for Cadiz Dunes is the old Cadiz Lake lake bed—an ancient, relict playa from the wetter Ice Age. The shifting sands create a constantly changing panorama of shapes and shadows. There is no water, so most people are likely to day hike into the area. However, given its relative isolation, an overnight camp in the dunes could be a rewarding experience.

The Borrego milk vetch (*Astragalus lentiginosus* var. *borreganus*)—a rare and endangered species in California—is known to occur in the dunes. Cadiz Valley is also a good habitat for the endangered desert tortoise. Other typical desert wildlife such as coyote, kangaroo rat, and jackrabbit are seen.

LOCATION: San Bernardino County; 40 miles east of Twentynine Palms, California

SIZE: 39,740 acres

ELEVATION RANGE: 1,000 to 1,500 feet

ADMINISTRATION: BLM Palm Springs Resource Area Office

MAPS: Desert Access Guide Sheephole Mountains #15; AAA San Bernardino County

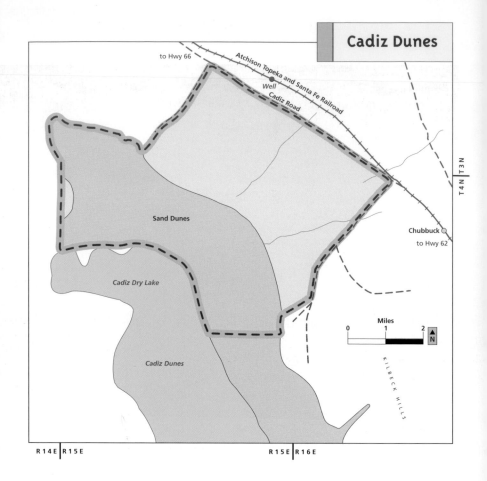

Cadiz Dunes

ACCESS

Access to the wilderness is along Cadiz Road, which is passable by 2wd vehicles. You can access Cadiz Road either from the north off Hwy 66 at Cadiz or from the south off Hwy 62 near Rice. I found the road from the north to be less challenging. The southern access tends to have more wind-blown sand and thus is less passable for 2wd vehicles. Cadiz Road follows a railroad right-of-way and pipeline route. It forms the eastern boundary of the wilderness for 5 miles.

The best access to the dunes is a sandy dirt road that forms the northern boundary of the wilderness, which lies just beyond pipeline orange sign marker 222. I was only willing to drive this road a short way before soft sand forced me to stop and walk. It is, however, no more than a 4-mile walk from Cadiz Road to the dunes themselves.

Chemehuevi Mountains Wilderness 41

Sunset on a rock outcrop in Chemehuevi Mountains Wilderness.

Chemehuevi Mountains Wilderness rises from the Colorado River to the summit of 3,697-foot Chemehuevi Peak. Although this may not seem like much elevation, the overall relief is quite substantial. The mountains, which include granitic rock and volcanic spires, form a horseshoe with the center facing eastward toward the Colorado River. The central valley is covered by dense stands of cholla, ocotillo, and agave.

Chemehuevi Mountains Wilderness is immediately adjacent to the Havasu Wilderness Area managed by the US Fish and Wildlife Service. Taken together, this is a biologically rich area. The Chemehuevi Mountains contain a mixture of Sonoran and Mojave Desert species. The close proximity to the Colorado River provides a habitat for riparian and water-dependent species as well, resulting in an unusually rich diversity of species for the California desert. Bighorn sheep and mule deer are reported for the area. Other unusual

LOCATION:
San Bernardino County;
12 miles southeast of
Needles, California

SIZE: 64,320 acres

ELEVATION RANGE:
500 to 3,716 feet

ADMINISTRATION:
BLM Needles Resource
Area Office

MAPS: Desert Access
Guide Needles #13,
Parker/Blythe #16; AAA
San Bernardino County

creatures include the Great Plains toad, Great Basin spadefoot toad, tree lizard, western ground snake, Sonoran lyre snake, and mountain lion.

The mountains contain light-colored granites and dark volcanic rocks. A number of large washes dissect the mountains, including Trampas Wash—a popular hiking route. The small but spectacular Sawtooth Range lies along the southwestern border.

The area was popular with native Americans, probably due to its proximity to the river. There are numerous cultural remains including campsites, fire rings, and rock art. Indeed, one of the best pictographs found in the California desert—a split red sphere about 3 feet across held by two black hands—is located in a cave in the southern part of the wilderness.

ACCESS

Drive south from Needles on Hwy 95 for 12 miles to the trailhead for Trampas Wash, which was a popular ORV route prior to wilderness designation. If you head southeast down the wash you reach the Colorado River in 12 miles or so.

Another potential destination is the 5-mile round-trip hike/scramble up 3,716-foot Chemehuevi Peak, the highest point in the wilderness. From Needles drive south on Hwy 95 for 23 miles. You pass the Sawtooth Range and cross a dirt power line road. This road is just north of the paved Havasu Lake Road, which parallels it to the southeast. Turn left on the dirt road, which is the southwestern border of the wilderness. Drive about 4 miles and park. Hike northeast across country, crossing several small washes until you come to a large wash draining a saddle northwest of Chemehuevi Peak. Follow the wash up to the saddle, then scramble up to the summit of the peak.

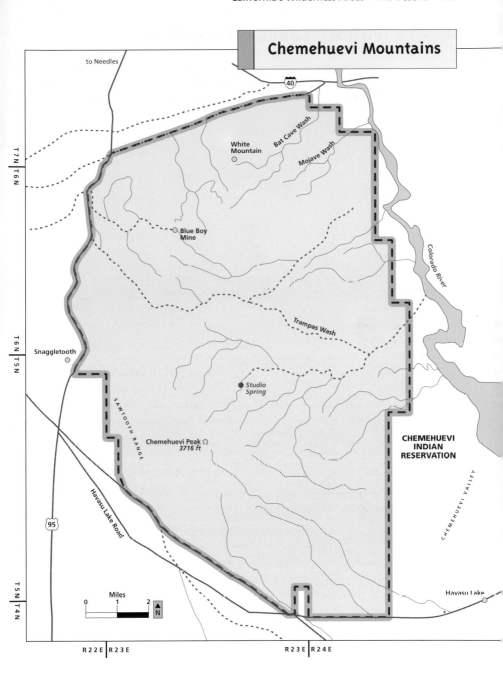

Chemehuevi Mountains

to Needles

40

White Mountain

Bat Cave Wash

Mojave Wash

T 7 N | T 6 N

Colorado River

Blue Boy Mine

Trampas Wash

T 6 N | T 5 N

Snaggletooth

Studio Spring

SAWTOOTH RANGE

Chemehuevi Peak
3716 ft

CHEMEHUEVI INDIAN RESERVATION

CHEMEHUEVI VALLEY

Havasu Lake Road

95

T 5 N | T 4 N

Havasu Lake

Miles
0   1   2
N

R 22 E | R 23 E

R 23 E | R 24 E

42 Cleghorn Lakes Wilderness

Granite outcrops of the Bullion Mountains, Cleghorn Lakes Wilderness.

LOCATION:
San Bernardino County; 16 miles northwest of Twentynine Palms, California

SIZE: 33,980 acres

ELEVATION RANGE:
1,400 to 4,100 feet

ADMINISTRATION:
BLM Barstow Resource Area Office

MAPS: Desert Access Guide Sheephole Mountains #15; AAA San Bernardino County

With a name like Cleghorn Lakes Wilderness one may be tempted to envision a shimmering blue oasis in the desert, however this wildland is named for normally dry lakes near the center of the wilderness. What one notices when visiting the area are not lakes but the granitic boulders and outcrops of the Bullion Mountains that give the area an appearance similar to Joshua Tree National Park.

The wilderness is divided into two different regions. The eastern portion is mountainous whereas the western end of the wilderness is a vast alluvial fan. The Twentynine Palms Marine Corps Base borders it on the north, and a road corridor for the base cuts off a small portion of the northwestern corner of the wilderness.

Bighorn sheep are known from the area, and desert tortoise are found on the valley floor. Occasionally spectacular wildflower displays occur on the dry lake beds. Barrel cac-

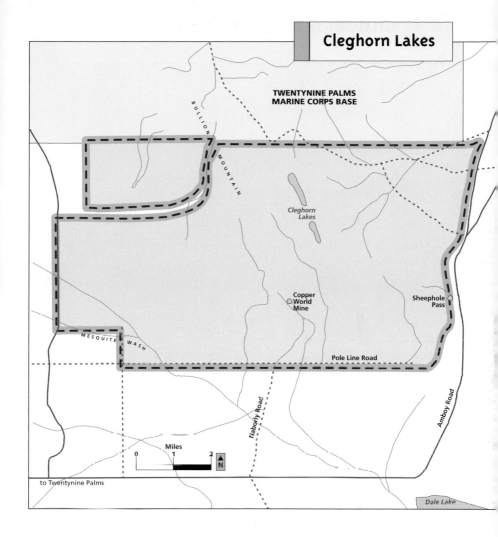

Cleghorn Lakes

TWENTYNINE PALMS
MARINE CORPS BASE

BULLION MOUNTAIN

Cleghorn
Lakes

Copper
○ World
Mine

Sheephole ○
Pass

MESQUITE   WASH

Pole Line Road

Naborly Road

Amboy Road

Miles
0   1   2
N

to Twentynine Palms

Dale Lake

tus gardens find nooks among the boulders, and smoke tree (a species common in the Colorado Desert) reaches its northern limits in this area. A disjunct population of crucifixion thorn, a species normally found in the Sonoran Desert, is found along the eastern border of the wilderness.

ACCESS

To reach the wilderness, head north and east out of Twentynine Palms on Amboy Road. The road marks the border of the wilderness from Sheephole Pass north for 5 miles. Just park and hike west from the road. Another potential trailhead lies off Amboy Road. From Twentynine Palms take Amboy Road until you intersect Naborly Road, which goes north 3 miles to the wilderness boundary. Here you can hike two more miles on an old road to ruins of the Copper World Mine.

43 Clipper Mountains Wilderness

Dawn at Clipper Mountains Wilderness.

LOCATION:
San Bernardino County;
50 miles west of
Needles, California

SIZE: 26,000 acres

ELEVATION RANGE:
2,000 to 4,600 feet

ADMINISTRATION:
BLM Needles Resource
Area Office

MAPS: Desert Access
Guide Providence
Mountains #12; AAA
San Bernardino County

The Clipper Mountains Wilderness lies just south of I-40 and the Mojave National Preserve. Walk this wilderness and you will be following in the steps of the Chemehuevis, who once hunted bighorn sheep in the area.

Consisting of a large mesa with canyons and hills, there are great views of Clipper Valley and Providence Mountains from the higher rims in this area. The "mountains" are oriented in a northeast-southwest alignment, with the most prominent ridge in the central region. Castle Dome, at 3,299 feet, is the highest named peak. Jagged buttes and spires are scattered throughout the region south of the main crest. Part of the area was once used as military training ground during World War II and the impact of these activities is still visible.

The area is known for its herd of bighorn sheep, which rely on the springs in the area as a water source.

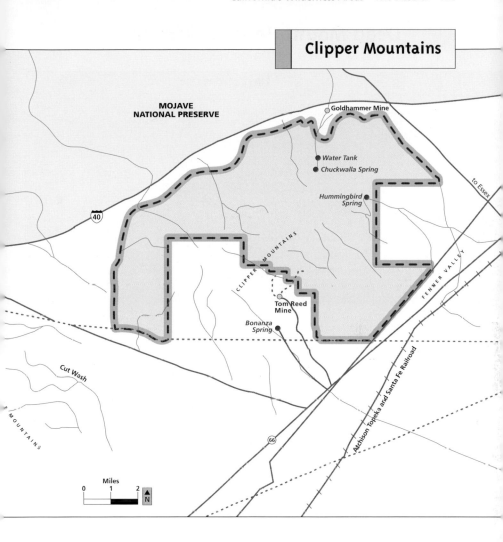

Clipper Mountains

MOJAVE
NATIONAL PRESERVE

Goldhammer Mine

Water Tank
Chuckwalla Spring

Hummingbird
Spring

to Essex

40

CLIPPER MOUNTAINS

FENNER VALLEY

Tom Reed
Mine

Bonanza
Spring

Cut Wash

MOUNTAINS

Atchison Topeka and Santa Fe Railroad

66

Miles
0   1   2
N

ACCESS

Access to the wilderness is somewhat problematic. One could park off I-40 and hike south to the wilderness, which lies less than a half mile from the highway in places. Or you could take Rte 66 west from Essex approximately 7 miles to where a rough dirt road goes north about 4 miles to the Tom Reed Mine. The mine is on the edge of the wilderness.

44 Dead Mountains Wilderness

Brittlebush frames the Dead Mountains in Dead Mountains Wilderness.

LOCATION:
San Bernardino County;
12 miles northwest of
Needles, California

SIZE: 48,850 acres

ELEVATION RANGE:
500 to 3,598 feet

ADMINISTRATION:
BLM Needles Resource
Area Office

MAPS: Desert Access
Guide Needles #13;
AAA San Bernardino
County

Hike in Dead Mountains Wilderness and you enter lands sacred to local native American tribes. Indeed the area was once a cremation site for local tribes, hence the origin of its name. The mountains form a jagged north-south range immediately adjacent to the Colorado River. The highest summit is 4,000-foot Mount Manchester. Large, winding canyons penetrate the mountains and afford secluded hiking opportunities, and sweeping bajadas flank the slopes.

There are several special plants associated with these mountains. The Piute Wash Smoke Tree Assemblage is the northernmost occurrence of this plant community in California. Springs in Picture Canyon and at Red Spring also host unusual plant communities.

Raptor use of these mountains is well established, with red-tailed hawk, prairie falcon, and golden eagle known to forage and sometimes nest in the area. A small resident

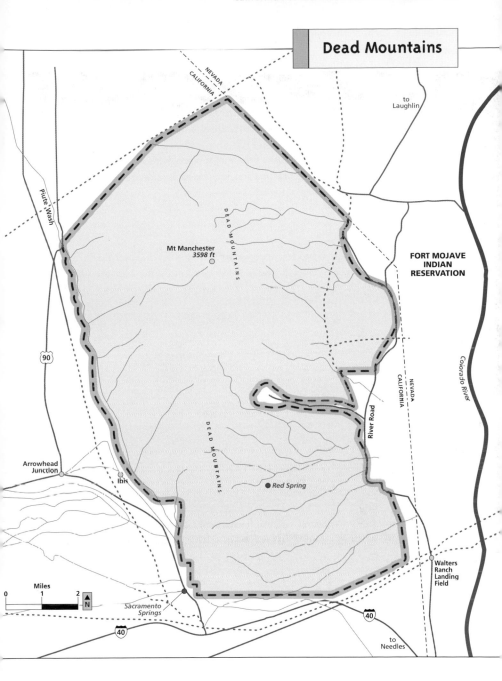

Dead Mountains

herd of desert bighorn sheep roam the area, and fairly high densities of desert tortoise have been documented.

The Dead Mountains play a significant role in native American traditions. The area is part of the Origin Myth of the Mojaves, and ceremonial sites abound. According to Mojave tradition, one spring (which shall remain nameless) in the wilderness is said to have healing power. Cremation sites, and even several battle sites between the Mojave and other tribes, are known in this area. Old aboriginal trails lie to the east and west of the mountains, and the aptly named Picture Canyon, which contains as many as 500 designs, is one of the major petroglyph locations in the entire eastern Mojave Desert. Other cultural artifacts include rock shelters, pottery shards, bedrock mortars, and projectile points.

ACCESS

To get to the wilderness, travel 16 miles north from Needles on River Road. Watch for a rock cairn adjacent to a wash, and proceed west toward the wilderness boundary.

Early morning on the Dead Mountains, Dead Mountains Wilderness.

Joshua Tree National Park 45

Evening light on Joshua tree, Joshua Tree National Park.

Joshua Tree National Park is a huge granitic wilderness. Domes, peaks, ridges, and boulders crop out of the landscape like mushrooms. The granite faces attract climbers from throughout the United States who come to clamber over the weathered, cracked stone. Adding to the scenic interest of the land are the twisted picturesque forms of the park's namesake—the Joshua tree.

The park was originally established as a national monument by presidential order in 1936. The 1994 California Desert Protection Act added 234,000 acres to Joshua Tree, enlarging it to 794,000 acres, and upgrading it from a national monument to a national park. Most of these new additions were in the Coxcomb Mountains and Eagle Mountains. The Eagle Mountains were originally part of Joshua Tree National Monument, but were "removed" during World War II to allow access to iron deposits. Altogether 70 percent, or some 585,040 acres, of the park are designated as wilderness.

LOCATION: San Bernardino County; 5 miles south of Twentynine Palms, California

SIZE: 794,000 total acres and 585,040 acres of wilderness

ELEVATION RANGE: 1,900 to 5,813 feet

ADMINISTRATION: Joshua Tree National Park

MAPS: Joshua Tree National Park; AAA San Bernardino County

As large as Joshua Tree National Park is today, it is still not as large as originally envisioned, when more than one million acres were proposed for protection. A much more effective biologic unit would extend the boundaries of the park northward to include Cleghorn Lakes Wilderness and Sheephole Mountains Wilderness, and eastward to the Colorado River by incorporating Palen-McCoy Wilderness, Rice Valley Wilderness, Big Maria Mountains Wilderness, and intervening lands into one park unit. The resulting 1.5-million-acre preserve would create a tremendous biologic reserve stretching from the Colorado River practically to the San Bernardino Mountains.

HISTORY

Members of the Serrano tribe were residents of San Bernardino County in the region of Joshua Tree National Park at the time of Spanish colonization of what is now California. They lived seasonally in the park area, gathering pinyon nuts from the higher peaks and hunting bighorn sheep among the rock formations. In 1867, the Chemehuevi, a people originally from the Colorado River, were forced from their homeland by the more aggressive Mojaves. The Chemehuevi settled in among the Serrano, intermarrying and sharing the meager resources of these desert highlands. Settlement focused on the few permanent water sources in the desert. One of these, within Joshua Tree (the Oasis of Mara), was an important native use area. Today the Twentynine Palms Visitor Center is located at the same oasis.

Food resources for these people, while meager, were varied. They included mesquite beans, yucca stems, juniper berries, pinyon nuts, cactus fruits, palm fruits, and other plants, augmented with wild game like antelope and bighorn sheep.

With the discovery of gold in the foothills of California's Sierra Nevada in 1848, prospectors fanned out across the state, including the deserts, looking for new mineral discoveries. The first mine in what would later be Joshua Tree National Park was established in 1865. By 1879, cattlemen were beginning to filter into the area. Several early ranching operations were established, including one in Queen Valley. Most of these early ranchers also held mining claims as well.

In 1910, Bill Keys (for whom Keys View is named) arrived in the Joshua Tree area to manage a mine. Eventually he came to own a ranch and a number of mining prospects. Keys has been glorified in many park historical accounts, perhaps because some attribute heroic dimensions to any old timer who managed to live in such an inhospitable environment. Yet Keys appears to have been prone to violent behavior. Keys acquired the Desert Queen Mine and other mining properties, often by what appears to be less than legal means. His half-wild cattle also ravaged the desert vegetation.

Keys might be forgotten except for his predilection for violent behavior. In 1932, during a dispute over the use of a water hole, Keys shot and wounded a local cowboy, who fortunately survived the encounter. In 1943, Keys again resorted to Old West violence in another argument over water by shooting and killing a neighboring rancher. Keys was sentenced to imprisonment in San Quentin. However, he was released 5 years later due to testimony by the dead man's ex-wife.

Apparently still bitter over their divorce, she claimed her husband had said he would kill Keys if he persisted in trespassing on his lands (so, supposedly Keys acted in self-defense). Keys died in 1969.

Joshua Tree, like most national parks, owes its existence to the efforts of a small group of dedicated supporters. In the case of Joshua Tree, the effort for protection was led by a Los Angeles socialite named Minerva Hamilton Hoyt. During the 1920s, increasing use of native desert vegetation for landscaping in southern California led to the removal of cacti and other plants from large areas of the desert. In addition, the expansion of automobile use, particularly on fragile desert landscapes, along with the impact of mining activities throughout the region led Mrs. Hoyt to fight for preservation of the desert landscape.

Starting in the 1920s she began to put together educational exhibits that extolled the virtues of the desert environment. By 1930 she had organized the International Deserts Conservation League to promote preservation of desert life and landscapes. In that same year she first broached the idea with public officials of creating a new national park in the California desert. Hoyt's proposal called for the creation of a million-acre national park stretching from present-day Joshua Tree all the way to the Colorado River.

As a consequence of her social connections, Hoyt was able to arrange a meeting with newly elected President Franklin Roosevelt and his Secretary of Interior, Harold Ickes, to present her case for a major desert park. Both Roosevelt and Ickes were impressed by Hoyt's presentation and withdrew 1,136,000 acres of public domain for potential designation as a desert park. After several more years of lobbying government officials, Mrs. Hoyt's dream was finally realized. On August 10, 1936, President Roosevelt signed a proclamation setting aside 825,000 acres as Joshua Tree National Monument.

The new monument was not welcomed by everyone. In particular, the mining and livestock industries were opposed to its establishment. They never really accepted the notion that any public lands should be off limits to their use and exploitation. These industries used their considerable political power to build opposition to the monument. In 1950, a bill was enacted that deleted 289,000 acres from the monument and reopened it to new mining claims. In 1961, more land was removed from the protection of the monument.

All these losses were largely reversed by the 1994 California Desert Protection Act. The bill reinstated protection for many of the lands "deleted" by the 1950 and 1961 bills, enlarging the park to 794,000 acres. Lands were added in the Coxcomb, Eagle, Cottonwood, Little San Bernardino, and Pinto Mountains. In addition, 70 percent (or 585,040 acres) were designated as wilderness.

GEOLOGY

The geologic structure of Joshua Tree consists of two major rock types—Pinto gneiss (a metamorphic rock that looks something like what everyone calls granite) and younger, lighter rocks that are granitic and are called quart monzonite and monzogranite. For example, monzogranite dominates the Wonderland of Rocks, Lost Horse, and Queen Valleys.

Granitic outcrop in Joshua Tree National Park.

These granitic rocks were created by the collision of gigantic plates that make up the outer mantle of the earth. Some 180 million years ago the western edge of the North American continental plate was located somewhere in the region of what is now Nevada. As the North American plate moved westward, it collided with the Pacific Ocean plate. The oceanic plate slid under the lighter North American plate and melted. Some magma rose up through cracks in the mantle to erupt at the surface of the earth as a series of volcanoes. (A similar geologic situation exists today in the Pacific Northwest, where the Cascades form a line of volcanoes where the Pacific plate is diving under the western edge of the North American plate.) Some of the magma never made it to the surface and cooled deep in the earth, creating the granitic plutons that now make up the Sierra Nevada, San Bernardino Mountains, and many of the other mountains ranges of southern California, including those in Joshua Tree National Park.

The subsequent pressures associated with plate movement cracked and fractured these rocks along faults. The faults also define many of the mountain ranges, which are usually associated with major faults. For instance, the Pinto Basin Fault separates Twentynine Palms Valley from the Little San Bernardino Mountains to the south.

Over time, the overlying rock was striped away by erosion, leaving behind the granitic ridges and peaks so characteristic of Joshua Tree. Some of the original overlying rock—the Pinto gneiss—remains in some parts of the park. These rocks, although significantly altered, were originally formed some 1.5 billion years ago. Good examples of this gneiss can be seen at Ryan Mountain and on other higher peaks in the park.

As the overburden of other rocks was removed by erosion, the underlying monzogranite and quart monzonite—the two rocks that make up most of the cliffs and domes in the park—were exposed to erosional processes. They were subsequently fractured and weathered into the fantastic shapes we see today.

Then, some 3 million years ago, new volcanic eruptions flowed out across the landscape, leaving behind a few nongranitic rocks in the park like those seen at Malpais Hill—a 400-foot-high hill of black basalt seen along the geology tour road.

The finishing touches to Joshua Tree's landscape are the result of geomorphologic erosive features associated with deserts. The creation of alluvial fans; rounded, granite boulders; and washes are all consequences of desert climatic conditions.

Deserts were created in southern California as a consequence of several factors, including the rise of the high wall of mountains to the west (the San Bernardino Mountains and San Jacinto Mountains). These high peaks block the flow of moist air from the Pacific, creating a rain shadow and restricting precipitation to 6 to 8 inches a year.

FAUNA AND FLORA

Joshua Tree National Park sits at a transition zone between the lower elevation Colorado Desert and the higher elevation Mojave Desert. In the southern part of the park there are plants like California fan palm, ocotillo, smoke tree, creosote bush, brittlebush, and cholla of the Colorado Desert, whereas Joshua tree dominates higher elevations. On the highest peaks there are even pinyon pine and juniper. An occasional oak from the coastal mountain plant communities sneaks into the park as well. Five palm oases are found in the park. These California fan palms are important from both an aesthetic perspective as well as for wildlife.

But the premier plant species found in the park is its namesake—Joshua tree. Joshua tree is found throughout the Mojave Desert and it reaches a southern limit in Joshua Tree National Park. This member of the lily family is also found in southern Nevada and just barely reaches into southwestern Utah and northwestern Arizona. Joshua tree was first described by American trapper Jedediah Smith, who trekked across the Mojave Desert in 1827. However, according to legend, the name Joshua tree was applied to the plant by Mormon pioneers crossing the California desert in 1851 en route to San Bernardino who thought the twisted arms of the plant looked like Joshua beholding the heavens.

True or not, Joshua tree is a remarkable plant with a shaggy bark, lovely white blossoms, and large, daggerlike leaves. The unusual branching of the plant results whenever the terminal bud of the branch is damaged or supports a flower. The branch then forks just before the old bud into two new branches. This continues throughout the life of the plant, resulting in the strange and unusual branching pattern seen on mature Joshua tree. The oldest of these plants are thought to be 800 years or more in age.

Joshua tree reproduce both by seed as well as by vegetative runner. The smaller "trees" found surrounding large, mature Joshua tree are typically genetic clones that grow from root suckers.

Numerous wildlife species are dependent on Joshua tree for existence. For instance, the yucca-boring beetle lays its eggs on the terminal bud of the plant. When the eggs hatch, the young larvae consume some of the plant tissue. This damage promotes new branching.

Another insect dependent on Joshua tree is the yucca moth. The moth gathers the sticky pollen of Joshua tree to fertilize the flowers of adjacent Joshua tree. Once fertilized, and thus ensuring the development of seeds, the moth lays her eggs on the seed pod. Not all the seeds are consumed by the moth larvae, and some survive to ensure new seedlings for the plant.

There is an even more complex insect-Joshua tree interrelationship. The small ichneumon wasp somehow detects which Joshua tree seed pods contain yucca moth larvae. It then bores into the seed pod, paralyzes the young moth larvae, then lays its own egg on it. The moth larvae then serves as the food source for the growing wasp.

Many other animals use Joshua tree for nest sites, feeding sites, and perch sites. At least 25 bird species are associated with the plant, including the ladder-backed woodpecker, Scott's oriole, loggerhead shrike, and red-tailed hawk. Other wildlife found in the park include mule deer, bighorn sheep, coyote, mountain lion, bobcat, badger, as well as 230 species of birds.

ACCESS

The easiest access to Joshua Tree is from the south. I-10 borders the park, and the Cottonwood entrance to the park is 52 miles east of Palm Springs. To the north is Hwy 62, with two entrances to the park. The north entrance is just south of Twentynine Palms and the west entrance is south of the town of Joshua Tree.

CAMPING

Cross-country hiking and camping are permitted in the park. Presently the park regulations require that you camp 1 mile off any road and 500 feet from any trail. Some areas of the park are designated day-use areas to protect sensitive wildlife such as bighorn sheep. You should inquire at park visitor centers to find out which areas are closed to overnight camping. Campfires are not permitted outside of campgrounds, hence any cooking requires the use of a backpacker stove. Finally,

Cholla cactus glow in evening light and Hexie Mountains, Joshua Tree National Park.

as in most national parks, dogs and other pets are not permitted outside of official campgrounds.

HIKING

Joshua Tree is well known among climbers who come to scramble up the granite boulders and outcrops. It is less appreciated as a good place for camping and hiking. Unlike most desert wildlands, there are established campgrounds and miles of trails that loop through the park. Currently there are 10 nature trails and six official trails. There are, however, unlimited opportunities for off-trail, cross-country hikes.

Most hikes in the park are day hikes, in part because water sources are almost nonexistent. It is possible to do longer overnight backpack trips either by carrying all the water you require—a heavy load—or by caching water in advance at road crossings. For instance, the California Riding and Hiking Trail crosses a number of park roads along its route where water caches could be hidden prior to a hike. Depending on how one strings a route together, you can also replenish water supplies by stopping at official campgrounds and ranger stations that provide water. Not all official campgrounds, however, have water. Potable water is available at the Twentynine Palms Visitor Center located at the Oasis of Mara, the Black Rock and Cottonwood Campgrounds, at the West Entrance station, and at the Indian Cove Ranger Station.

A more chancy means of doing an extended hike depends on the weather. The higher elevations of Joshua Tree do occasionally experience snowfall. On winter desert trips I have melted snow for water. Finding enough snow can be a problem, plus getting it into the pot without dragging in some sand and dirt is often difficult. Nevertheless, if you don't mind drinking slightly gritty soup or tea, you may be able to plan on camping beyond the roads for an extended time. Keep in mind that melting snow consumes a lot of fuel, so bring plenty if you plan to exercise this option. Remember, a minimum of 1 gallon of water per day per person is recommended.

The longest trail in Joshua Tree National Park is the California Riding and Hiking Trail. There are 35 miles of trail within the park. Many shorter trails for a one-day or shorter exploration are available. Pick up an information sheet at one of the two visitor centers.

Among the more interesting short trails is the 1.1-mile jaunt to Barker Dam. The nearly level trail loops past petroglyphs. The 2-mile Lost Horse Mine leads to remnants of old buildings, a mine, and a mill. The Ryan Mountain Trail is a strenuous 3-mile round-trip (two to three hours) to a great panorama of park valleys and Wonderland of Rocks, San Jacinto, and San Gorgonio Peaks. The 3-mile round-trip hike to Fortynine Palms Oasis features a palm-ringed oasis in a rocky canyon. The somewhat longer 8.5-mile round-trip to Lost Palm Oasis leads to a stunning view of another oasis. This hike is particularly spectacular during wildflower season. From the same trailhead as the Lost Palm Oasis one can hike the Mastodon Peak Trail, which leads past gold mine ruins to an overlook and the panorama of Eagle Mountains and the Salton Sea in the distance.

DAY HIKE: LOST PALM OASIS
One-way length: 4.2 miles
Low and high elevations: 3,000 to 3,400 feet
Difficulty: moderate

The Lost Palm Oasis contains the largest group of California fan palms found in Joshua Tree National Park. The oasis is used by bighorn sheep as a watering hole, consequently backcountry camping near the palms is not permitted. The trail is located southeast of the Cottonwood Visitor Center. To find the trailhead, leave I-10 at the Cottonwood exit. Go north 8 miles to the Cottonwood Visitor Center. Turn right and travel 1.5 miles to the Cottonwood Springs parking area.

This is one of the better marked trails in the park, with mileage markers and sign posts. It offers a good introduction to desert hiking for those with less experience in desert travel.

The trail follows the undulating topography of ridge and wash. The constant up-and-down, rolling gait of the trail can get to be somewhat tiring—to the point that you wonder if you will ever reach the oasis. But most hikers agree that the anticipation and time spent hiking is worth the effort for the view of the final destination, with its tropical-looking cluster of palms. The palms, combined with willow thickets and tranquil pools of water, create a refreshing contrast to the surrounding desert. The oasis is a good place to bird watch or just to rest and enjoy a picnic lunch.

DAY HIKE: MASTODON PEAK
One-way length: 3-mile loop
Low and high elevations: 3,000 to 3,440 feet
Difficulty: moderate

Miners named Mastodon Peak for its presumed resemblance to that Ice Age creature. The hike to Mastodon Peak begins at the same trailhead as Lost Palm Oasis and passes some old mining sites located in the southeastern corner of the park. The trail is clearly marked. In a fifth of a mile from the trailhead you reach the first mining ruin, which includes the old foundation for the Winona mill site. The trail then winds up a hill to the old mine, which operated between 1919 and 1932. Some of the ore assayed out at $744 a ton, but the vein petered out quickly and the mine never lived up to its potential. Beyond the mine site there is a short (0.1-mile) "use" trail to the summit of Mastodon Peak that requires some minor boulder scrambling. From the summit, depending on weather and smog conditions, you may be able to see the Salton Sea. Whether you climb up Mastodon Peak or not, the main trail continues south approximately 0.5 mile to a trail junction with the Lost Palm Oasis Trail. Here you turn west (right) to head 1 mile back to the parking area.

DAY HIKE: GOLDEN BEE MINE
One-way length:	2 miles
Low and high elevations:	2,200 to 2,900 feet
Difficulty:	moderate

The hike to the Golden Bee Mine provides a close-up of old mining ruins and debris, plus outstanding panoramic views of the Pinto Basin. The trailhead is located along Pinto Basin Road between the Cottonwood Visitor Center and the White Tank Campground. To find the trailhead, drive Pinto Basin Road to Cholla Garden. The trail is on the south side of the road just a quarter-mile west of the Cholla Garden Nature Trail.

The trail—an old, abandoned mining road that is washed out in numerous places—heads south toward the mountains. The first mile or so is relatively flat. After hiking 1.3 miles you come to the base of the Hexie Mountains. The last 0.7 mile of the hike to the mine ruins is fairly steep and strenuous.

DAY HIKE: LOST HORSE MINE
One-way length:	2 miles
Low and high elevations:	4,600 to 5,313 feet
Difficulty:	moderate

The Lost Horse Mine is the best preserved old mining operation in the park. There are ruins of old buildings and a stamp mill, and great views from the mine site. The trail follows an old, abandoned road. The trailhead is located off Keys View Road. From Park Road 12 travel 2.6 miles on Keys View Road to the signed turnoff to the Lost Horse Mine Trailhead. Follow the dirt road for 1 mile to the parking area. From the trailhead it is a moderate 2-mile climb on an old mining road (now a good trail), through juniper, nolina, and yucca to the mine site.

The mine, which was established in 1896, was one of the most profitable mines ever to operate in the park, producing 9,000 ounces of gold. Equipment, including a stamp mill, were brought to the site by horse and wagon all the way from the Colorado River. Legend has it that the mine was discovered by a German named Frank Diebold. Diebold was unable to mark the claim properly because cowboys working for one of the local ranchers, Jim McHaney, continually threatened his life. Another prospector named Johnny Lang met Diebold while searching for his "lost" horse in the vicinity of the mine. Lang and his father, George, purchased the discovery rights to Diebold's mine. The Langs, along with several other partners, eventually managed to overcome the intimidation of McHaney's cowboys and located their claim in 1893. In 1895 all the partners except Johnny Lang sold their interests in the mine to the Ryan brothers. The Ryan brothers developed the mine, employing at one time up to 25 men at the mine site.

After viewing the mine site, most people simply return the way they came. It is possible, however, to continue southeast on the old road past the mine for another 0.4 mile to the top of a pass. Here you find a "use" trail that leads south

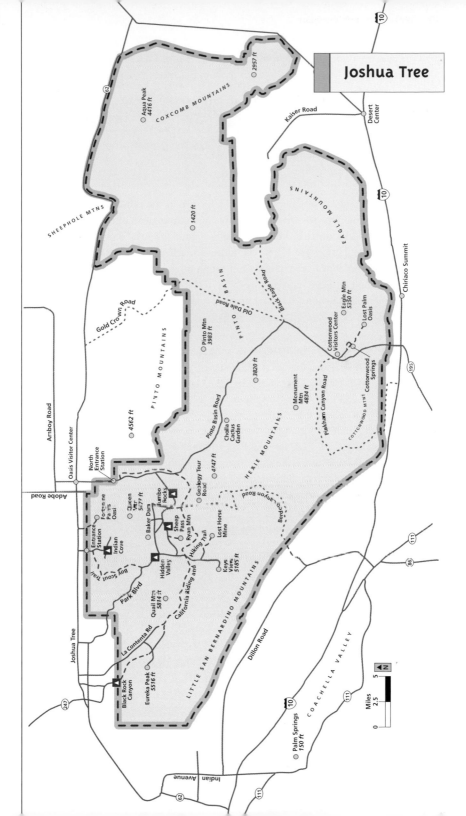

Joshua Tree

of the pass up a ridge 0.3 mile to the top of 5,313-foot Lost Horse Peak. There are tremendous views from the top of the mountain of Queen Valley and Pleasant Valley.

DAY HIKE: RYAN MOUNTAIN HIKE
One-way length: 1.5 miles
Low and high elevations: 4,400 to 5,461 feet
Difficulty: moderate

The whale-shaped top of Ryan Mountain is located at the center of the park and offers panoramic views from its summit, including views of the snow-capped San Bernardino Mountains. The mountain is named after the Ryan brothers who once owned the Lost Horse Mine. The route is a well-built park trail that winds gradually up the slope of the mountain through pinyon and juniper woodlands. The mountain consists of ancient, 1.5-billion-year-old Pinto gneiss—the host rock into which the younger, lighter granitic rocks were intruded.

DAY HIKE: QUAIL MOUNTAIN
One-way length: 7.5 miles
Low and high elevations: 4,200 to 5,813 feet
Difficulty: strenuous

At 5,813 feet, Quail Mountain in the Little San Bernardino Mountains is the highest peak in Joshua Tree National Park and makes a good destination for more experienced hikers. Most of the route is via the California Riding and Hiking Trail, however the final climb to the summit of Quail Mountain is a cross-country scramble. A map is handy to have. With no water on the entire hike, make sure you carry plenty with you.

The vista from the summit is expansive and includes good views of the towering, often snow-covered peaks of the San Bernardino Mountains. Whether one chooses to climb the mountain or not, the hike along the California Riding and Hiking Trail makes for a good day trip into the western section of the park. Signs of wildlife, including deer, bighorn sheep, coyote, and jackrabbit, are often evident.

There are three options for the hike to Quail Mountain. One can make it a long day hike and go in and out by the same route. If you can arrange a shuttle, you can also make it a long 15-mile one-way hike. A third option is to make the ascent of Quail Mountain part of an overnight backpack trip.

Most people make the ascent of Quail Mountain a long day hike. There are two potential trailheads. The easiest access point is from Joshua Tree via West Entrance Road. From Joshua Tree drive 5 miles to the West Entrance Station then continue 10 more miles on Park Road 12 to its intersection with Keys View Road. Turn right on Keys View Road and go 1 mile to the Juniper Flats Trailhead, where the California Riding and Hiking Trail crosses the road. The trail heads west from the road. It is well defined and marked, and gradually climbs through a Joshua tree forest toward Quail Mountain. There are good views of the surrounding landscape all along this trail.

After hiking about 5 miles from the trailhead you reach milepost 23 on the California Riding and Hiking Trail. Here you can look north and see the summit of Quail Mountain. You can turn around at this point and retrace your steps to the trailhead, making for a good 10-mile round-trip hike, or if you are in good shape and ambitious you can climb to the summit of Quail Mountain, which at this point is another 2.5-mile one-way cross-country scramble. Although there is no "defined" trail to the summit, most people choose to follow the wash that intersects the California Riding and Hiking Trail at this point. Hike the wash upstream until it peters out on the southeastern ridge of the summit, which you then follow the rest of the way to the naked mountaintop. The distance from the Juniper Flat Trailhead to the summit and back is 15 miles. This makes for a long day, so many people opt to do this as an overnight backpack trip. Hike in and set up camp somewhere below Quail Mountain on the first day, then climb to the summit early in the morning and return to the trailhead in the afternoon.

One can also hike to Quail Mountain from the Upper Covington Flat Trailhead. The area around Upper Covington Flat is exceptionally good for the development of large Joshua trees. The largest Joshua tree in the park is a short walk from the trailhead. It is 14 feet in circumference and 36 feet high.

The Upper Covington Flat Trailhead at 4,820 feet is higher in elevation than the Juniper Flat Trailhead. To reach the trailhead, travel west from Joshua Tree on Hwy 62 for 3.4 miles to La Contenta Road. Follow this south for 2.9 miles to Lower Covington Flat Road. Go 6.1 miles on this road to an intersection, where you turn right at a sign for Backcountry Trailhead. Continue to follow the signs. Go another 1.8 miles to another junction. Turn left and travel 1.9 miles to the trailhead. It is an undulating 5-mile hike along the California Riding and Hiking Trail to milepost 23, and the beginning point for the cross-country scramble up Quail Mountain. One can turn around at this point and retrace your steps to the Upper Covington Flat Trailhead. If you have previously arranged for a shuttle, skip the side trip to the top of Quail Mountain and continue hiking directly to Juniper Flat Trailhead. This makes for a 10-mile one-way hike. If you add Quail Mountain onto this, the total hike is a long 15-mile trek.

DAY HIKE: FORTYNINE PALMS OASIS

One-way length:	1.5 miles
Low and high elevations:	2,600 to 3,080 feet
Difficulty:	moderate

The hike to Fortynine Palms Oasis (there are actually more than 50 palms at the oasis) follows an old Indian trail to the oasis. Pools of water and the riparian vegetation are a great attraction to birds. Although the trail is short, it has a bit of up-and-down terrain, with climbs over a number of ridges covered with barrel cactus. Views to the north from the trail include Twentynine Palms and the Bullion

Mountains within the Marine Corps Air Ground Combat Center stretching out into the distance.

To reach the trailhead, go 4 miles west of Twentynine Palms on Hwy 62. Turn south on Canyon Road at the sign for Fortynine Palms Canyon Road. It is 1.8 miles to the trailhead parking area.

DAY HIKE: BARKER DAM LOOP
One-way length: 1.1 miles
Low and high elevations: 4,251 to 4,320 feet
Difficulty: easy

Barker Dam creates the only "lake" in the park. Nestled among granite boulders, the lake, when filled, covers 20 acres and looks remarkably like an alpine lake resting in a timberline bowl. The water attracts a host of wildlife, including an abundance of birds. Barker Dam was constructed in a natural catch basin around the turn of the century by ranchers C.O. Barker and William Shay as a water storage facility for their livestock. Later, the infamous Bill Keys added another 6 feet of concrete to the dam to raise the water level.

The trail is easy to follow and leads through intimate coves among the granite boulders. En route you pass stands of turbinella oak and pinyon pine. The acorns and pine nuts from these trees were once a source of food for local natives. Indeed, there are seed-grinding holes worn in the granite rocks that can been seen along the trail. The lake is reached in about a half-mile. You may see such nondesert bird life as heron and coot using the water hole. Bighorn sheep are also occasionally spotted here.

From the lake, if you continue on the loop another 0.4 mile, you come to a short spur trail that leads to a large outcrop that contains native American rock art. From the petroglyphs it is another 0.3 mile back to the parking area.

DAY HIKE: DESERT QUEEN MINE
One-way length: 0.75 mile
Low and high elevations: 4,440 to 4,600 feet
Difficulty: easy

The hike to the Desert Queen Mine is an easy jaunt along a sandy trail to an overlook of the old mine site that is located on a hillside above the canyon. It is about a 0.75-mile hike, mostly a downhill descent into the canyon, to reach the mine site. To reach the trailhead from Twentynine Palms, head south on Utah Trail for 8.2 miles to the junction with Pinto Basin Road. Bear right and head toward Jumbo Rocks Campground. Go 5.1 miles to the signed beginning of the geology tour on the south (on the left). On the opposite side (to the north) of the road there is a narrow dirt road that leads 1.4 miles to the Pine City/Desert Queen Mine trailhead.

Looking to San Bernardino mountains from Quail Mountain, Joshua Tree National Park.

The Desert Queen Mine was owned by the McHaney brothers, and was one of the more productive mining operations in the region. The McHaney brothers were forced to sell the mine in 1896 after a bank foreclosed on a loan the brothers had received to develop the mine. The new owner, William Morgan, hired Bill Keys to manage it. After Morgan's death in 1915, Keys successfully argued that ownership of the mine should pass to him as partial payment for back wages that Morgan owed him. The mine operated intermittently from 1896 until 1961.

DAY HIKE: PINE CITY
One-way length: 1.5 miles
Low and high elevations: 4,440 to 4,560 feet
Difficulty: easy

Pine City is the site of an old mining camp that got its name from the abundance of pinyon pine in the surrounding hills. There are, however, no structures left from this mining encampment. Nevertheless, this easy hike leads to a nice boulder-strewn area with numerous nooks and crannies shaded by oak, pine, and juniper. For the desert, this is a "lush" spot. Good views of the snow-capped San Bernardino Mountains are seen along the trail.

To reach the trailhead from Twentynine Palms, follow Utah Trail south for 8.2 miles to the junction with Pinto Basin Road. Bear right and head toward Jumbo Rocks Campground. Go 5.1 miles to the signed beginning of the geology tour on the south (on the left). On the opposite side (to the north) of the road there is a narrow dirt road that leads 1.4 miles to the Pine City/Desert Queen Mine Trailhead. Make sure you take the left path that leads to Pine City. The right path is the trail to the Desert Queen Mine.

The hike crosses several washes in the first part of the route. After 1.3 miles you arrive at an open, sandy flat surrounded by a large group of granite boulders that once was the location of Pine City. Another 0.2 miles beyond the "town site" is a mine shaft—the only evidence that mining occurred in this location. Return by the same route.

DAY HIKE: WALL STREET MILL
One-way length: 0.75 mile
Low and high elevations: 4,280 to 4,320 feet
Difficulty: easy

The remains of the Wall Street Mill and mining effort makes a good short destination for anyone interested in the mining era or anyone out to get a bit of exercise before taking on a more difficult hike. The trailhead is reached by driving from any of the entrances to Hidden Valley Campground in the center of the park. Turn east off the paved park road and bear right on a signed dirt road immediately after entering Hidden Valley Campground. Continue east another 1.5 miles on this dirt road, passing the turnoff north to the Barker Dam parking area. Just beyond the Barker Dam turnoff you reach an unsigned dirt spur to the left. Take this 0.3 mile to a parking area on the edge of the Wonderland of Rocks.

From the trailhead, the path leads through woodlands of Joshua tree and past rusting hulks of old cars and trucks. The Wall Street Mill was built by Bill Keys to process ore from the Desert Queen Mine. You can visit the ruins of an old ranch house by taking the left fork in the trail immediately after leaving the trailhead. This fork eventually swings back 0.3 mile ahead and joins the main trail to the mill site.

Just beyond where the two trails reunite, there is a short spur that leads to the gravesite of Worth Bagly. Bagly homesteaded land adjacent to Bill Keys' Desert Queen Ranch. Keys continued to cross Bagly's land to reach his mill site in defiance of Bagly's numerous protests about trespass. Finally, the quarrel came to a head and Keys shot Bagly to death. Keys claimed that Bagly shot first and that he killed Bagly in self-defense. Keys was convicted and spent 5 years in prison before intervention on his behalf by a number of high-profile political friends led to his parole and eventual pardon. The mill lies 0.2 mile beyond the gravesite and is set among large (for the desert) oaks.

DAY HIKE: EUREKA PEAK LOOP

One-way length:	10.5-mile loop
Low and high elevations:	3,980 to 5,518 feet
Difficulty:	moderate

This is a well-marked loop trip in the western part of the park that offers outstanding vistas from the summit of Eureka Peak. There is road access to Eureka Peak via Upper Covington Flat Road, so the final destination is not like being in the "wilderness," however the hike—both coming and going—is through wonderful undeveloped country.

The hike starts at the Black Rock Campground. To get to the campground/trailhead, travel south from Hwy 62 in Yucca Valley on Avalon Avenue. Follow this for 3 miles (the name changes to Palomar Drive) to Joshua Tree Lane. Turn left and go 1 mile to San Marino Avenue, where you turn right. Follow San Marino for 0.3 mile to Black Rock Road. Turn left again and continue until the road ends at the campground.

From the trailhead, head east up a wash (which serves as both the trail for Eureka Peak and the California Riding and Hiking Trail) for 2 miles to a sign marking the junction with the Eureka Peak Trail. Turn south and proceed up this wash for 2 miles, where you encounter another sign pointing to Eureka Peak. You proceed nearly a mile up a ravine to the summit ridge, which you then follow 0.1 mile to the peak. In winter there are spectacular views of the snow-covered San Bernardino Mountains.

After enjoying the views from the summit, follow the trail to Upper Covington Road and the parking area. Hike down the road approximately a half-mile to its intersection with the California Riding and Hiking Trail. There is a trailhead sign off the road that marks the beginning of the trail. Turn left (north) onto the trail, which you then follow for approximately 5 miles back to the Black Rock Campground Trailhead, completing the loop.

46 Kelso Dunes Wilderness

Creosote bush flats and the Bristol Mountains. There are no dunes in the Kelso Dunes Wilderness.

LOCATION: San Bernardino County; immediately west of Mojave National Preserve

SIZE: 129,580 acres

ELEVATION RANGE: 1,000 to 3,223 feet

ADMINISTRATION: BLM Needles Resource Area Office

MAPS: BLM Desert Access Guide Irwin #8, Johnson Valley #11, New York Mountains #9, Providence Mountains #12; AAA San Bernardino County

Despite its name, the Kelso sand dunes are largely outside of the wilderness. This dune system, the second highest in California, lies to the east within the adjacent Mojave National Preserve. Most of the wilderness consists of broad, sweeping bajadas that drape the slopes of the rolling Bristol Mountains. The Bristols are dominated by volcanic rocks and some granitic outcrops, and the highest named summit is McGorman Peak (elevation, 3,223 feet). Other significant topographical features include Broadwell Mesa and a natural arch found in the western third of the wilderness. Broadwell Dry Lake lies on the western border of the area. Despite these interesting geologic features, one is likely to encounter few other recreationalists. Most of the vegetation consists of grasses and creosote bush.

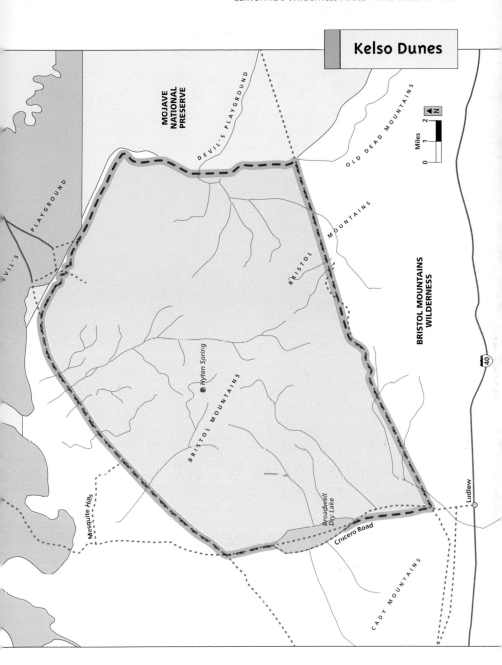

Kelso Dunes

MOJAVE NATIONAL PRESERVE

DEVIL'S PLAYGROUND

DEVIL'S PLAYGROUND

OLD DEAD MOUNTAINS

N

Miles
0   1   2

BRISTOL MOUNTAINS

BRISTOL MOUNTAINS WILDERNESS

Hyten Spring

BRISTOL MOUNTAINS

Mesquite Hills

Broadwell Dry Lake

Crucero Road

Ludlow

40

CADY MOUNTAINS

One water source, Hyten Spring, was used by native peoples and is a known archeological site.

ACCESS

To reach the southwestern corner of the wilderness, take the Ludlow exit off I-40. Go north on Crucero Road (a sandy track that heads north) 2 miles to an intersection with an east-west pipeline road. Continue north on Crucero Road, the intersection beyond which becomes the western boundary of the area. You can also turn east on the pipeline road, which forms the southern border of the wilderness. Hike from either road. Although the slightly sloping bajada with nothing more than creosote bush would seem to provide little topographical screening, it is surprising how quickly you can lose sight of your vehicle.

Beware that these access roads are very sandy. I got stuck in loose sand and spent an hour digging myself out. Drive slowly so that you don't get too emerged in a sand trap before you realize its unstable consistency. Carry appropriate tools—like a shovel and carpet for traction—needed for extraction from loose sand.

Mojave National Preserve

Kelso Dunes frames the Providence Mountains in Mojave National Preserve.

The 1.4-million-acre Mojave National Preserve takes in the eastern portion of the Mojave Desert, a vast empty quarter where boundless space and limitless vistas dominate. I-10 forms the northern border and I-40 is the southern boundary for the newly established Mojave National Preserve. Within these bounds are lava fields, cinder cones, sand dunes, playas, mesas, and at least seven mountain ranges, with nearly 700,000 acres designated as wilderness.

There are a number of notable features within the preserve. Cima Dome is a gently rounded granitic dome covered with one of the finest Joshua tree woodlands in the world. The highest point, Teutonia Peak, is a popular hiking destination. The Cinder Cones consist of at least 32 extinct volcanoes and have been designated a National Natural Landmark.

LOCATION: San Bernardino County; sandwiched between I-10 and I-40, 40 miles east of Barstow, and directly south of Baker, California, 50 miles west of Las Vegas, Nevada

SIZE: 1.4 million total acres and 695,200 acres of designated wilderness

ELEVATION RANGE: 900 to 8,000 feet

ADMINISTRATION: Mojave National Preserve

MAPS: Recreation Map of the Mojave National Preserve; AAA San Bernardino County

Clark Mountain, just north of I-15, at 7,929 feet, is the highest mountain in the Mojave Desert. Among the limestone crags of its summit grow one of two isolated white fir forest stands in the entire California desert.

The Granite Mountains are noted for their rugged beauty and diverse plant community, with more than 400 species recorded for the area. The Research Natural Area, operated by the University of California, occupies a small part of the range.

The creosote-covered Ivanpah Valley, which lies between the New York Mountains and Ivanpah Mountains, contains some of the best desert tortoise habitat in the California desert, with as many as 100 tortoise per square mile reported.

The Kelso Dunes are located at the southern end of the Devil's Playground. The dunes are the third tallest in North America.

The New York Mountains form the central spine of the preserve. Rising to 7,200 feet in elevation, the New York Mountains are among the highest mountains in the Mojave Desert. The mountains consist of two different regions. The area west of Ivanpah Road has a steep, deeply eroded north face. Long canyons like Caruthers and Fourth of July are on the southern flank, and are known for their unusual live oak and chaparral plant communities. To the east of Ivanpah Road are the Castle Peaks, which are striking reddish spires of volcanic rock.

The Mid Hills area of the New York Mountains contain both granitic boulder outcrops and volcanic crags and canyons. Dense stands of sagebrush, along with pinyon and juniper woodlands give the area more a Great Basin feel than other parts of the preserve.

Adjacent to the New York Mountains lie the scenic Providence Mountains. This limestone-dominated range has sheer cliffs on its northern face along with dense stands of cacti. Within the Providence Mountains lies the Providence Mountain State Recreation Area.

The Piute Range in the southeastern corner of the preserve contains the region's only perennial stream. Because of the year-round supply of water, there are numerous archeological remains found in this area. In addition the ruins of Fort Piute, an Army outpost, is found here.

Soda Lake, in the northwestern corner of the preserve, is a relict Ice Age playa. Three springs in this area support the endangered Mojave tui chub.

The area within today's national preserve was originally managed by the BLM. Driven by a growing concern that the California desert was being overrun by ORVs and was suffering from mining, overgrazing, and general neglect, Congress set up a 25-million-acre California Desert Conservation Area in 1976 and directed the BLM to come up with a cohesive management scheme to protect the resource values on the 12.1-million public acres under its jurisdiction in the region. One result of this effort was the designation of the BLM in 1985 of a 1.5-million-acre East Mojave National Scenic Area.

Despite the name change, conservationists still complained that the BLM was unable or unwilling to monitor and control damaging activities effectively. They argued that the desert's fragile tapestry was being unraveled piece by piece.

Pressure mounted to place the East Mojave National Scenic Area under Park Service management. When Senator Alan Cranston introduced the first version of the

California Desert Protection Act in 1986, it included the proposed designation of a new national park in the East Mojave. After numerous revisions and amendments, the California Desert Protection Act was passed by Congress in 1994 and was signed into law by President Clinton. The Act, among other things, created the 1.4-million-acre Mojave National Preserve in the heart of the Mojave Desert, and transferred the lands known as the East Mojave National Scenic Area from the BLM to the National Park Service.

The name Mojave National Preserve may be confusing to some people. Why isn't it called Mojave National Park? Preserves are essentially the same as national parks. Both are managed by the National Park Service. The main difference is that sport hunting is permitted in preserves. The idea of preserves originated in Alaska in the 1970s during the debate over the creation of new national parks in that state. To pacify opposition from hunting organizations to the establishment of new park units, most of the better big-game hunting lands in the state were excluded from Alaska's newly established national parks. But rather than leave these lands open to industrial development, a new land management category was created—the preserve. Preserves do not permit habitat degradation, but they are open to legal hunting. Hence in Alaska you find park units with names like Denali National Park and Preserve, Wrangell-St. Elias National Park and Preserve, and the Yukon-Charley Preserve. All include lands open to sport hunting, but not resource extraction.

As originally written in the California desert legislation, the East Mojave area was going to be redesignated a national park. Opposition to park establishment from hunting organizations like the Safari Club and the National Rifle Association held up the desert bill in Congress. The opposition was based more on principle than genuine concern about the loss of hunting opportunities. Almost no one hunted in the proposed preserve anyway, and the number of game animals is limited to a few hundred deer and bighorn sheep. Rather than lose the entire bill over this one issue, environmentalists agreed to create a national preserve instead of a park so that the hunting argument could not be used to jeopardize protection of the area.

However, another last-minute compromise with significant ecological consequences centered on livestock grazing. Environmentalists wanted to phase out livestock grazing in the new preserve unit. They argued that no other human activity negatively affected more of the California desert than grazing. Given the meager productivity of the desert, any removal of vegetation by nonnative animals affects native species. One reason for the decline of desert tortoise, for instance, is the competition between this reptile and domestic cattle for forage. Trampling of fragile desert soil crusts, destruction of riparian areas and wetlands, the expropriation of water sources for livestock at the expense of wildlife (many wildlife species will not use water sources dominated by livestock), and removal of fine fuels (grasses) that once supported periodic wildfires are just a few of the negative ecological consequences of livestock grazing. But grazing interests strongly opposed any limitations to livestock use, and under the final legislation that created the Mojave National Preserve, grazing will continue indefinitely in the park.

HISTORY

Evidence of the people who have lived and made a living from the desert and its resources is scattered across the region. The earliest record is of people associated with the large glacial lakes that once covered the California desert. This cultural tradition dominated from 10,000 to 7,000 years ago. As the climate dried, people were forced to migrate more frequently to find a diverse supply of food sources. Around 4,000 years before present (BP), the grinding of seeds and seed storage dominated survival strategies. This adaptation, which created food surpluses, resulted in population growth for the region.

Around 1,500 BP several other major technological innovations were introduced to the region, including the bow and arrow, and ceramic pottery. Then about 700 BP Paiute-Shoshone groups moved into the area and forced the Mojaves to the Colorado River. The Paiute dominated the desert until the advent of the European exploration. Petroglyphs and pictographs, etched and drawn on the rocks throughout the region, are evidence of a long history of the peoples who followed the natural cycles of plants and animals, gathering and hunting.

The earliest account of historic exploration was a Spanish expedition led by Francisco Garces and Juan Bautista Anza (for whom Anza Borrego Desert State Park is named). Looking to establish an overland route from the Spanish settlements in New Mexico and the California coast, the Garces and Anza expedition crossed the Mojave in 1775 and 1776 following the Mojave Trail, an Indian path that traveled from water hole to water hole. The trail crossed Piute Creek, and followed the edge of the New York and Providence Mountains and the Kelso Dunes. The first American to enter the region was Jedediah Smith (for whom Jedediah Smith Redwoods and the Smith River in northern California are named), a mountain man of some fame who crossed the Mojave in 1826 and 1827 during a exploratory trapping expedition. Other expeditions followed. In 1857 Edward Beale established a wagon route across the Mojave, and soon Prescott, Arizona, and San Bernardino were linked with regular mail and freight service.

By the 1860s mineral exploration was in full swing. Prospectors were fanning out across the desert looking for veins of gold and silver. Within the boundaries of the Mojave National Preserve, mining camps were established at Ivanpah, Hart in the Castle Mountains, and Providence along the slopes of the Providence Mountains. By the 1920s falling gold prices and played out mines led to the abandonment of most of these camps and towns.

GEOLOGY

The Mojave National Preserve takes in the easternmost section of the Mojave Desert. The desert is roughly delineated by two major faults—the San Andreas and the Garlock. These faults mark the stress points on a landscape that has been in formation for hundreds of millions of years. Plate tectonics holds the secret to today's desert. As much as a half-billion years ago, the western coast of the North American plate ended somewhere near today's Nevada-Arizona border. Sediments from this

Granite boulders in the Granite Mountains, Mojave National Preserve.

continental mass were washed into the sea, creating shale and sandstone. Ocean-based sediments created limestone and dolomite, such as those now found in the Providence Mountains within the Mojave National Preserve.

Between 245 million to 65 million years ago the North American continent began to override the oceanic plate. The pressure of this collision crumpled the western edge of the continent and promoted the resulting uplift of the ancestral Sierra Nevada as well as the highlands in the Mojave. As the oceanic plate dove under the North American continent, the rock melted and magma flowed up toward the surface. Some flows erupted as volcanoes, but other molten rock cooled slowly deep in the earth to create a very erosion-resistant plutonic rock that we know as granite. The rocks that comprise the core of the Granite Mountains and the New York Mountains in the Mojave National Preserve were formed during this period.

Then about 25 million years ago the San Andreas Fault began rifting California apart, sliding northward. This opened up the Gulf of California and stretched apart the Basin and Range Province. Mountains rose along faults and valleys dropped. This extension is ultimately responsible for the uplift of nearly all the mountains in the California desert. The stretching of the earth also permitted magma to find its way to the surface, and volcanic eruptions poured out lava across the landscape. In the Mojave National Preserve, eruptions of rhyolite flowed across the landscape, capping softer volcanic ash. The Mid Hills area, particularly the Hole in the Wall, are exposed volcanic rock formations. Even younger volcanic flows and cinder cones are evident in the Cinder Cones area just south of Baker. Here there are more than 30 extinct volcanoes, although the most recent eruptions ended less than 1,000 years ago.

The finishing touches on the Mojave landscape occurred during the past 20,000 years during the tail end of the Ice Age. Wetter conditions resulted in the formation of large lakes in the California desert. A giant glacial-age water body, Lake Mojave covered much of the eastern Mojave. But as the climate dried during the past 10,000 years, most of these lakes disappeared and left behind only salt pans and seasonally flooded playas. Soda Lake Playa near Baker is a relict of this lake.

Another geologic feature associated with Lake Mojave is the Kelso Dunes. This unique and isolated dune system rises more than 600 feet above the desert floor. The dunes were created by southeasterly winds that blew fine-grained residual sand from the Mojave River sink (Soda Lake), which lies to the northwest. The color of the dunes is created from many golden rose quartz particles. When the dry sand grains slide down the steep upper slopes, a notable booming sound is produced. In some years the dunes offer a nice spring wildflower display.

Another indirect consequence of the higher precipitation during the glacial period is the caves and passages at Mitchell's Caverns in the Providence Mountains. Mitchell's Caverns are now part of Providence Mountains State Park. The state park is completely surrounded by the Mojave National Preserve. The caverns are named for Jack Mitchell, the first owner and promoter of the caves.

The caverns were formed when sedimentary limestone and metamorphosed limestone (marble) were dissolved by groundwater high in carbonic acid. The continued dripping of highly mineralized groundwater into the caverns produced stalactites (dripstone deposits extending downward from the ceiling) and stalagmites (dripstone deposits building upward in mounds from the floor).

Mitchell's Caverns consists of three basic caves: El Pakiva, or the Devil's House; Tecopa, named for one of the last chiefs of the Shoshone; and the deep and vertical Winding Stair Cave.

FAUNA AND FLORA

The desert in the Mojave National Preserve ranges in elevation from less than 1,000 feet to almost 8,000 feet. The park lies at the confluence of three major American deserts: the Great Basin, the Mojave, and the Sonoran. Although the Mojave National Preserve lies officially in the Mojave Desert, the area contains floral elements from all three deserts. Nearly 70 percent of the vascular plants known to occur in the California desert can be found in this preserve.

In addition to the ubiquitous creosote bush and other typical desert vegetation, there are many unusual plant communities or occurrences. For instance, the New York Mountains host manzanita, California lilac, oak, and silk tassel—all characteristic of coastal plant communities. At the same time, the Mid Hills support sagebrush and Utah juniper—species usually associated with the Great Basin. At the other extreme, smoke tree and ocotillo, typical Sonoran Desert species, reach into the southeastern corner of the preserve.

Other unusual plant occurrences include the westernmost known stands of white fir in southern California. These relict stands are found in the New York Mountains and on Clark Mountain in the Clark Mountains.

Mojave yucca, up to 10 feet tall, occur on the slopes of the Woods, Providence, and Hackberry Mountains. The Woods and Hackberry Mountains also support extensive stands of desert succulents, including silver cholla, buckhorn cholla, barrel, hedgehog, pin-cushion, beavertail, and prickly pear cactus. Piute Creek, the only perennial stream in the eastern Mojave, supports cottonwood and other riparian vegetation.

Wildlife is nearly as varied as the plant life. More than 300 different species of animals roam the area. This includes 47 mammalian species such as 500 to 600 desert bighorn sheep, mule deer, porcupine, mountain lion, bobcat, rock squirrel, and wood rat. In addition there are 36 species of reptiles including the Gila monster, Mojave fringe-toed lizard, regal ring-necked snake, and desert striped whip snake. The endangered desert tortoise is also found here in good numbers. Some 200 species of birds have been recorded and these include golden eagle, several types of hawk, Bendire's thrasher, crissal thrasher, gray vireo, and Lucy's warbler. The elf owl, a state endangered species, was reintroduced into Piute Creek Canyon to reestablish the species in this region.

ACCESS

Mojave National Preserve is relatively easy to access. It is less than 50 miles west of Las Vegas and about 50 miles east of Barstow, California. I-15 and I-40 create a prong, with the preserve located between them. Several paved roads cross the

preserve including Kelbaker Road from Baker, California, and Kelso-Cima Road, which goes from the Kelso Depot east and then north to link with I 15.

HIKING

There are currently no facilities in the preserve. You must bring all the gas, food, and other supplies you need with you. You can obtain water in a few locations, including the Post Office at Cima, Providence Mountains State Recreation Area, and Hole in the Wall Campground. Regulations often change. Be sure to inquire at the visitor centers in Baker or Barstow and get the most up-to-date information.

I've hiked in the Mojave National Preserve in all four seasons. Winter can be darn cold. I've had water freeze in water bottles at night. And due to the mountains, which exceed 6,000 to 7,000 feet, summer temperatures are moderated somewhat from the low-desert country so that hiking in July and August is not as stupid as it first sounds. Just bear in mind that hiking at high noon is not recommended. Wear a hat and drink plenty of water. The best time to visit, however, is between October and May. October and November may be the best months because the days tend to be clear and are not as windy as the spring months.

Like most desert wilderness areas, there are few established trails in Mojave National Preserve. Most of the hiking involves walking up a wash or climbing a ridge. There are no paths. There are, however, a few old mining roads that now serve as trails, some of which are described in the following pages.

DAY HIKE: CARUTHERS CANYON—NEW YORK MOUNTAINS	
One-way length:	1.5 miles
Low and high elevations:	5,570 to 6,150 feet
Difficulty:	moderate

Caruthers Canyon lies in the New York Mountains and provides access to the granite heart of the range. Due to its higher elevation, there is more water here than elsewhere in the desert, supporting some unexpected plant distributions. For instance, species exist here that are more typical of the California coast, including manzanita, ceanothus, and oak. Pinyon pine and juniper are plentiful. The hike up the canyon follows an old mining road to the Giant Ledge Mine—an abandoned copper mine.

To reach the canyon from the north, drive east from Baker on I-15 for 25 miles to the Cima exit. Turn south on Cima Road and drive 28.5 miles to Cima Junction. Turn southwest (right) on Kelso-Cima Road and go 4.9 miles to the dirt Cedar Canyon Road. Turn southeast (left) onto Cedar Canyon Road and follow it across the New York Mountains for 22.3 miles to Ivanpah/Lanfair Road. Turn north (left) on Ivanpah Road and go 5.7 miles to the OX Ranch. Watch for New York Mountain Road on the west (left), which you then take for 5.9 miles to an intersection and turn right to Caruthers Canyon. It is 1.8 miles to a wash. Park there and begin hiking.

Looking to Providence Mountains at dawn, Mojave National Preserve.

If you are coming from the south, exit I-40 at the Fenner exit. Gas up here then follow old Rte 66 to Goffe, where you take a left onto the paved Ivanpah/Lanfair Road. The road becomes a good dirt road after 9.6 miles. Continue on the dirt road for approximately six more miles until you reach the intersection with Cedar Canyon Road described earlier. Continue straight for another 5.7 miles to the OX Ranch and then follow the directions provided in the previous paragraph.

The hike follows the old mining road. Avoid side spurs leading to campsites and just continue up the main canyon. You cross the wash several times about halfway to the mine, and often there is water in the wash in winter and spring. As you walk, there is plenty of opportunity to admire the oddly shaped granite boulders that line the ravine and sometimes almost block the old, deteriorating road—making for slow going at times. Once you reach the mine area there are a number of open mine shafts and an old wooden chute to investigate, then return back down the canyon to your vehicle.

DAY HIKE: CIMA DOME—TEUTONIA PEAK

One-way length:	2 miles
Low and high elevations:	5,020 to 5,643 feet
Difficulty:	moderate

Until you are practically on top of Teutonia Peak, it is hard to tell where the dome is really located. Cima Dome is shaped like an inverted gold pan. Huge, more than 10 miles in diameter, the nearly circular swelling of monzonite (granitic rock) rises 1,500 feet above the surrounding desert. It is considered the most symmetrical, natural domed feature in the United States. The dome was formed when a molten plume of magma rose toward the earth's surface and cooled in place as a giant mushroom-shaped granite bubble that erosion has subsequently exposed.

The surface of this dome is covered with the world's largest Joshua tree woodland. The species here, *Yucca brevifolia jaegariana,* is a slightly different subspecies from those seen at Joshua Tree National Park. This species possesses a greater number of bisymmetrical branches and attains an overall larger size.

To get to the trailhead, take the Cima Road exit off I-15 and head 11 miles south toward Cima. If coming from the south, go 6 miles north from Cima on Cima Road. Trailhead parking for the 2-mile hike to Teutonia Peak lies on the west side of the road.

The trail climbs gently uphill across a sandy landscape dotted with cholla, Joshua tree, and yucca. Along the way you pass several fences—an indication that this area is grazed by domestic livestock. At a half-mile you cross a dirt road. At 0.9 mile you cross another road (neither road is marked on my topographical map), which you follow past some mining ruins to a marked path leading off to the west. The path climbs briefly to a ridge. Follow the path south and watch for cairns that signal the way to the rocky summit. Great views of the Ivanpah Mountains are directly east of the summit. Scramble around the summit boulders to get views in other directions.

> ### DAY HIKE: SILVER PEAK—GRANITE MOUNTAINS
> One-way length: 4.3 miles
> Low and high elevations: 4,000 to 6,375 feet
> Difficulty: moderate

Silver Peak is the highest point in the northern portion of the Granite Mountains and affords one of the best views in the entire preserve. The hike to the summit follows an old mining road most of the way. Those attaining the summit are rewarded with sweeping vistas north across the Kelso Dunes and Devil's Playground, and intimate views of the rugged Providence Mountains to the east and the Clipper Mountains to the south beyond I-40.

To reach the trailhead, take the Kelbaker exit off I-40 some 78 miles east of Barstow. Go north 10.1 miles, crossing Granite Pass en route. Just a few hundred feet beyond the pass watch for a dirt road heading west. Follow this rough, narrow road as far as you dare or until you come to the wilderness boundary some 1.8 miles from Kelbaker Road. You can also reach the trailhead coming from the north. Just find your way to the "town" of Kelso. Continue on Kelbaker Road to Granite Pass, then follow the same directions given previously.

From the parking area, follow the old mining road up Cottonwood Wash. It is 4.6 miles to the end of the road near the summit of Silver Peak. Lovely Cottonwood Wash Valley has oak and other vegetation you might not expect to find in the desert. It is also one of the places where cattle are still grazed, so you may see some of these hoofed locust en route. Don't be confused by the numerous cattle trails that wander here and there about the valley. The old road eventually curves uphill and up the northern slope of the valley as it winds up toward the peak. The road ends at an elevation of 6,075 feet just below the summit. A "use" path climbs the last 300 feet to the summit. Cattle seldom climb such steep slopes, hence there are beautiful grasslands beneath the scattered pinyon and juniper stands about the summit. I lingered on the peak until sunset. Nevertheless, I was able to follow the old road quite easily back to my vehicle with the aid of moonlight.

> ### DAY HIKE: HOLE IN THE WALL—MID HILLS
> One-way length: 8.4 miles
> Low and high elevations: 4,265 to 5,600 feet
> Difficulty: moderately strenuous

The Hole in the Wall Trail is only one of two official trails in the preserve. The path crosses rolling terrain with canyons and pinnacles, and sagebrush mixed with pinyon and juniper woodlands. It is well marked and distinct, and can either be hiked as an overnight backpack trip or a long point-to-point trek if a vehicle shuttle or pickup has been previously arranged. If you don't mind walking down a dirt road for several miles, at about the halfway point one can also leave the trail and follow an old mining road to Black Canyon Road (which doesn't have too much traffic) to hike back to the starting point. It's difficult to get too terribly lost since

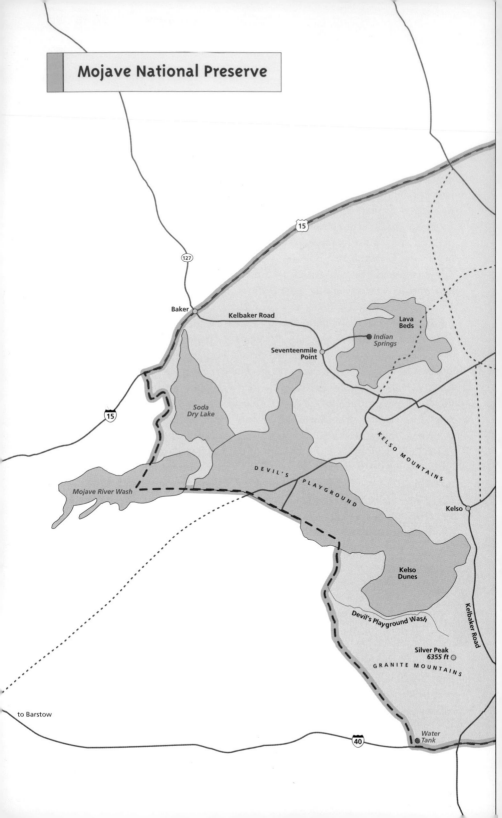

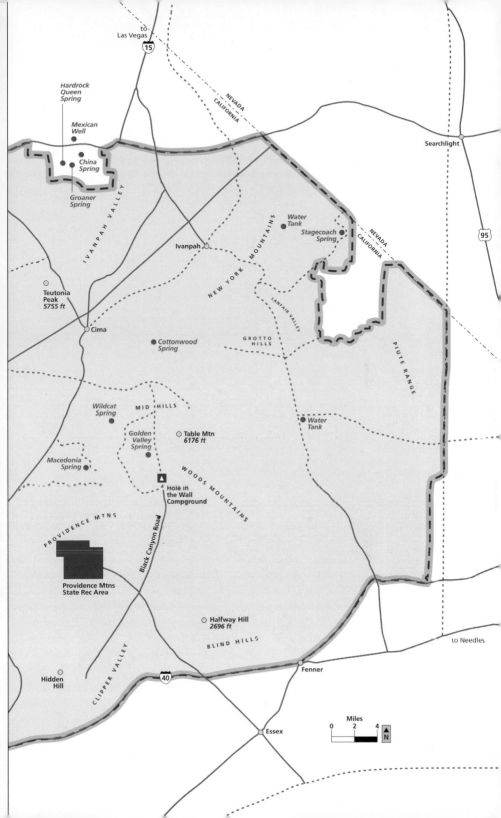

dirt roads lie a couple of miles north and south of the hiking route on either side of the trail.

To find the trailhead, take I-40 44 miles west from Needles to the Essex Road exit. Turn north and head toward the Providence Mountains State Recreation Area. Go 9.7 miles to the intersection of Essex Road and Black Canyon Road. Turn northeast (right) on Black Canyon Road, which you then follow 8.5 miles to the Hole in the Wall Campground and Visitor Center. The trailhead is located at the picnic area just beyond the visitor center.

The first part of the "trail" may be intimidating to some, particularly if you are accompanied by small children. Immediately on leaving the parking area you must descend 215 feet in less than 0.2 mile into Banshee Canyon—a narrow slot in the volcanic rocks. To aid in the descent there are metal rings imbedded in the rock walls as handholds. In very short order you come out of the canyon and into an open wash. For those not inclined to take on the narrows of Banshee Canyon, you can drive to this point and begin the hike here. The trail continues across cholla- and yucca-covered rolling terrain to a wash. Follow the wash (there are signs) to a trail junction about 1 mile from the trailhead. If you turn left you reach the Wild Horse Canyon Trailhead to the Hole in the Wall Trail (yet another optional starting point) some 0.25 mile south. To continue the hike, turn right (north) and head upslope. At 1.7 miles you reach a low pass (elevation, 4,460 feet) surrounded by barrel cactus and boulder outcrops. You soon cross a gate with a sign that reads "6.2 miles to Mid Hills." You descend to the wash and continue to an old road, which you follow for 0.3 mile, then the signed trail takes off to the left. The trail follows a wash, then climbs among granite boulders. At 4.3 miles you cross a road that leads to the abandoned Gold Valley Mine.

If you are not inclined to hike to Mid Hills or you wish to make a loop of the trip, you can turn to the right at the road intersection and follow Gold Valley Mine Road east and southeast back to Black Canyon Road, which you then follow southwest back to the Hole in the Wall Campground and Trailhead.

If Mid Hills is your goal, continue heading north up the path. You pass through another gate that states the remaining mileage to Mid Hills. You soon intersect another abandoned road, which you follow for 1.3 miles. Just after passing another gate marked "Mid Hills 3.1 miles," there is sign that points to a trail that heads off to the right. Continue following the signs and the trail to the high point of the hike (elevation, 5,600 feet)—some 8.0 miles from the Hole in the Wall Trailhead. At this point you can see the windmill that lies near the end of the trail. From the high point it is only another 0.4 mile to Mid Hills.

View north from Granite Mountains towards Kelso Dunes in evening, Mojave National Preserve.

48 Newberry Mountains Wilderness

Newberry Mountains from Kane Wash, Newberry Mountains Wilderness.

LOCATION: San Bernardino County; 15 miles east of Barstow, California

SIZE: 22,900 acres

ELEVATION RANGE: 2,200 to 5,100 feet

ADMINISTRATION: BLM Barstow Resource Area Office

MAPS: Desert Access Guide Johnson Valley #11; AAA San Bernardino County

The Newberry Mountains are just south of I-40. Camp Rock Road bounds it on the west and Kane Wash Road defines the eastern border. These rugged volcanic-sedimentary mountains, cut by deep canyons, rise abruptly on the north but are gentler in the south. Views from the peaks of this wilderness give one a sense of being on top of the world. Creosote bush dominates, along with a variety of cacti.

ACCESS

As with many desert wildernesses, there are no designated trails or trailheads. Hikers merely find an interesting point of departure from an access road and begin hiking. To get to the wilderness from Barstow, head east on I-40 for 6 miles to the Daggett exit and take Camp

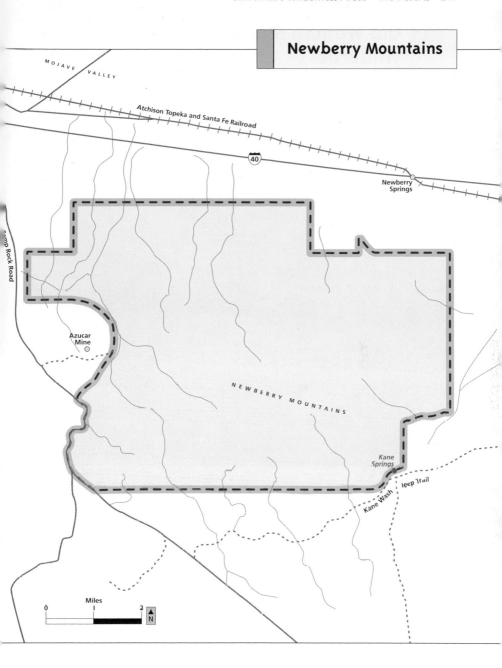

Newberry Mountains

Rock Road south. After 4 miles Camp Rock Road becomes the western border of the wilderness. Although access is easier from Camp Rock Road, the canyons are more spectacular along Kane Wash Road. Be forewarned that Kane Wash Road has some steep sections that are probably best run in a 4wd vehicle, although I successfully negotiated the road in a 2wd pickup.

49 Old Woman Mountains Wilderness

Cholla cactus frames the Old Woman Mountains near the Golden Fleece Mine.

LOCATION: San Bernardino County; 35 miles southwest of Needles, California

SIZE: 146,020 acres

ELEVATION RANGE: 800 to 5,300 feet

ADMINISTRATION: BLM Needles Resource Area Office

MAPS: Desert Access Guide Providence Mountains #12, Sheephole Mountains #15; AAA San Bernardino County

The Old Woman Mountains lie just south of the newly established Mojave National Preserve. Named for a granitic rock outcrop—Old Woman Statue (elevation, 5,000 feet)—that presumably resembles a woman, these mountains are among the more spectacular in the California desert. Although granite outcrops dominate the range, dolomite and limestone outcrops occur in the northeastern portion of the wilderness, as evidenced by 5,200-foot Carbonate Peak.

The range of these rugged, fault-block mountains stretches 35 miles in a north-south direction and at times it is up to 28 miles wide. Such an expanse provides plenty of opportunity for solitude. Jagged peaks with numerous washes and some natural springs (don't rely on these springs for water) make this an attractive place for extended back-packing trips.

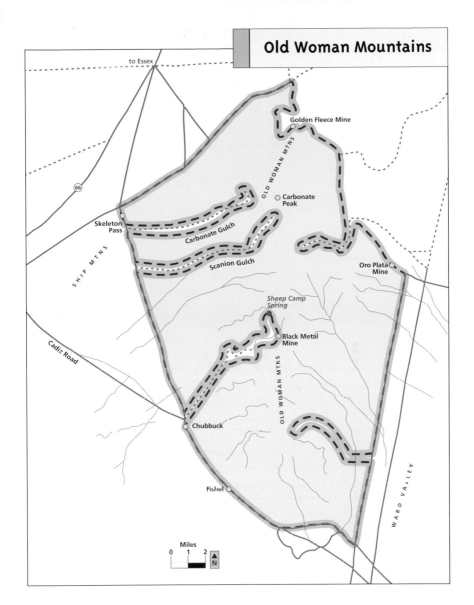

The wilderness lies at a transition zone between the Colorado Desert and Mojave Desert, and sports plant communities representative of both regions. Creosote bush dominates the lower elevations and the mid elevations contain a cactus-shrub mix including some magnificent barrel cactus gardens. Pinyon pine and juniper woodlands are found on the highest peaks.

Like many mountain ranges in the California desert, the Old Woman Mountains were extensively explored by miners, and evidence of old mining operations abound. Most of the mines were operated between 1889 and 1902. A number of cherry stem roads penetrate the wilderness and nearly all of them access old mining operations. Historically, tungsten, lead, antimony, and mercury were all produced here. Limestone has also been mined. Gold was mined at the Blue Eagle, Long Shot, and Black Beauty Mines; and silver, lead, and zinc came from the Jumbo Tungsten, How, Hidden Value, and Udsogn Mines.

Due to the variety of terrain and wildlife habitats, there was historically more hunting here than in many other desert wilderness areas, with quail, chukar, and deer the primary prey. Bighorn sheep also inhabit the range. Sheep are known to associate with Dripping Springs and Long Spring in the northern portion of these mountains, and Sheep Camp Spring (named for obvious reasons) is another area popular with wild bighorns. The presence of water and desert woodlands along washes provides considerable habitats for songbirds, and the area has higher densities of these birds than other wilderness areas.

Evidence of past native American occupation and use abound, including the occurrence of rock shelters, middens, and potsherds, and petroglyphs and pictographs near the wilderness boundary.

Like most desert wildernesses, there are no formal trails. However, many of the old mining roads make for excellent hiking and are seldom used by vehicles. In addition, opportunities for cross-country hiking/backpacking abound—if you carry the appropriate amount of water.

ACCESS

Take the Essex exit off I-40 and head south through Essex. Cross the Atchison, Topeka, and Santa Fe Railroad tracks onto the dirt Sunflower Springs Road. Continue south 7 miles to reach the northeastern corner of the wilderness. There are roads beyond this point, but many are best driven by 4wd vehicles or ridden on mountain bike.

Another point of access is Scanlon Gulch. This is probably best driven by a 4wd high-clearance vehicle because you have several washes to cross. From I-40 take the Essex exit and go 6 miles south to the town. Turn west (right) onto Rte 66 (National Trails Highway) and proceed 9 miles or so to the turn south for Danby. From Danby, go south 1.7 miles and cross the Atchison, Topeka, and Santa Fe Railroad tracks and bear right at the dirt road heading south to Skeleton Pass. Take this road 9 miles to the entrance of Scanlon Gulch, which due to erosion often looks like a wash. You can proceed 5 miles up this "road" if you have the appropriate vehicle; beyond this point it degenerates to a trail. The entire road from its mouth to the end is 9 miles long and makes for a good hiking/mountain biking route, with many places to camp. Scanlon Gulch also puts you within hiking/scrambling distance of Old Woman Statue (although reaching the top requires serious climbing skills).

Sheep Camp Spring, within the heart of the mountains and accessible by another old mining road (best used as a trail) that leads to the Black Metal Mine, is also a popular destination for hikers and campers. Visitors should be mindful of camping too close to the spring so as not to hinder access to water by bighorns. To reach the turnoff for Black Metal Mine Road, continue south 10 more miles on the same dirt road that leads to Scanlon Gulch. It is 8.5 miles from Black Metal Mine Road to the end of the road by Sheep Camp Spring.

Palen-McCoy Wilderness 50

The vast expanse of desert in the Palen-McCoy Wilderness frames the Granite Mountains.

Palen-McCoy Wilderness is one of the largest roadless areas in the California desert. It encompasses parts of five mountain ranges, including the metasedimentary and metavolcanic Palen Range, the metasedimentary McCoy Range, the granitic Granite Range, and the limestone-dominated peaks of the Little Maria and Arica Ranges. The wilderness is easily large enough to provide for extensive backcountry exploration—if you can carry enough water. However, as large as it is, this wildlands complex could potentially be enlarged by 100,000 to 370,000 acres by closing a few dirt roads. It would be even more valuable ecologically if it, along with Rice Valley Wilderness, Riverside Mountains Wilderness, and Big Maria Mountains Wilderness, were combined with Joshua Tree National Park to create a

LOCATION:
Riverside County;
25 miles northwest
of Blythe, California

SIZE: 270,629 acres

ELEVATION RANGE:
600 to 3,600 feet

ADMINISTRATION:
BLM Palm Springs
Resource Area Office

MAPS: Desert Access
Guide Sheephole
Mountains #15, Parker/
Blythe #16, Chuckwalla
#18; AAA Riverside
County

wildlands stretching from the Colorado River to the San Bernardino Mountains. This idea is for future environmentalists to promote.

Even without expansion, the diversity of landforms in the Palen-McCoy Wilderness is exceptional and includes secluded canyons, untouched desert pavement, interior valleys, jagged peaks, sweeping bajadas, and even some small dunes. The Palen Mountains in particular are very rugged.

The largest pristine wash system in the California desert is contained in this wilderness. Lying near the edge of the Colorado Desert, the area supports substantial riparian vegetation along the washes that includes smoke tree and palo verde. The Midland Ironwood Forest is the largest in the California desert. These woodlands are among the most productive wildlife habitats in the California desert. The bajadas are dominated by creosote bush, whereas ocotillo, barrel cactus, cottontop cactus, and brittlebush are common on rocky slopes.

Wildlife known to inhabit the area include gray fox, kit fox, bighorn sheep, mule deer, and bobcat.

Native use of the area includes remains of a permanent village site and burial locations. Later, during World War II, General Patton trained troops along the northern slope of the Granite Mountains. Camp Granite, a relict of this era, lies just north of the wilderness. In some places fading tank tracks are still evident in the desert pavement areas, demonstrating how long it can take for a desert landscape to recover from disturbance.

ACCESS

As in most California desert wildernesses, there are no formal trails, although some old, now-abandoned jeep tracks do penetrate the mountains and serve as "trails." In most instances one simply drives to the edge of the wilderness and hikes up a promising wash or crosses a bajada to the mountains.

There are a number of ways to access this wilderness. Hwy 62 west of Vidal Junction lies just north of the Granite and Arica Mountains. Probably the easiest way to gain the heart of the wilderness is to take the cherry stem dirt road from Hwy 177 on the western border that travels 12 miles to Palen Pass, which separates the Palen Mountains from the Granite Mountains. The wilderness borders either side of this road and you can simply take off hiking from the road.

If you are in Blythe, California, access to the southeastern part of the wilderness can be gained by driving a number of dirt roads that leave the paved Midland Road.

Access to the southern boundary of the wilderness can be gained by taking the Wileys Well exit off I-10, 30 miles west of Blythe. Take the dirt road north from the exit and travel 4 miles to the wilderness border.

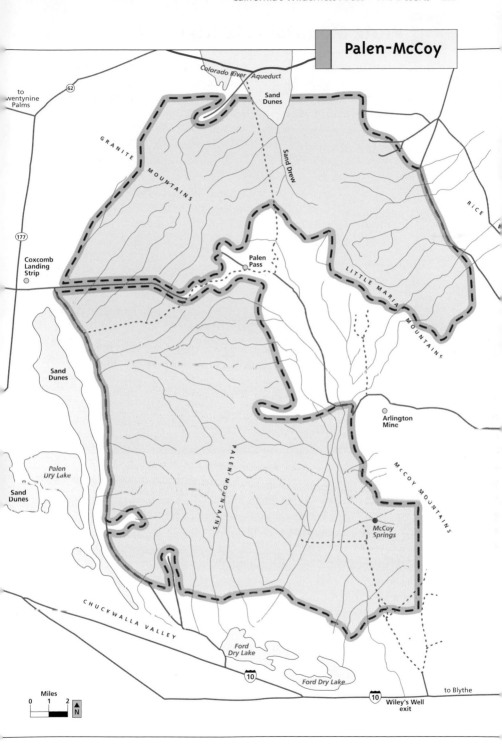

Palen-McCoy

51 Piute Mountains Wilderness

Barrel cactus frames Piute Mountains near Fenner Spring, Piute Mountains Wilderness.

LOCATION:
San Bernardino County;
30 miles west of
Needles, California

SIZE: 36,840 acres

ELEVATION RANGE:
1,000 to 3,700 feet

ADMINISTRATION:
BLM Needles Resource
Area Office

MAPS: Desert Access
Guide Providence
Mountains #12; AAA
San Bernardino County

The Piute Mountains were called *Kwikantsoka* by the Mojaves and were considered a sacred place. Today, we give protection to this area as a sacred place within our social and political system by officially protecting the area as wilderness.

As a wildlands the Piute Mountains may not seem all that outstanding, nevertheless this range of volcanic rock has its spiritual as well as scenic appeal. The wilderness lies just south of the Mojave National Preserve and I-40. A dirt road splits the wilderness into two nearly equal segments. The central core mountain area is cut by many canyons and washes surrounded by sloping bajadas and an apron of unconsolidated alluvium. Vegetation consists of barrel cactus, yucca, and creosote bush.

The flats are dominated by loose soils and are an ideal habitat for the endangered desert tortoise. A tortoise density of up to 50 tortoise per square mile is recorded for this area. Bighorn sheep occasionally wander into the region as well.

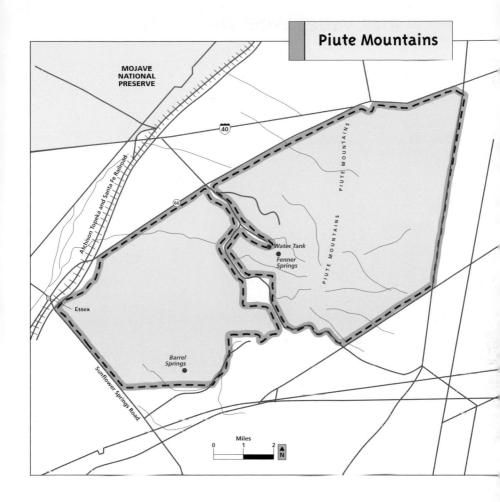

ACCESS

The best access is from Rte 66 (the National Trails Highway). The town of Essex lies at the northwestern corner of the wilderness. Just south of Essex is the gravel Sunflower Springs Road, which forms the western border of the wilderness. Hike east from the road. Another access point is the unnamed dirt road that bisects the range. To find this road, go east from Essex approximately 4.2 miles along Rte 66. Just past a sign for the Essex Sand and Gravel Mine, look to the south for a single-track dirt road. There is a gate and you'll know you have the right road if you see the brown, plastic BLM wilderness markers on either side of the road. You can easily make it to the second major wash crossing in a 2wd vehicle, however travel beyond this wash should only be attempted by those in 4wd vehicles. The road then becomes an exceptional trail leading through the heart of the wilderness, with a number of closed side roads also providing a "trail" for hiking. One of these side roads leads to Fenner Spring in the heart of the mountains and is a good destination for a one-day hike.

52 Rice Valley Wilderness

The creosote bush flats of Rice Valley with the Big Maria Mountains in the distance.

LOCATION:
Riverside County;
26 miles northwest
of Blythe, California

SIZE: 40,820 acres

ELEVATION RANGE:
500 to 2,000 feet

ADMINISTRATION:
BLM Palm Springs
Resource Area Office

MAPS: Desert Access
Guide Parker/Blythe
#16; AAA Riverside
County

Rice Valley Wilderness is one of those areas that is designated wilderness largely because it is roadless. For the most part, the broad, flat creosote-covered plain is not likely to attract many recreationalists. The BLM, in doing its analysis of the area, did suggest that the unconfined nature of the landscape may provide visitors with a sense of "vastness and desolation." If you are in need of a little isolation and desolation, then Rice Valley may be the place for you.

Not all of the wilderness is flat plain. A small portion of the rugged, volcanic peaks of the Big Maria Mountains are contained within the borders of the wilderness, but overall this is a pretty unexciting area.

A small band of sand dunes 30 to 40 feet high bisects the middle part of the valley. These dunes are part of the much larger Cadiz-Ward Valley dune system.

During World War II, Rice Valley was used for military training. Rice Air Base, which was located just

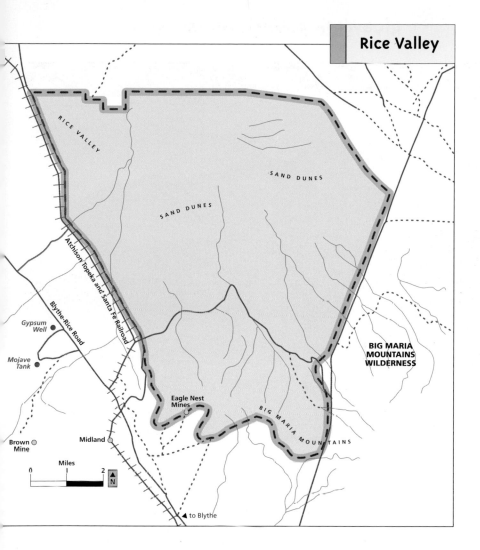

north of the wilderness, was used to train pilots. The valley was used for bombing and strafing practice, and may still contain unexploded ordinances.

If unexploded bombs and generally flat terrain aren't enough to discourage you, the BLM also notes (quite correctly) that there's little in the way of wildlife habitat in this area, hence little opportunity for bird watching, hunting, or wildlife viewing. There is also no water, and with almost nothing for shade, daytime temperatures outside of the winter months can be grueling. All in all, this is not the first place I would pick to spend time in the California desert.

ACCESS

For those of you who can't resist going someplace no one else wants to visit, the best access is via Midland Road north of Blythe. There several dirt roads that lead northeast off this paved road to the border of the wilderness.

53 Riverside Mountains Wilderness

Big Wash on the southern border of Riverside Mountains Wilderness provides a good access point into the wilderness.

LOCATION: Riverside County; 10 miles north of Blythe, California

SIZE: 22,380 acres

ELEVATION RANGE: 400 to 2,200 feet

ADMINISTRATION: BLM Palm Springs Resource Area Office

MAPS: Desert Access Guide Parker/Blythe #16; AAA Riverside County

The aptly named Riverside Mountains hug the Colorado River on the Arizona-California border. Indeed, the eastern boundary of the wilderness is less than one-half mile from the river and it is possible to hear "river-associated sounds" like waterfowl, frogs, and other wildlife. The mountains themselves are rugged, with numerous canyons and jagged peaks, and gentle bajadas that sweep down toward the Colorado River. These sloping bajadas are cut by numerous washes including Big Wash, which marks the southern border of the wilderness.

Vegetation consists of ocotillo, creosote bush, beavertail cactus, cholla cactus, barrel cactus, and burrobush. Palo verde and ironwood woodlands are found along the washes. Two sensitive species known from the area include foxtail cactus and California barrel cactus. Wildlife includes mule deer, bobcat, coyote, and other typical desert residents.

Evidence of past mining efforts are found in the wilderness, and some of the old mining roads are now used as

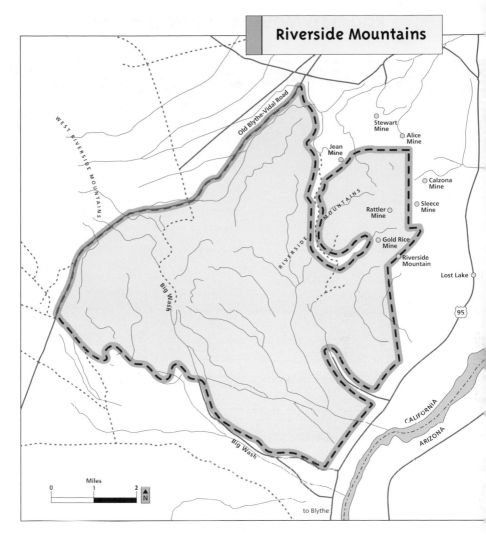

Riverside Mountains

trails. Most of these human disturbances are confined to the edge of the wilderness, with the rugged interior remaining essentially natural.

Due to their overall low elevation, high summer temperatures, and lack of surface water, recreational use of the Riverside Mountains is essentially a winter, late fall, and early spring activity. Travel here in the summer can be fatal.

ACCESS

State Hwy 95 provides access to the eastern border of the wilderness. Two non-wilderness cherry stem roads intrude into the wilderness. One is the dirt road to the Gold Rice Mine in the northeastern corner of the wilderness. The turnoff for this dirt road is off Old Blythe-Vidal Road, which can be reached in Vidal. To find the second dirt road, head west from Hwy 95 about 3 miles south of Lost Lake. Finally, a 4.5-mile dirt road up Big Wash provides access to the southern border of the wilderness.

54 Rodman Mountains Wilderness

Granite outcrops in Rodman Mountains Wilderness.

LOCATION:
San Bernardino County;
30 miles southwest of
Barstow, California

SIZE: 27,690 acres

ELEVATION RANGE:
2,000 to 5,000 feet

ADMINISTRATION:
BLM Barstow Resource
Area Office

MAPS: Desert
Access Guide Johnson
Valley #11; AAA San
Bernardino County

Rodman Mountains Wilderness lies just south of I-40 and immediately east of Newberry Mountains Wilderness. Taken together (a single dirt road separates them) they create a much larger wildlands unit than either alone.

The Rodman Mountains consist of fault-block ridges that rise up 5,000 feet. A lava flow, now appearing as a flat-topped mesa, slopes down from the aptly named Cinder Mountain near the southern border of the wilderness. Deep canyons and wide washes cut through the ridges, and sloping bajadas sweep away from the central core of peaks. Several natural water holes, known as tanks, litter the lava flow, some of which hold thousands of gallons of water. These tanks are critical for wildlife.

Sheep Spring is located in the center of the wilderness, and it no doubt commemorates the past presence of bighorn sheep in these mountains. The sheep have been

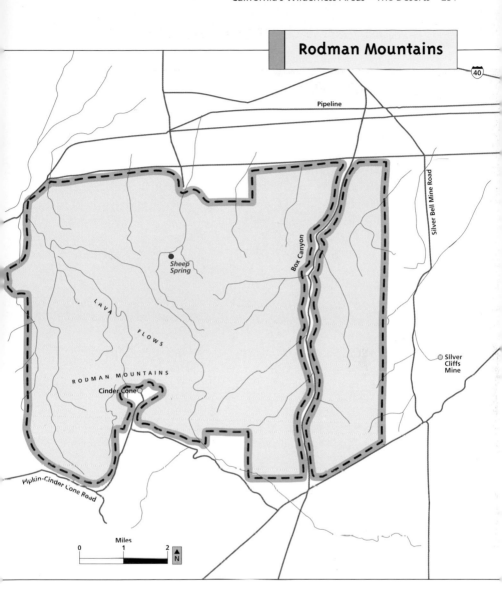

extirpated, but are found in the adjacent Newberry Mountains Wilderness and could be reintroduced into this area. The Rodman Mountains are also an important breeding area for raptors. Golden eagle and prairie falcon use the cliffs as nesting sites.

Many petroglyphs are found in this area. In fact, some archeologists believe they are some of the best preserved and one of the densest concentrations of petroglyphs in the entire Mojave Desert. Several thousand individual rock art drawings are found on cliffs within the wilderness and include representations of deer, bighorn sheep, lizards, tortoise, snakes, and abstractions. Some 2,500 acres are part of an Archeological District on the National Register of National Historic Places.

ACCESS

A primitive road up Box Canyon on the eastern edge of the wilderness actually splits the area into two units. The road also provides access to the interior of the range. To reach Box Canyon Road, take Rte 66 by exiting I-40 at the Fort Cady exit. Head east 3 miles to the turn south for Box Canyon. The bottom part of this route goes up a wash.

For those with 2wd vehicles there is good road access to the southern border and highest point at Cinder Cone. Take the Camp Daggett exit off I-40 and drive the gravel Camp Rock Road to the Camp Rock Mine. Camp Rock Road veers southwest here. To reach Cinder Cone, go straight on Road OJ228, which is sometimes called Pipkin-Cinder Cone Road. It is another 4 miles to Cinder Cone.

San Gorgonio Wilderness

55

Yucca frames San Gorgonio Wilderness.

The San Bernardino Mountains aren't your typical desert range. For one, they are well watered and forested. They are also extremely high, rising like a fortress and walling in the eastern edge of the Los Angeles Basin. This is the rooftop of southern California, with a number of ridges and peaks that rise above treeline including 10,806-foot Charlton Peak, 11,205-foot Jepson Peak, 10,624-foot San Bernardino Peak, 10,630-foot East San Bernardino Peak, and 11,502-foot Mount San Gorgonio—the highest peak in southern California. On a clear day from the broad summit plateau of Mount San Gorgonio, exquisite views are possible, with the Sierra Nevada and much of the Mojave Desert visible. The peak is also the southernmost glaciated landscape in California and includes the glacial landforms of Dollar Lake, Dry Lake, and Poopout Hill.

The San Bernardino Mountains are fault-block mountains defined by very active faults, including the San

LOCATION: San Bernardino and Riverside Counties; 2 miles north of Morongo Valley

SIZE: 94,702 total acres (37,980 acres of which is BLM land)

ELEVATION RANGE: 2,300 to 11,502 feet

ADMINISTRATION: BLM Palm Springs Resource Area Office; San Bernardino National Forest

MAPS: Desert Access Guide Yucca Valley #14, Palm Springs #17; AAA San Bernardino County; San Bernardino National Forest

Andreas Fault along the southern edge of the mountains. The Mill Creek Fault slices through the range, providing an easy target for erosion and hence the deep canyon of Mill Creek. A mix of rocks including granite, gneiss, and limestone can be found in the range.

The San Bernardino Mountains have one of the most diverse species of flora of any southern California mountain range. At lower elevations on the eastern slopes there are Joshua tree, pinyon pine, and juniper, whereas the western low-elevation slopes are dominated by chaparral. Higher up are magnificent forests of Coulter pine, ponderosa pine, Jeffrey pine, white fir, incense cedar, sugar pine, black oak, California dogwood, and bigleaf maple. At the highest elevations grow lodgepole pine and ancient limber pine, often forming open forests of barely-alive gnarled and twisted snags. Quaking aspen reaches its southernmost US distribution in the Fish Creek drainage and Arrastre Creek, whereas narrowleaf cottonwood (a Rocky Mountain species) is found in Holcomb Creek. A few meadows dot the range, adding to the attractive mix. Wildlife includes bighorn sheep, mule deer, mountain lion, and black bear.

Mormon settlers from nearby San Bernardino were the first whites to exploit the mountains. They cut timber on the slopes and crest, setting their first sawmills in Mill Creek—hence its name. By 1854 there were six sawmills operating in the mountains. In 1859, William Holcomb discovered gold in his namesake valley near Bear Valley, setting off a minor rush to the area. More gold was discovered in Bear Valley, and by 1860 several gold rush communities with as many as 2,000 residents dotted the crest of the San Bernardino Mountains. Eventually, the placer deposits gave out and most of the miners moved away. However, hard-rock underground mining continued well into this century.

In the 1880s, water was the new lure of these mountains. Several major dams were constructed to hold back water, including Big Bear Lake and Lake Arrowhead. Roads were built to bring supplies and people to build the reservoirs, and later to enjoy the lakes. The Rim of the World Highway was completed in 1915, setting the stage for the latest and last major rush—recreation. Several ski areas were proposed for development in what eventually became the San Gorgonio Wilderness. Fortunately wilderness proponents won out and the ski developments were never constructed. Although heavily used by hikers, the impact from recreationalists is minor, very concentrated, and nothing more than cosmetic compared with the effects of logging, mining, and housing development that has influenced the rest of the range.

The area now encompassed by the San Gorgonio Wilderness was first part of the San Bernardino Forest Reserve set aside in 1893. Its special qualities were recognized when the Forest Service chief designated the high country around San Gorgonio a primitive area in 1931. Its name changed to San Gorgonio Wild Area in 1956, and again in 1964 when it was officially designated the San Gorgonio Wilderness. In 1984 the wilderness was enlarged by 23,720 acres. The 1994 California Desert Protection Act added another 37,980 acres (managed by the BLM) to the southeastern corner near the Whitewater drainage. Today the San Gorgonio Wilderness encompasses 94,702 acres. More than 100 miles of trails, most in the highest elevations, are managed by the Forest Service and allow for everything from day hikes to extensive multiday treks. Yet much of the wilderness is trailless, particularly the upper Whitewater and Hell For Sure drainages, offering potential solitude for the more intrepid hiker.

The recent addition of BLM wilderness lands on the southeastern corner of the existing Forest Service wilderness has increased the amount of low-elevation terrain, which is covered with chaparral and other shrub communities like rabbit-brush. These lands are of scientific interest because they lie at a transition zone where the Mojave and Sonoran Deserts overlap with coastal vegetative communities. The mixture and diversity of plants found in this area is unusual as a consequence. Additionally, important riparian habitats including beautiful groves of cottonwood are found along Whitewater Canyon, Cottonwood Canyon, and Mission Creek. During bird migration these riparian habitats are populated with dozens of different species.

The area also supports some unique intergrades between desert and coastal reptile species. For instance, the banded gecko, glossy snake, and gopher snake all exhibit morphological characteristics of both coastal and desert variations. Two sub-species of collared lizards (*Crotaphytus insularis vestigium* and *C.i. bicinctores*) are located here, and some scientists believe they warrant separate species status.

ACCESS

There is an extensive trail system within the wilderness. Most of the trailheads are located off Hwy 38 between Mill Creek and Bear Lake. The other major access is off I-10 at Whitewater Creek.

HIKING

There are many opportunities for day hikes, as well as longer backpacking excursions. The following are only a few suggestions.

DAY HIKE: SAN BERNARDINO PEAK

One-way length:	8.0 miles
Low and high elevations:	6,000 to 10,624 feet
Difficulty:	moderate

A popular destination is the 8-mile hike to the summit of San Bernardino Peak (elevation 10,624 feet). This hike is long and climbs more than 4,600 feet, so it makes for a tough day hike but the rewards are the worth the effort. The views from the summit of San Bernardino Peak are tremendous. To find the trailhead from I-10 in Redlands, take Hwy 38 and travel 20 miles to the trailhead at the end of a short spur road by Camp Angelus.

The first part of the hike follows switchbacks up through a lovely forest of fir and pine, and comes to the wilderness boundary 2 miles from the trailhead. Although the grade moderates occasionally, most of the time you are hiking uphill, passing campsites at Columbine Spring and Limber Pine Bench — both with springs nearby that contain water. The trail continues its climb to where a short spur trail takes you to the final summit at 10,624 feet.

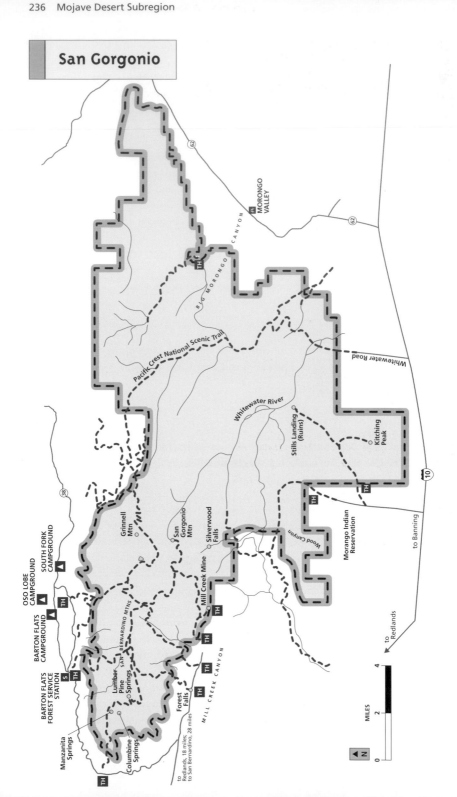

San Gorgonio

MILES

0   2   4

N

to Redlands

to Banning

10

62

62

MORONGO VALLEY

Whitewater Road

BIG MORONGO CANYON

Pacific Crest National Scenic Trail

Whitewater River

Stills Landing (Ruins)

Kitching Peak

Morango Indian Reservation

Wood Canyon

Grinnell Mtn

San Gorgonio Mtn

Silverwood Falls

Mill Creek Mine

38

SAN BERNARDINO MTNS

MILL CREEK CANYON

OSO LOBE CAMPGROUND

SOUTH FORK CAMPGROUND

BARTON FLATS CAMPGROUND

BARTON FLATS FOREST SERVICE STATION

Manzanita Springs

Lumber Pine Springs

Columbine Springs

Forest Falls

to Redlands, 18 miles; to San Bernardino, 28 miles

DAY HIKE: SAN GORGONIO PEAK

One-way length:	7.0 miles
Low and high elevations:	7,200 to 11,502 feet
Difficulty:	moderate

San Gorgonio Peak, also known as Old Grayback, is the highest peak in the San Gorgonio Wilderness and—like the hub of a wheel—more than a half dozen trails converge on its lofty summit. The Vivian Creek Trail, however, is considered by many to be the best way to the top.

Be ready for some climbing, because you must ascend more than 1 mile in elevation between the trailhead and the summit. To reach the trailhead, take Hwy 38 from Redlands east to Forest Home Road, which you follow for another 5 miles to the parking lot.

The first part of the hike follows Vivian Creek to Vivian Creek Trail Camp, where lovely pine and fir shade the stream. The route then passes through small meadows and open pine forests all the way to High Creek Camp (elevation 9,000 feet)—a good, potential overnight campsite. The trail continues climbing, with increasingly better views as you pass some old ancient limber pine and lodgepole pine, reaching timberline at 11,000 feet. You pass two more trail junctions and reach the summit, where on clear days expansive views south to Mexico and north to the Sierra Nevada are possible. Mount San Jacinto, just to the south, seems so close you can almost reach out and touch it.

DAY HIKE: KITCHING PEAK

One-way length:	4.7 miles
Low and high elevations:	4,400 to 6,598 feet
Difficulty:	moderate

Kitching Peak lies at the headwaters of Whitewater Creek on the southern edge of the San Gorgonio Wilderness, accessible from the I-10 corridor by Banning Pass. The peak offers great views of both Mount San Gorgonio and Mount San Jacinto. To reach the trailhead, leave I-10 in Banning Pass at Fields Road and drive north through the Morongo Indian Reservation. Take Morongo Road into Millard Canyon and follow it to Forest Road 2S05. At the first junction make a hard right, then at the second junction take a left to reach the parking area at the end of the road.

The hike follows Little Kitching Creek up the east branch of Millard Canyon, ascending through oak and Douglas fir. After 2 miles the trail leaves the creek and climbs to a ridge where a signed junction is located. Keep your eyes open for bighorn sheep. Turn right and take Trail 2E24 south along the ridge line through chaparral, and occasional fir and sugar pine to the summit, where exceptional views of the surrounding countryside await you.

DAY HIKE: PACIFIC CREST TRAIL
One-way length: 14 miles
Low and high elevations: 2,000 to 9,000 feet
Difficulty: moderate

The best access into the newly added BLM wilderness lands on the southern part of the San Gorgonio Wilderness is via the Pacific Crest Trail. The Pacific Crest Trail crosses I-10 at Banning Pass and continues through the San Gorgonio Wilderness via Whitewater Creek. To find the trailhead, turn off I-10 at Whitewater Canyon Road some 40 miles east of San Bernardino. Go north up the canyon for 4 miles to a parking area on the western side of the creek. The trail follows the creek and crosses a ridge into Mission Creek and eventually enters the higher elevation forested sections of the San Bernardino National Forest.

Sheephole Valley Wilderness

56

A wash frames granite outcrops in Sheephole Valley Wilderness.

Sheephole Valley Wilderness is one of the larger desert wildernesses in California. It encompasses two mountain ranges—the Sheephole Mountains and Calumet Mountains —plus an intervening valley. The Sheephole Mountains resemble the granitic parts of Joshua Tree National Park, and indeed were part of Joshua Tree National Park until 1950 when this area was "deleted" to allow mineral development. It is nice that protection for this area has been restored. Scenically the Sheephole Mountains are steeper and more dramatic than any of the other mountains in the park. The highest point in the Sheephole Mountains is 4,613 feet. The Calumet Mountains, although also of granitic origin, are lower and less rugged, with a high point that only rises to 3,723 feet. There is a small sand dune area in the southwestern corner of the wilderness. The combination of sweeping valleys, rugged mountains, and sandy dunes gives this wilderness a classic desert feel.

LOCATION:
San Bernardino County; 20 miles east of Twentynine Palms, California

SIZE: 174,800 acres

ELEVATION RANGE: 2,000 to 4,613 feet

ADMINISTRATION: BLM Needles Resource Area Office

MAPS: Desert Access Guide Sheephole Mountains #15; AAA San Bernardino County

The Sheephole Mountains support bighorn sheep. Several transplants of the animals in the 1980s supplemented the existing relict herd. Desert tortoise are numerous in Sheephole Valley, with densities of up to 50 animals per square mile. The rare Alverson's pincushion cactus (*Coryphantha vivipara* var. *alversonii*) is reported in the northwestern corner of the wilderness, otherwise vegetation is similar to that found in other nearby desert areas, including cholla cactus, creosote bush, and numerous wildflowers in the spring.

ACCESS

The easiest way to gain entry to this wilderness is off paved Hwy 62, which forms the southern boundary for 12 miles. You can also easily hike into the wilderness from the paved Amboy Road, which makes up the western border of the wilderness and separates it from Cleghorn Lakes Wilderness to the west. As with other desert wildernesses there are no formal trails, although there are numerous washes and old mining roads that serve as potential routes for cross-country travel.

Sheephole Valley

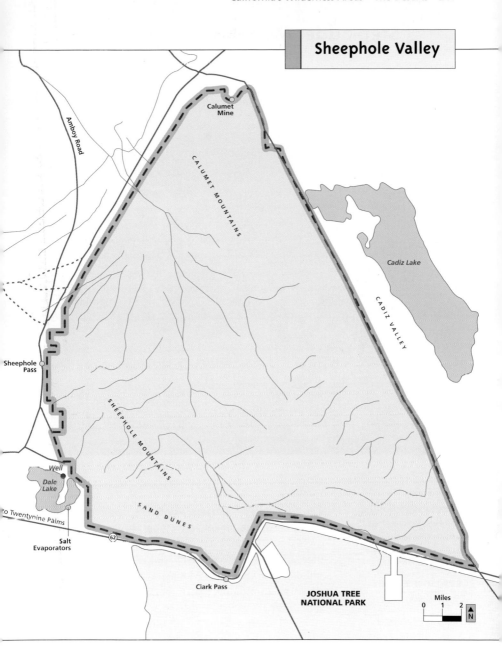

Calumet
Mine

Amboy Road

CALUMET MOUNTAINS

Cadiz Lake

CADIZ VALLEY

Sheephole
Pass

SHEEPHOLE MOUNTAINS

Well

Dale
Lake

to Twentynine Palms

SAND DUNES

Salt
Evaporators

62

Clark Pass

JOSHUA TREE
NATIONAL PARK

Miles
0   1   2

N

57 Stepladder Mountains Wilderness

Sunlit cholla cactus near Chemehuevi Wash, Stepladder Mountains Wilderness.

LOCATION:
San Bernardino County;
15 miles southwest of
Needles, California

SIZE: 81,600 acres

ELEVATION RANGE:
1,500 to 2,400 feet

ADMINISTRATION:
BLM Needles Resource
Area Office

MAPS: Desert Access
Guide Parker/Blythe
#16, Needles #13; AAA
San Bernardino County

The Stepladder Mountains Wilderness, despite its name that refers to mountains, consists mostly of creosote bush-covered bajada and desert riparian woodlands along washes. Indeed, only 15 percent of the wilderness has any mountains. Although the Stepladder Mountains do not rise that high above the surrounding desert, they are rather rugged in appearance.

The most significant feature in this wilderness is Chemehuevi Wash. Lined with palo verde woodland, this wash is attractive to both wildlife and hikers alike. The wide expanse of gentle bajadas is also a superb desert tortoise habitat, and densities up to 100 tortoise per square mile are found here. Bigelow cholla cactus is also found here, covering some 45 square miles of the wilderness, and a small stand of crucifixion thorn (*Holacantha emoryi*), common in Arizona but rare in California, occurs along Homer Wash.

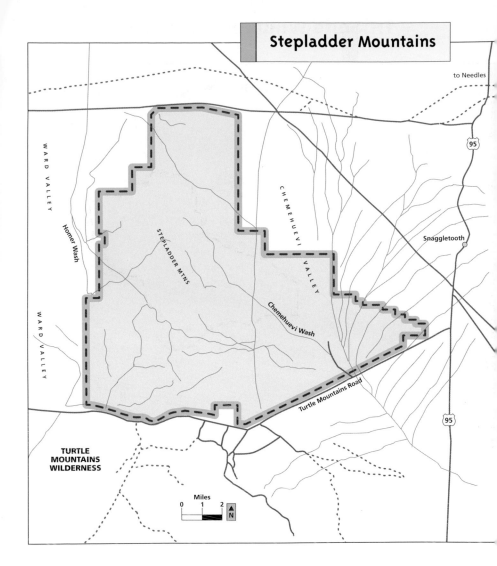

Archeological sites are located in the mountain portion of the wilderness. This includes rock shelters, petroglyphs, and a network of ancient trails most recently used by the Chemehuevis.

More recently the area was used during World War II for training of troops, and there is the potential for live explosives in the area.

ACCESS

To access the southern boundary of the wilderness, take US Hwy 95 south from Needles for 25 miles to Turtle Mountains Road. After going 2 miles west, the wilderness lies just north of the road for 17 miles. Chemehuevi Wash can sometimes present an obstacle to 2wd vehicles, otherwise the road is a washboard, but drivable.

58 Trilobite Wilderness

Wash in the Trilobite Wilderness.

LOCATION: Riverside County; 50 miles west of Needles, California

SIZE: 31,160 acres

ELEVATION RANGE: 1,000 to 3,500 feet

ADMINISTRATION: BLM Needles Resource Area Office

MAPS: Desert Access Guide Providence Mountains #12; AAA San Bernardino County

Trilobite Wilderness encompasses the Marble Mountains. Its name is a reference to the trilobite fossils—extinct Paleozoic marine arthropods—that are found embedded in the rocks of these mountains. Although there are outcrops of marble, the name of the mountains is a reflection of its marbled appearance of light and dark rock layers that have been swirled by geologic forces. Most of the range is of volcanic origin but there are outcrops of sedimentary sandstones near the center of the range.

The area is home to one of the more rapidly growing bighorn sheep herds in the Mojave Desert. Desert tortoise are found on the bajadas, and raptors like prairie falcon and golden eagle are reported to nest in the area.

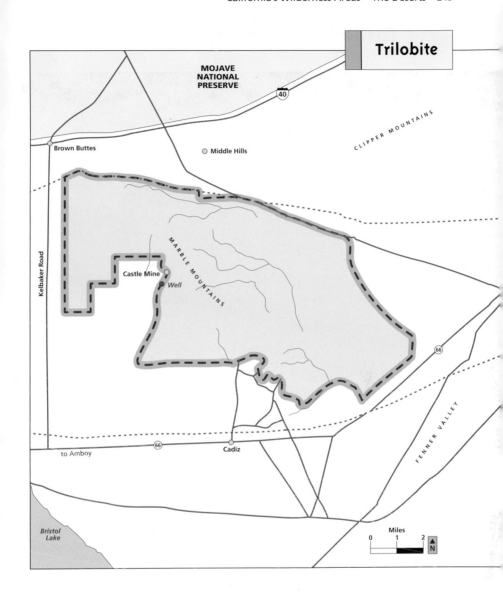

ACCESS

Turn south off I-40 at the Kelbaker Road exit. Go south for approximately 10 miles to the National Trails Highway (Rte 66). Go east 5 miles to the loose collection of buildings that is Cadiz. Once in "town," look for a sign for the Cadiz Land Company. Turn at this sign and travel 0.25 mile to a barrel with a hand-painted sign that says "Mountains that way." Make a slight jog to the right, then head north on a dirt track to the mountains. This road is narrow but passable with a 2wd vehicle. Where the road ends, it is possible to scramble up the slope to a saddle, which offers access to the crest of the range.

59 Turtle Mountains Wilderness

The turreted peaks of Turtle Mountains Wilderness.

LOCATION:
San Bernardino County;
30 miles south of
Needles, California

SIZE: 144,500 acres

ELEVATION RANGE:
1,000 to 4,231 feet

ADMINISTRATION:
BLM Needles Resource
Area Office

MAPS: Desert Access
Guide Parker/Blythe
#16, Sheephole
Mountains #15; AAA
San Bernardino County

With 144,500 acres within its boundaries, the Turtle Mountains Wilderness is one of the largest wildernesses in the eastern portion of the California desert. Yet it could be much larger. Since only a dirt road separates the Turtle Mountains from the 81,600-acre Stepladder Mountains Wilderness to the north, the effective size of this wildlands is considerably greater than even its significant acreage may indicate. Not only is this wilderness area spacious, but it is also one of the most dramatic. Volcanic cliffs, granitic spires, and deep canyons all surrounded by broad bajadas and numerous washes make this a wildlands worthy of extensive exploration. Many of the highest peaks are volcanic plugs—the necks and relicts of large volcanoes that were active in this area millions of years ago. Among the more spectacular named peaks are Horn Peak (elevation 3,866 feet), Castle Rock (elevation 2,979 feet), the twin Mopah Peaks (elevations 3,541 and 3,514 feet) and 4,231-foot Bolson Peak—the highest in the range.

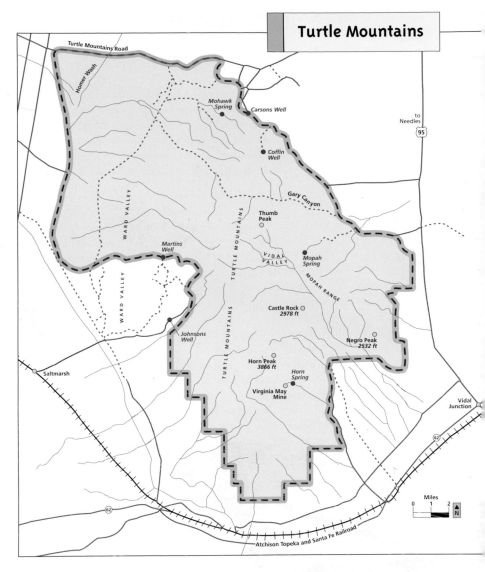

Turtle Mountains

The northern Turtle Mountains consist of colorful volcanics with jagged spires, whereas the southern Turtle Mountains are more rounded. Between the two sections is a large interior valley bisected by numerous washes. Homer Wash, another major drainage, cuts across the northwestern corner of the wilderness and has a rich desert woodland riparian zone with palo verde, ironwood, smoke tree, and other desert wash species.

Unlike most of the California desert wildernesses, which are completely waterless, the Turtle Mountains harbor 11 springs, including Horn Spring, Martins Well, Mopah Spring, Carsons Well, Mohawk Spring, and Coffin Spring. However the BLM recommends that anyone hiking in this wilderness bring their own water because the springs may not be reliable. Mopah Spring supports the most northern California fan palm oasis in the California desert, although the palms are not native to the range, having been planted there in 1924.

Vegetation consists of typical desert species like creosote bush, barrel cactus, and palo verde located along streams. Wildlife include desert bighorn sheep, desert tortoise, golden eagle, and prairie falcon.

The Turtle Mountains possess significant archeological resources and are a designated National Natural Landmark. Cultural remains include rock shelters, rock art, rock alignments, quarry sites, and tool production sites. Mopah Springs in particular has an extensive collection of petroglyphs, trail shrines, and habitation sites.

The Turtle Mountains are also well known among rock hounds for jasper, agate, and Mopah Roses—a chalcedony thought to resemble the folded petals of a rose.

ACCESS

The easiest way to reach the boundary of Turtle Mountains Wilderness is along the northeastern corner. From Needles go approximately 25 miles south on Hwy 95 to Turtle Mountains Road. Turn west onto this road and go 10 miles to a fork in the road. Turtle Mountains Road can be driven (carefully) by a 2wd vehicle to this point. You might want to park and hike from here. If your vehicle can handle it, turn south (left) and travel another 3 miles to the road end at Carson's Well. There are a few ruins of houses here. Mohawk Spring makes for a good hiking destination from this location. It is about 1 mile distant on an old jeep trail. Don't get your hopes up by the name; the spring is more of a seep than a gushing fountain. Near the spring is an unusual petroglyph. It is an abstract design that looks like a blueprint more than anything else. Outstanding specimens of chalcedony roses have been found here by the spring.

Another good hike destination is Mopah Spring. From Needles go south on US Hwy 95 for 34.4 miles and turn west onto the dirt road marked with a rock cairn. Travel 2.75 miles west until you see a red road closure sign in the center of the road; park here. This is usually passable in a 2wd vehicle. From the road closure, walk along the south extension of the fork for about 1.1 miles to the ruins of a stone cabin. Here at the canyon mouth you are about 3.5 miles from Mopah Spring, which is southwest up the canyon wash. Mopah Peak is about the same distance away, but a little farther to the south. To reach the spring, hike up the wash.

Mopah Spring, which lies northwest of the massive monolith of Mopah Peak, has a small pool of clear water approximately 4 feet across. A clump of California fan palms grows at the spring. (This is an excellent spot for bird watching.) The five mature palms were burned in 1983, and now dozens of seedlings have appeared. Like nearly all of the palm oases in the southwest, this one is growing in size.

Those with good map and compass skills may consider doing an overnight cross-country backpack loop of 16 to 18 miles that goes up to Mopah Springs and eventually comes back out the north fork of Gary Wash. Follow the directions to Mopah Spring then continue another 0.5 mile west to a saddle, which you cross to enter Vidal Valley—the Turtle's interior valley. Hike northwest up the valley to another saddle about a half-mile east of Thumb Peak—a prominent spire on the northern horizon. Once over this saddle you enter the wide expanse of Gary Wash, which can be followed east and south on an old 4wd route back down to your starting point.

Whipple Mountains Wilderness   60

Eroded volcanic turrets in Whipple Mountains Wilderness.

The rugged and extremely dissected Whipple Mountains lie adjacent to the Colorado River. The highest peak—Whipple Peak—rises to 4,130 feet. Spires, horns, cliffs, natural bridges, and countless deep canyons and washes all make this a visual treat. Indeed, the Whipples are among the most scenic mountains in the California desert. The Whipple Mountains are oriented in an east-west direction. The eastern half is composed of brick red volcanics and highly scenic eroded formations. Large areas of desert pavement cover portions of the western part of the wilderness. Fourteen-mile-long Whipple Wash cuts through the heart of the range, has walls more than 1,000 feet high, and is sometimes compared with the canyons found in Zion National Park.

Diverse vegetation covers these mountains, including ocotillo, brittlebush, and a wide variety of cactus such as Bigelow cholla, prickly pear, plus an occasional saguaro—one of three places in California where this cactus is found.

LOCATION:
San Bernardino County;
10 miles north of
Parker, Arizona

SIZE: 77,520 acres

ELEVATION RANGE:
500 to 4,130 feet

ADMINISTRATION:
BLM Needles Resource
Area Office

MAPS: Desert
Access Guide Parker/
Blythe #16; AAA San
Bernardino County

Along the washes there are dense woodlands of palo verde, smoke tree, and ironwood. Wildlife include mule deer, desert bighorn sheep, and the endangered desert tortoise. On bajadas in the western part of the wilderness, tortoise densities of as many as 100 per square mile have been recorded.

The Whipples have also assumed some importance for climatic research, since pack rat middens in these mountains provide a record of past vegetative changes for the last 40,000 years.

The Whipples contain one of the greatest concentrations of cultural sites in the California desert. These mountains have great mythological significance for the Chemehuevi, Mojave, and Halchidhoma tribes. There are numerous burial and religious ritual sites found in the area. In 1981, the BLM designated part of the eastern Whipple Mountains an ACEC to protect the important archeological treasures found here.

ACCESS

The easiest route to the wilderness lies along the eastern margin. From Parker, Arizona, cross into California on Hwy 62. Turn right on Parker Dam Road and go north approximately 15 miles. One mile before the dam, turn left onto Black Meadow Landing Road. Follow this road for 6 miles to a left turn onto a dirt road signed for Havasu Palms. Drive another 2.1 miles on this road to a power line road on your left. This steep, rough road forms the eastern border of the wilderness for the next 8 miles. If you have a 2wd vehicle, I recommend that you walk or ride a mountain bike on this road.

Whipple Mountains

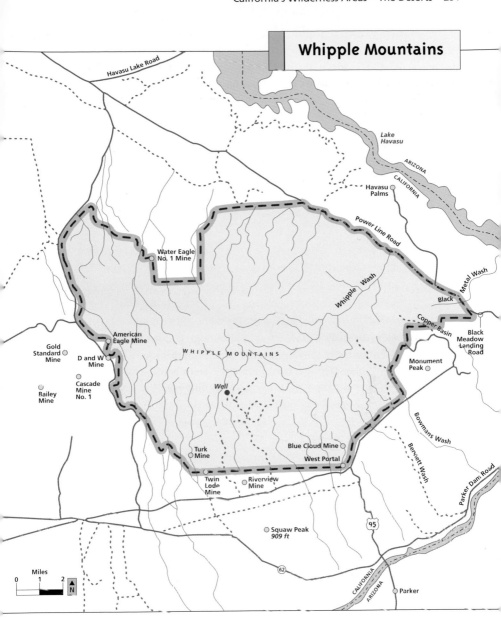

Colorado Desert Subregion

The Colorado Desert is the northwest extension of the famous Sonoran Desert of Arizona. It occupies the hottest, lowest, driest part of the California desert. For the purposes of this book, it is the area sandwiched between the Mexican border and I-10, although technically, and from a purely botanical perspective, it should curve northward toward Needles to include the Whipple, Turtle, and Chemehuevi Mountains, among others.

Anza Borrego Desert State Park is the largest wildlands reserve in the region. Although Anza Borrego is a large wildlands complex, in general compared with areas further north, most of the wildernesses in this sub-region are small in size. Perhaps this is a reflection of the greater nearby development by a large human population. The Imperial and Coachella Valleys are both used for irrigated farming, and numerous cities and small towns dot the landscape.

Much of the Colorado Desert occupies the Salton Trough. This trough, which lies below sea level, is the northern extension of the Gulf of California and was created by movement along the San Andreas Fault.

Like other California deserts, precipitation falls primarily in the winter. However, occasional summer moisture gives this desert a biseasonal source of moisture.

Due to the hot temperatures, creosote bush dominate most flats and slopes as it does in the Mojave Desert to the north. There are, however, far more cacti and succulents like agave growing in this desert than further north. The whiplike ocotillo is one defining plant of the Colorado Desert.

Perhaps the most biologically rich community of the Colorado Desert is the desert wash woodlands of palo verde, ironwood, smoke tree, and mesquite that line all the waterways. California fan palm oases are another unique feature of this desert.

Cactus below the San Ysidro Mountains, Anza Borrego Desert State Park.

61 Anza Borrego Desert State Park

Mountain Palm Canyon, Anza Borrego Desert State Park.

LOCATION: San Diego county; 80 miles east of San Diego, California

SIZE: 600,000 total acres (378,000 areas of designated wilderness)

ELEVATION RANGE: Sea level to 6,193 feet

ADMINISTRATION: Anza Borrego Desert State Park

MAP: AAA San Diego County

Anza Borrego Desert State Park is one of the "crown jewels" of the California State Park system. At 600,000 acres, this sweep of badlands, palm canyons, rugged mountains, and desert washes is one of the largest state parks in the country. It is approximately 60 miles north-south, and up to 30 miles wide. Elevations range from near sea level up to 6,193 feet at Combs Peak. Some 63 percent of the park is designated state wilderness and is managed essentially the same way as federal wilderness areas. It is a good place for those new to the desert to get acquainted with the desert environment. It has a good visitor center, several designated campgrounds, and well-marked trails.

About two thirds of the park is mountainous, with a number of named mountain ranges. Starting in the north and working south, they are the Santa Rosa Mountains, San Ysidro Mountains, Vallecito Mountains, Laguna Mountains, In-Ko-Pah Mountains, and the Coyote Mountains. There are also significant badlands, including the Borrego Badlands and the Carrizo Badlands. The community of Borrego Springs, a large parcel of private land, lies in the middle of the park.

HISTORY

The park takes its name from the Spanish explorer Juan Bautista de Anza, who led several expeditions across this region in 1774 and 1775. After the Anza exploration the area was traversed by the Butterfield Overland Mail stages that linked San Francisco, California, to St. Louis, Missouri.

Anza Borrego Desert State Park was established in 1933 and was carved out of what was then federal land. The acquisition of federal land for state park purposes is the result of one of the strange twists of fate that so often determine the course of history. The Anza Borrego area was first identified as a potential park site by Frederick Law Olmsted, a renown landscape architect. Olmsted was hired in the early 1930s by the newly established California State Parks Commission to survey the state and report back to the commission on recommended state park sites. Olmsted identified 125 sites deserving state park status or acquisition, but in particular he noted that the desert offered a special opportunity for park designation.

Ray Lyman Wilbur, one of the original members of the State Parks Commission, was appointed Secretary of Interior in 1929. Wilbur immediately placed a temporary halt to homesteading, mining claims, and other forms of federal public land acquisition to permit development of a long-term park plan for California. In 1933, a highly unusual piece of legislation was introduced in Congress. With Wilbur's backing, the legislative bill permitted California to acquire 189,000 acres of federal land in the Borrego Valley area for a state park.

Expansion of the park continued throughout the 1930s, facilitated by the additional acquisition of federal land that was obtained for the price of one dollar per 80 acres, or the cost of the federal filing fee. Not surprisingly, mining and grazing industries fought to block any expansion of the park. Public hearings were held by both the state and federal governments, but despite local objections, expansion of the park proceeded.

GEOLOGY

The mountains and badlands that make up the bulk of the Anza Borrego region are a complex mix of rock types. This mixture has been influenced by plate tectonics and the local manifestation of various major faults, including the San Andreas Fault. The oldest rocks exposed in the region are metasedimentary rocks that were deposited in an ocean basin during the Paleozoic era some 500 million years ago.

These old marine sediments, including shale, sandstone, and limestone, were once 8,000 feet thick. With the later emplacement of the Peninsula Batholith (molten rock that later cooled into the granitic rocks so abundant in the region), these sedimentary rocks were "cooked" and metamorphosed into schist, gneiss, marble, and quartzite—all of which are visible in the San Ysidro, Santa Rosa, and

Coyote Mountains. These metasedimentary rocks can be seen in Carrizo Peak in the Coyote Mountains and Indianhead Mountain by Borrego Palm Canyon.

About 150 million years ago, the Farallon plate collided with the westward-moving North American plate. The result was an extensive period of mountain building and uplift in the western United States. The Farallon plate dove under the North American plate and melted. Magma rose toward the surface of the earth, but did not erupt as lava. Instead this rock hardened slowly, forming a large granitic body known as a batholith.

Some 65 to 70 million years ago (approximately the time that the dinosaurs went extinct) the Peninsula Mountains were uplifted. As they rose, the overlying sedimentary and metasedimentary rocks were striped away by erosion, eventually exposing the granitic rocks so common in Anza Borrego Desert State Park today.

Around 20 million years ago Baja, Mexico, began to split off from the mainland of Mexico, and the Gulf of California opened up in its wake. As Baja became "unzipped" from Mexico, a deep trough formed and filled with water—an area we now call the Sea of Cortez. The northern end of this basin is known as the Salton Sea Trough or Depression. This structural depression stretches north from the Mexican border through the Coachella Valley to San Gorgonio Pass. (The Salton Sea is 274 feet below sea level.) Volcanic eruptions occurred at the same time, depositing ash and lava still evident in the region today in portions of the Fish Creek Mountains and Volcanic Hills.

Then about four to five million years ago an inland sea filled the Salton Sea Trough and lapped against the Vallecito and Fish Creek basins. The gypsum now mined near the Fish Creek Mountains was deposited during this period. Sediments accumulated during this era, and the buried fossil remains of more than 100 large mammals have been found in the Vallecito Badlands. At one time there were ground sloth, camels, horses, and zebras grazing in this region, and they were preyed upon by saber-toothed tigers and American lions.

By 1.5 million years ago the climate had cooled and the Pleistocene Ice Age engulfed the region. The cooler temperatures prompted the establishment of woolly mammoths and giant bears.

From one to two million years ago the mountains of the region were rising rapidly, which increased erosion and downcutting. The uplift also began to block airflow from the ocean, creating a rain shadow to the east.

FAUNA AND FLORA

The park is home to a wide diversity of animals, including 60 mammalian species, 270 avian species, 27 species of snake, and 31 species of lizard. The park also harbors several varieties of the rare desert pupfish.

One of the more special animals of Anza Borrego Desert State Park is the desert bighorn sheep. Indeed, *borrego* means wild sheep in Spanish. Bighorn were once common throughout the desert ranges of California, but they were decimated

Vallecito Mountains at dawn in Anza Borrego Desert State Park.

by a combination of market hunting during the mining era and the introduction of domestic livestock, which transmitted disease to the sheep and usurped their food and water resources. Anza Borrego Desert State Park is now home to 300 to 400 of these animals. There are a number of species of desert sheep, and the animals inhabiting Anza Borrego are Peninsula bighorns. Anza Borrego is home to two thirds of all Peninsula bighorn in the world. The park's bighorn are distributed in five separate herds—in the Santa Rosa Mountains, the Vallecito Mountains, Carrizo Gorge, Coyote Canyon, and Palm Canyon.

The park is also home to a wide variety of plant species. California fan palms, the only native palm in California, are found wherever water seeps to the surface—usually along faults. Another unusual tree species is the thick-trunk elephant tree. Relatively common in Baja, the elephant tree reaches it most northern distribution here. Adding to the diversity of vegetation are tree species such as smoke tree and mesquite, along with 22 species of cactus. At the higher elevations grow pinyon pine and juniper. Anza Borrego is also famous for its spring time floral displays. The intensity of blooms depends on the fall rainfall. The park maintains a special phone line that informs visitors about the status of the flower season.

ACCESS

The park is located just off I-8, 80 miles east of San Diego. California Hwy 78 provides access to the center portion of the park.

CAMPING

Unlike most parks, Anza Borrego Desert State Park has no entrance fee. Nor is a backpacking permit needed, although it is always good to let someone (such as a relative or friend) know of your approximate, planned itinerary. There are 11 state campgrounds as well as private campgrounds in or near the park. The park also allows car camping almost anywhere in the park as long as you remain within one car length of the road. However when backpacking or camping, avoid camping near water sources so that wildlife has access to water.

HIKING

Most of the hikes in the park are short day hikes. There are, however, six longer segments of the Pacific Crest Trail that traverse the park, offering potential multi-day hikes.

California fan palms in Borrego Palm Canyon, Anza Borrego Desert State Park.

DAY HIKE: SOMBRERO PEAK

One-way length:	3 to 4 miles
Low and high elevations:	1,000 to 4,229 feet
Difficulty:	moderate

The hike to the top of Sombrero Peak in the southwestern corner of the park provides panoramic views of the Carrizo Badlands and Laguna Mountains. To find the trailhead, drive County Road S2 north 18 miles from I-8. Turn west onto the dirt Indian Gorge Road. In 2.8 miles you reach a fork. At the fork go left (southwest) into South Indian Valley. Drive as far as your vehicle permits. A 4wd vehicle can go approximately 3 miles. Hikers in 2wd vehicles should park sooner and walk or ride your mountain bike.

Proceed up South Indian Valley Canyon until you come to a branch of the canyon that heads north. At the mouth of the branch is a palm tree and water. Hike up to the ridge line north of the canyon and follow the rolling plateau to the peak.

DAY HIKE: TOROTE CANYON—ELEPHANT TREES

One-way length:	0.6 mile
Low and high elevations:	1,100 to 1,300 feet
Difficulty:	easy

This short hike takes in several groves of elephant tree—one of the rarest trees in California. *Torote* is the Spanish word for twisted and it refers to the tortured growth habit of the elephant tree. The trailhead is located off County Road S2 in the southern portion of the park. To reach the trail, take County Road S2 north from I-8. After passing the Carrizo Badlands overlook and the sign for the Mountain Palm Springs Campground, you come to the signed turn, at which you turn west (left) onto Indian Gorge Road. Drive 1.8 miles up the sandy road to the mouth of Torote Canyon.

The hike up Torote Canyon is straightforward. Just follow the wash upstream, scrambling over a few boulders en route. The first elephant trees are reached in 0.4 mile, but the bigger and more spectacular grove is another 0.2 mile upcanyon. After savoring the trees, turn around and retrace your steps back to the trailhead.

DAY HIKE: WILSON TRAIL

One-way length:	5.5 miles
Low and high elevations:	4,000 to 4,400 feet
Difficulty:	moderate

The high elevation of this trail makes it a good hike when the temperatures are high in the lower desert around Borrego Springs. The end of the hike rewards you with a good view of Borrego Valley. To find the trailhead, take County Road S22 and travel 8 miles southwest from Borrego Springs until you come to the turnoff heading south on Old Culp Valley Road. You might want to park near the turnoff and walk or mountain bike to the trailhead because Old Culp Valley Road is steep and sandy. This road is not recommended for 2wd vehicles. It is 3.1 miles from County Road S22 to the signed trailhead. If you decide to walk from the main highway, bear in mind that the round-trip hike totals 17.2 miles—a bit excessive for all but the most experienced hikers. It does, however, make for a good overnight hike if you are prepared to carry all your water.

The trail is a former jeep road that is now closed. From the trailhead, climb up a moderate slope 0.6 mile to the ridge top with good views of the surrounding mountains. Descend 0.5 mile to a swale full of cholla and agave, then climb again for another 0.5 mile to another granite-studded ridge. The next mile or so of the route crosses rolling terrain, with some ups and downs, while climbing gradually to a saddle by 4,573-foot Mount Wilson. Five miles from the trailhead, the old jeep trail deteriorates to a more primitive path marked by cairns. After another 0.3 or 0.4 mile the path begins to drop eastward. At this point turn north and walk about 100 yards to get a good view of Borrego Springs Valley and the Salton Sea. Retrace your steps back to the trailhead.

DAY HIKE: MOUNTAIN PALM SPRINGS CANYON
One-way length: 1.5 miles
Low and high elevations: 750 to 1,190 feet
Difficulty: moderate

The hike up Mountain Palm Springs Canyon offers a relatively easy stroll up a sandy wash to several groves of California fan palms. To find the trailhead, take County Road S2 north from I-8 past the Carrizo Badlands overlook and the turnoff for the Bow Willow Ranger Station, just before mile marker 47 there is a sign indicating the turnoff to the west for the Mountain Palm Springs Trailhead. The trailhead is 0.5 mile beyond County Road S2.

From the trailhead head west, and in less than 0.5 mile you come to a small grove of four palm trees. In another 0.4 mile you reach a second, larger grove known as Pygmy Grove (so named because of the short stature of the trees). You pass a third group of five palms, after which you bear left up the main valley. At 1.2 miles you come to a fork in the trail. Go right for 0.3 mile to arrive at Southwest Palm Grove—the largest collection of palms in this canyon. Linger here to enjoy the pools of water and the nearby elephant trees.

If you have more energy, you can visit some other palm groves and make a loop trip out of this by going north to the next canyon. From Southwest Palm Grove head north 1 mile to Surprise Canyon on a faint but distinct trail that crosses a rocky ridge. Once you reach the canyon floor, head up the wash 0.5 mile to Palm Bowl—the largest palm grove in the complex. From Palm Bowl retrace your steps toward Surprise Palm Grove, and continue east down the wash, passing another palm grove en route. You reach the trailhead in about a mile.

DAY HIKE: BORREGO PALM CANYON TRAIL

One-way length:	3.5 miles
Low and high elevations:	800 to 1,300 feet
Difficulty:	moderate

This hike is a signed nature trail that follows a seasonal creek past one of the largest palm groves in the park and ends by a small waterfall. Hummingbirds are common along this trail in the spring, and bighorn sheep are sometimes encountered. The trail is a good introduction to the geology, plants, and animals of the region. The trailhead is located at the Borrego Palm Canyon Campground and Picnic Area 1 mile north of the park visitor center. The trail is well marked and easy to follow. For all these reasons it is also popular and likely to be well used on weekends. Even in the middle of June with the temperature higher than 105°F, I encountered several other hiking parties! From the trailhead it is 1.5 miles to the palm grove, with an overlook of the oasis another 0.25 mile beyond that.

At first the canyon appears somewhat barren and rocky, but eventually you begin to encounter more water, particularly in the spring, and hence more vegetation. The majority of palms are upstream from this overlook. It is possible to scramble upstream beyond the first palms, but the trail is much rougher with more dense stands of brush, and it requires some wading. If you choose to turn around at this point you can either follow the main trail back down the canyon or take an alternative return route that climbs up the south slope and provides a different perspective of the canyon.

DAY HIKE: COYOTE CANYON—LOWER WILLOWS— BOX CANYON

One-way length:	2 miles or a 4-mile loop
Low and high elevations:	1,140 to 1,350 feet
Difficulty:	moderate

This is a good hike on a warm day because it follows Coyote Canyon Creek, one of the loveliest clear streams in the desert. It does, however, require numerous crossings in muck and water. The trail is used by horseback riders as well, so the trail may be somewhat torn up. However, the lush riparian vegetation harbors many birds and makes for excellent birding in the spring months.

To find the trailhead, take Palm Canyon Drive east from the visitor center to Di Giorgio Road. Turn left (north) on Di Giorgio Road and continue north 5 miles on pavement. Continue north on the gravel Coyote Canyon Road, crossing the creek several times. If you have a 4wd vehicle, go past Second Crossing (signed) to the parking area at Third Crossing. The trailhead for Lower Willows Trail begins just before you reach the signed Third Crossing. Those with low-clearance vehicles may wish to park at Second Crossing and walk the last mile to Third Crossing. Bear in mind that this section of the park is closed between June 1 and September 30 to minimize disturbance of bighorn sheep in the area.

Cholla along Alcoholic Pass Trail, Anza Borrego Desert State Park.

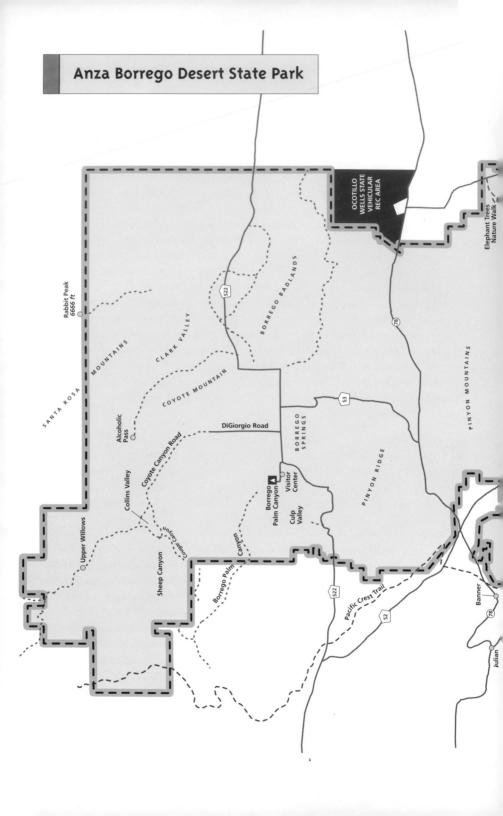

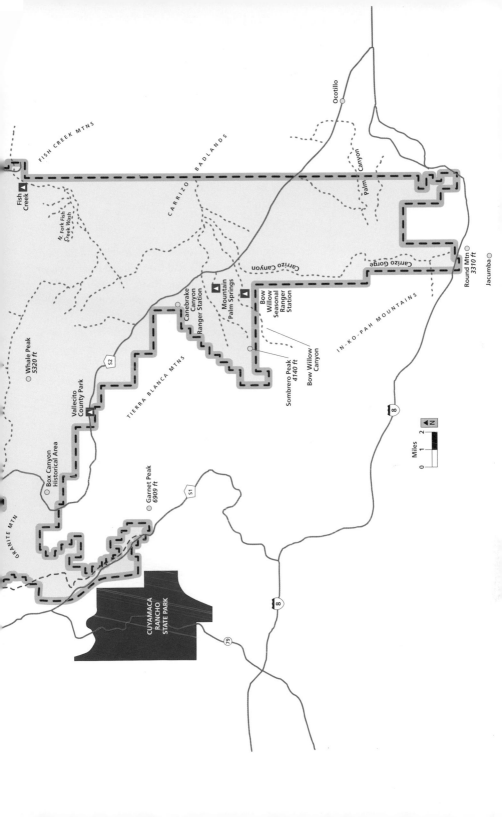

The "trail" basically follows the creek upstream, and there are repeated crossings. After 2 miles you emerge into a wide, sandy wash. Here you can turn around and retrace your steps back down the creek or follow yellow-topped white posts out of the wash to the west to reach Coyote Canyon Road. Turn east (left) and follow the dirt road back to the Lower Willows Trailhead.

DAY HIKE: ALCOHOLIC PASS

One-way length:	1.1 miles
Low and high elevations:	800 to 1,500 feet
Difficulty:	moderate

Alcoholic Pass Trail climbs quickly from Coyote Creek Valley and offers outstanding views of the surrounding mountains. To find the trailhead from Borrego Springs, drive east on Palm Canyon Drive to Di Giorgio Road. Turn north (left) on Di Giorgio Road and travel 5 miles on pavement. Continue on a gravel road for 2.6 miles to the signed trailhead and small pullout, which is on the right.

The trail goes up a wash a short way, past cholla cactus. It then climbs up a ridge rather steeply. Eventually the trail reaches a plateau that leads to a low notch in the mountains—the pass. You can turn around at this point, but you really won't have seen the best view. To get a commanding vista of Clark Valley to the northeast you need to go beyond the pass another half mile or so. To return, retrace your route.

DAY HIKE: COUGAR CANYON

One-way length:	5 miles
Low and high elevations:	1,140 to 2,300 feet
Difficulty:	moderate

The hike up Cougar Canyon takes you along a stream and past a palm grove to a waterfall. There is delightful riparian vegetation, including sycamore and willow. This hike also makes for a moderate overnight backpack trip. Getting to the canyon mouth requires hiking about 4 miles up Coyote Canyon Road—a very rough but somewhat drivable 4wd road. On weekends, you may encounter jeep traffic.

To get to the trailhead, head east on Palm Canyon Drive to Di Giorgio Road. Take Di Giorgio Road north 5 miles until the pavement ends and the dirt Coyote Canyon Road begins. Follow Coyote Canyon Road, crossing the creek several times. If you have a 2wd vehicle, it is best to stop at Second Crossing (signed). If you have a 4wd vehicle you can usually reach Third Crossing, which is another mile further up the road. Here it is best to park and walk or use a mountain bike to access the trailhead. The distance from the parking area at Third Crossing to the trailhead is 4 miles.

From Collins Valley, Cougar Canyon looks like any other dry wash. But within a few twists and bends of the canyon you begin to hear water gurgling over rocks. There are sandy beaches and small, clear pools of water. Riparian vegetation is lush. The trail eventually fades after about 1.5 miles. To return, retrace your route.

Carrizo Gorge Wilderness 62

View of Carrizo Gorge Wilderness.

Carrizo Gorge Wilderness is a long, narrow (barely a half-mile wide in some places) wildlands that ironically doesn't contain its namesake gorge. Nevertheless, the view from the wilderness of the gorge and beyond is spectacular. On a clear day it is possible to see the Salton Sea and south into Mexico.

The wilderness encompasses the eastern slope of the In-Ko-Pah Mountains and the steep transition zone from the coastal mountains of southern California and the Colorado Desert beyond. Although the In-Ko-Pah Mountains contain few dramatic peaks, this broad, rolling upland area is strewn with numerous, large granite rock formations that tower above the chaparral-covered landscape. A series of earthquake faults related to the San Andreas Fault extends along the eastern edge of the coastal mountains. Over a period of 150 million years, the landmass west of the fault system has been pushed up to form the mountains, while the landmass east of the fault system has dropped down to form the Salton Trough, of

LOCATION:
San Diego County;
60 miles east of San
Diego, California; Just
west of Anza Borrego
Desert State Park

SIZE: 15,700 acres

ELEVATION RANGE:
1,500 to 4,600 feet

ADMINISTRATION:
BLM El Centro
Resource Area Office

MAPS: Desert Access
Guide McCain Valley
#19; AAA San Diego
County

which the Imperial Valley is a part. Movement along the faults in the zone between the two landmasses has produced the Jacumba Mountains, a series of north-south ridges and canyons at progressively lower elevations that lie between the In-Ko-Pah Range and the lower desert country of Imperial County. Carrizo Canyon is the most spectacular of the north-south canyons, and it forms the dividing line between the In-Ko-Pah and Jacumba Ranges.

Vegetation includes chaparral species like red shank, chamise, and shrub oak. These chaparral species gradually give way to desert natives like brittlebush, catclaw, and agave. California fan palms are found along some washes in the area. Several herds of Peninsula bighorn sheep and the San Diego coast horned lizard inhabit the area.

The Carrizo Gorge area was home to the Kumeyaay or Southern Diegueno Indians. These natives hunted game and gathered plant resources in the In-Ko-Pahs until the early 1900s. Each spring they moved from winter settlements at lower elevations into the coastal mountains, following wildlife. They also harvested acorns, and other seeds and plant materials as they became available. In the fall they returned to hunting-and-gathering areas in the inland mountains. Signs of native American occupation are fairly common in the McCain Valley-Carrizo Gorge area. Bedrock morteros, or grinding holes, are some of the most interesting and readily identified cultural remains.

The gorge and canyon also provided an access route for early Spanish, Mexican, and American travelers, including those on the Butterfield Overland mail stage. In 1852 George McCain homesteaded and began grazing livestock in the valley that now bears his name. During the 1860s and 1870s additional settlers arrived in the McCain Valley region due, in part, to the discovery of gold near Cuyamaca and Julian. Today with the growing urban population in nearby San Diego, recreation is now the dominant land use of the area.

ACCESS

The easiest access to the wilderness is off I-8. Take the Boulevard exit (70 miles east of San Diego). Once on old Hwy 80, go east for 1.8 miles to McCain Valley Road. Follow signs for McCain Valley Resource Conservation Area and Sacatone Springs Overlook some 11 miles from the highway. There is a picnic area right on the edge of the canyon. If you look across the gorge you can see a portion of the San Diego-to-Arizona Railroad, also referred to as The Impossible Railroad. With binoculars you may see some old railroad cars that have been abandoned on the hillside below the track. Near the overlook point is an old, abandoned mine called The School Mine.

The Sacatone Springs Overlook provides the easiest access to the edge of the wilderness, although there are no maintained trails. There are, however, "use" trails that work their way down into the canyon.

Another potential cross-country hiking destination is the palm grove in Four Frogs Canyon. Only those with good backcountry travel skills should attempt this hike, and a good topographical map is helpful. Keep in mind that most maps are outdated with regard to "roads" and "jeep trails." To access this route drive further north along McCain Valley Road. Go 0.8 mile beyond the

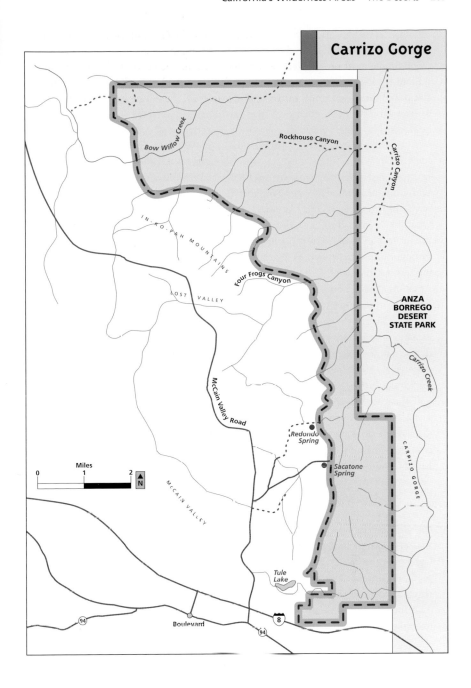

Carrizo Gorge

Rockhouse Canyon

Bow Willow Creek

Carrizo Canyon

IN-KO-PAH MOUNTAINS

Four Frogs Canyon

LOST VALLEY

ANZA BORREGO DESERT STATE PARK

Carrizo Creek

McCain Valley Road

Redondo Spring

Sacatone Spring

CARRIZO GORGE

Miles
0   1   2

N

McCAIN VALLEY

Tule Lake

94

Boulevard

8

94

intersection of McCain Valley Road and old Lost Valley Road where there is an unmarked "jeep road" (now a trail) that heads east. Follow the abandoned road east 0.5 mile to a meadow, then head north for another half-mile on an old jeep trail, over a slight hill, and down into a wide draw. Follow the draw northeast for about 2.5 miles, detouring around a sharp drop-off. You eventually reach the head of Four Frogs Canyon. Pick your way down into the canyon among house-size boulders. The largest palm grove grows at an elevation of 2,200 feet.

The headwaters of Rockhouse and Bow Willow Canyons are located in the Carrizo Gorge Wilderness. Access to these canyons, however, originates in Anza Borrego Desert State Park to the east. A loop of 7.5 miles that takes in portions of both canyons is possible. Following the "trail" is sometimes difficult, and it helps to have a topographical map. The hike begins at Bow Willow Campground. From the Ocotillo exit on I-8 follow County Road S2 northwest approximately 16 miles to the turnoff for Bow Willow Campground. Take the dirt road west 1.7 miles to the campground. The site where the campground is located has been a favorite camping spot for centuries, and long before Europeans entered the region, native Americans used the area as a base camp. Evidence of their occupation includes morteros in the granite boulders and pottery shards scattered about the area.

Once at the campground walk 0.5 mile up Bow Willow Canyon. Just past the first ridge from the campground watch for an alluvial fan on the south (left as you head up the canyon). Clamber a couple hundred feet up the rocky draw, past a single palm to a sandy wash. Follow the wash for a mile or so, watching for ducks or trail cairns marking the route south-southwest over an almost indistinct watershed divide at 1,600 feet. Head downhill into Rockhouse Canyon. Head upstream into a valley cloaked with cholla and ocotillo. In 0.5 mile you reach the remains of an old cowboy line shack—the "rock house" for which the canyon is named. From the rock house go north over a low divide known as Saddleback Ridge (elevation 1,700 feet), which will take you back into Bow Willow Canyon. Follow the canyon east back to your starting point at the campground.

If you want to delay your return to the campground you can head up Bow Willow Canyon and explore its various branch canyons, most of which contain California palm groves.

A longer hike either as a loop or as an in-and-out hike to Rockhouse Canyon begins on County Road S2 where it crosses Carrizo Wash just south of the road that leads to Bow Willow Campground. Carrizo Wash is a wide, sandy arroyo covered with a smoke tree forest. Head southwest up the wash. The wide, sandy mouth of Rockhouse Canyon comes in from the west in 2.5 miles. It is 3.3 miles from the mouth of the arroyo up to the rock house line shack.

Chuckwalla Mountains Wilderness 63

Palo verde along Corn Wash, Chuckwalla Mountains Wilderness.

The Chuckwalla Mountains Wilderness rises from a vast sea of sand and rock just south of I-10. Steep-walled canyons, washes, rocky outcrops, the vastness of the desert, and a palm oasis at Corn Springs all contribute to make this a special place.

Wildlife include bighorn sheep, mule deer, coyote, and mountain lion. There is at least one prairie falcon nest site. The southwestern corner of the wilderness has been identified as a particularly critical desert tortoise habitat, with as many as 150 of the reptiles per square mile recorded. The last antelope in the California desert once ranged here until extirpated, and could be reintroduced to the wilderness. Ocotillo, cholla, yucca, nolina, and barrel cactus cloak the landscape. Ironwood line the washes. The occurrence of Munz cholla (the largest known cholla), found only here and in the Chocolate Mountains, is only one of a number of rare plants found in this wilderness area.

LOCATION: Riverside County; 40 miles west of Blythe, California

SIZE: 80,770 acres

ELEVATION RANGE: 800 to 4,600 feet

ADMINISTRATION: BLM Palm Springs Resource Area Office

MAPS: Desert Access Guide Chuckwalla #18, Salton Sea #10; AAA Riverside County

Chuckwalla Mountains

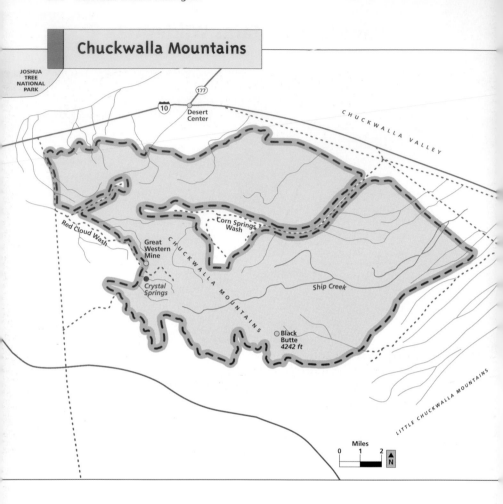

The Chuckwalla Mountains were roamed by native Americans, and evidence of their passage still remain, including rock quarry sites and petroglyphs.

Rock hounding in this area is popular, with chalcedony, geodes, jasper, and petrified wood the main attractions.

ACCESS

The best access to this wilderness is at Corn Springs Road off I-10, which leads into the heart of the mountains. Another access route includes Bradshaw Trail to the south. The occurrence of some springs makes longer treks possible, however most people opt for day hikes.

Coyote Mountains Wilderness 64

Fossil Canyon area, Coyote Mountains Wilderness.

The Coyote Mountains Wilderness borders the southeast corner of Anza Borrego Desert State Park and has been characterized as a "wonderland of geology." It encompasses both the Coyote Mountains as well as the forbidding, gullied Carrizo Badlands. Badlands, sandstone formations, and dissected terrain give this area plenty of topographical relief. Sandstone formations in the Coyote Mountains harbor marine plant and invertebrate (mostly shellfish) fossils from a sea that covered the region some six million years ago. Recently whale bones have been uncovered in the area as well.

The lower elevations are covered with creosote bush, which gives way to succulent agave and other desert vegetation at slightly higher elevations. The barefoot gecko, a rare reptile, is known to inhabit this wilderness area.

An unusual petroglyph consisting of pits and grooves etched into sandstone has been found in the wilderness. It is

LOCATION: Imperial County; 35 miles west of El Centro, California

SIZE: 17,000 acres

ELEVATION RANGE: 100 to 1,980 feet

ADMINISTRATION: BLM El Centro Resource Area Office

MAPS: Desert Access Guide Imperial Valley #22; AAA Imperial County

Coyote Mountains

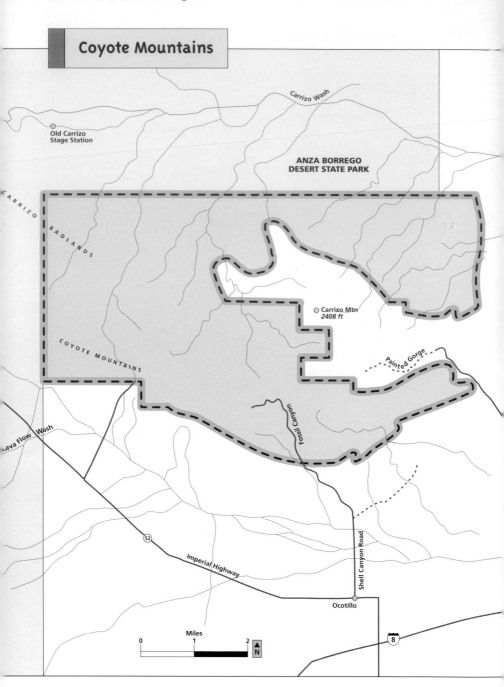

Carrizo Wash

Old Carrizo
Stage Station

**ANZA BORREGO
DESERT STATE PARK**

C A R R I Z O

B A D L A N D S

C O Y O T E   M O U N T A I N S

Carrizo Mtn
2408 ft

Painted Gorge

Lava Flow Wash

Fossil Canyon

52

Imperial Highway

Shell Canyon Road

Ocotillo

8

Miles

0   1   2

N

similar to others found in Baja, Mexico, but is not previously known in the United States.

ACCESS

To access the wilderness, turn off I-8 at the Ocotillo exit and take County Road S2 north toward Anza Borrego Desert State Park. In less than a mile, Shell Canyon Road (a graded gravel road) heads off to the north. In about 3 miles the gravel road turns off onto a dirt road that leads to Fossil Canyon (also known as Shell Canyon or Alverson Canyon). You can drive a 2wd drive vehicle up into the mouth of a canyon a short distance before you come to a locked gate. If you look closely at the canyon walls you will find shells embedded in the sandstone—hence its alternative name of Shell Canyon. The shells are from organisms that lived in two ancient lakes, the oldest of which was formed six million years ago. You can hike up Fossil Canyon, which starts out narrow then opens up into a multitributary basin with colorful rock strata. It is also possible to hike up and out of the canyon onto the surrounding ridge lines.

A second access point is Painted Canyon. From Ocotillo take old Hwy 80 and travel 4 miles east to a graded dirt road heading north, marked by a sign labeled Painted Gorge (Y181 on BLM Desert Access Guide Imperial Valley South #22). After 6 miles or so you enter a colorful landscape of orange, red, and purple rocks that are the result of iron, copper, and sulfur in the ancient marine sediments and igneous rock.

65 Fish Creek Mountains Wilderness

Ocotillo frames the Fish Creek Mountains.

LOCATION: Imperial County; 50 miles west of Brawley, California, adjacent to Anza Borrego Desert State Park

SIZE: 25,940 acres

ELEVATION RANGE: Sea level to 2,400 feet

ADMINISTRATION: BLM El Centro Resource Area Office

MAPS: Desert Access Guide Salton Sea #20, Imperial Valley #22; AAA San Diego County

The Fish Creek Mountains rise as a limestone plateau above the Salton Trough. Because this wilderness is contiguous with state wilderness in Anza Borrego Desert State Park, its effective size is much larger than its acreage might indicate. From the highest ridges it is possible to see into Mexico and across Imperial Valley to the Chocolate Mountains.

At one time Lake Cahuilla, formed 50,000 years ago during the wetter Ice Age, occupied the Salton Trough and lapped against these mountains. The lake evaporated some 500 years ago, leaving behind terraces that are still visible and mark the ancient shorelines. Aboriginal stone fish weirs, some as old as 2,500 years, are located in the northeastern portion of the wilderness along these old shorelines.

The Fish Creek Mountains are 10 miles long by 5 miles wide. From a distance the mountains appear to have little relief, but carved into the flanks of the range are numerous twisting, water-smoothed canyons. These

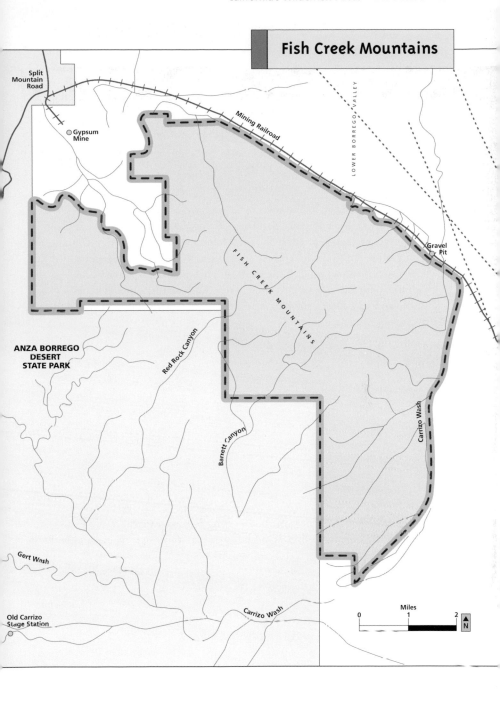

Fish Creek Mountains

Split Mountain Road

Gypsum Mine

Mining Railroad

LOWER BORREGO VALLEY

Gravel Pit

F I S H   C R E E K   M O U N T A I N S

ANZA BORREGO DESERT STATE PARK

Red Rock Canyon

Barrett Canyon

Carrizo Wash

Gert Wash

Old Carrizo Stage Station

Carrizo Wash

Miles

0   1   2

N

canyons provide natural hiking pathways that penetrate the limestone ridges. Natural catch basins carved into the stone by swirling water from flash floods have created tanks important to desert wildlife such as Peninsula bighorn sheep, which are known to roam the area.

Other unique species include the barefoot gecko, a species common in Baja, Mexico, but rare in California. Prairie falcon are known to nest in the area as well.

Ocotillo, creosote, bur sage, cactus, and other desert vegetation is present, but sparse.

ACCESS

To reach the wilderness, follow Hwy 78 through Anza Borrego Desert State Park. Just 3 miles west of the Imperial-San Diego county line and 2 miles east of Ocotillo Wells Ranger Station, turn south on Split Mountain Road. Go 9 miles south to the Gypsum Mine Railroad tracks. These tracks form the northeastern boundary of the wilderness. A dirt road parallels the tracks and provides access to the wilderness, which lies south and west of the road. Carrizo Wash on the southern boundary of this wildland also offers a good hiking route into the mountains with several tributary canyons to explore.

Imperial Wilderness 66

Sunset on the Colorado River and Imperial Wilderness.

Imperial Wilderness lies along the Colorado River and borders the BLM's Little Picacho Peak and Indian Pass Wilderness areas, which are part of the 25,765-acre Imperial National Wildlife Refuge that lines both sides of the Colorado River for 30 miles (one of the last unchanneled sections of the lower Colorado River). The refuge was created in 1941 after Imperial Dam, an irrigation project, backed up water along the Colorado River. The Arizona side of the refuge was given protection as wilderness in 1990 and the California side was protected as part of the 1994 California Desert Protection Act.

The wilderness protects both Sonoran Desert vegetation as well as riparian-marsh habitats immediately adjacent to the river. An abundance of palo verde, smoke tree, ironwood, and other Sonoran vegetation cloak the rugged, highly scenic volcanic hills. This is considered to be one of the best winter birding areas in Arizona and California.

LOCATION: Imperial County; 20 miles north of Yuma, Arizona

SIZE: 15,056 total acres; 5,836 acres in California

ELEVATION RANGE: 500 to 600 feet

ADMINISTRATION: Imperial National Wildlife Refuge

MAPS: AAA Imperial County, AAA Colorado River Guide

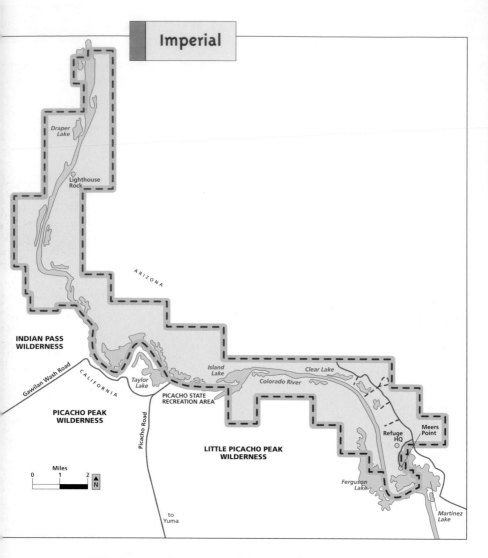

Fishing is a popular activity, with largemouth bass and channel catfish the primary targets of fishermen.

ACCESS

There is no road access to the California side of the wilderness. To reach this "desert" wilderness you have to travel by watercraft on the river. It is possible to take a canoe from Martinez Lake Marina (on the Arizona side of the river) to various sites along the river that are suitable for hiking. Access to the river is also possible from Picacho State Recreation Area. One can also hike to the wilderness from Picacho State Recreation Area as well. Overnight camping, however, is not permitted, and those wanting to spend the night should consider camping at Picacho State Recreation Area.

Indian Pass Wilderness

Ocotillo frames the volcanic peaks of Indian Pass Wilderness.

Indian Pass Wilderness is one of the more dramatic and spectacular scenic areas in the entire California desert. A sub-unit of the Chocolate Mountains, the volcanic turrets, with jagged peaks and deep, twisting canyons make this wilderness a visual feast. The Colorado River borders the area on the east. Quartz Peak, at 2,177 feet, is the highest summit in the wilderness. In the heart of the wilderness lies Julian Wash—a broad, tree-lined desert canyon. In reality the more appropriate name for this area is Julian Wash Wilderness because Indian Pass is actually outside of the wilderness area.

The lands immediately adjacent to the Colorado River and just east of Indian Pass Wilderness are part of Imperial Wilderness. These lands are closed to camping. Nevertheless, one can easily paddle a canoe over the river to access the mouth of tributary canyons like Julian Wash, then hike up the canyon to camp within the BLM portion of the wilderness.

LOCATION: Imperial County; 35 miles north of Yuma, Arizona

SIZE: 33,855 acres

ELEVATION RANGE: 300 to 2,177 feet

ADMINISTRATION: BLM El Centro Resource Area Office

MAPS: Desert Access Guide Midway Well #21; AAA Colorado River Guide

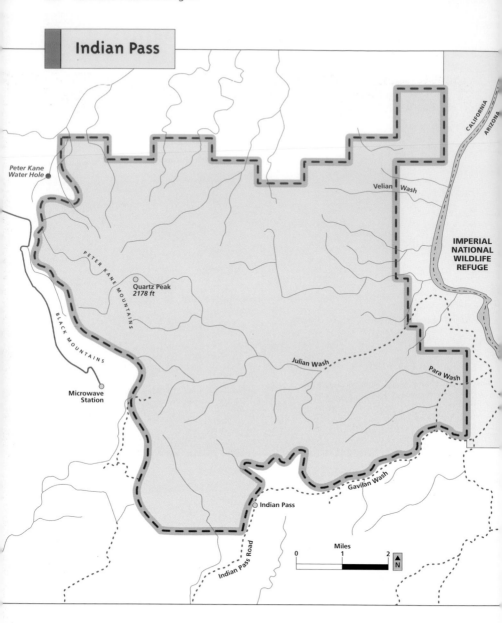

Indian Pass

Wildlife include desert bighorn sheep and mule deer. One rare plant, California ditaxis, has been found in Gavilan Wash on the border of the area.

ACCESS

From I-8 west of Yuma take County Road S34 north (Ogilby Road) to Indian Pass Road. Drive 9 miles northeast on Indian Pass Road. Once over Indian Pass you begin the descent to Gavilan Wash. The border of the wilderness lies just north of the road.

Jacumba Mountains Wilderness 68

Granite outcrops in Jacumba Mountains Wilderness.

The scenic Jacumba Mountains lie on the Mexico-United States border along the eastern flank of southern California's Peninsula Range. Granitic boulder outcrops reminiscent of Joshua Tree National Park litter this plateaulike region of rolling topography. In particular, many have compared the granitic outcrops in the Valley of the Moon in the southwestern corner of the wilderness to the more famous national park. Although granite dominates the wilderness, limestone crops out in the Myer Valley and upper Davies Canyon area. A series of ridges, each slightly lower in elevation, marches eastward from the western border to lowlands in the Colorado Desert. Intervening valleys lie between each ridge. Davies Valley is the largest valley in the wilderness. Skull Valley on the east is a closed basin with a playa on the valley floor.

The wilderness is an area of remarkable biologic diversity, marking the transition zone between the coastal vegetative communities and the Colorado subdivision of

LOCATION: Imperial County; right on the Mexico-United States border south of I 8, 30 miles west of El Centro, California

SIZE: 33,670 acres

ELEVATION RANGE: 500 to 4,000 feet

ADMINISTRATION: BLM El Centro Resource Area Office

MAPS: Desert Access Guide Imperial Valley #22; AAA Imperial County

the Sonoran Desert, along with northern incursions of typically Mexican species. The western flank of the wilderness harbors oak and chaparral species like chamise, mixed with more typically desert species like pinyon pine and agave. California fan palm and cottonwood grow in the Pinto Canyon/Myer Valley area. Ocotillo, brittlebush, cholla, and mesquite are found in the lower, eastern portion of the wilderness.

Rare plant species include a locoweed (*Astragalus doglasii* var. *perstrictus*). Other sensitive and relatively rare species include *Ayenia compacta*, San Diego monkeyflower (*Diplacus aridus*), Mountain Springs lupine (*Lupinus excubitus* var. *medius*), Jacumba gilia (*Ipomopsis tenufolia*), elephant tree (*Bursera microphylla*), *Pholisma arenarium*, *Mentzelia hirsutissima* var. *stenophylla*, *Geraea viscida*, and Cleveland penstemon (*Penstemon clevlandii* var. *connatus*). One of the best preserved stands of crucifixion thorn in California is found in Skull Valley.

Wildlife include mule deer, Peninsula bighorn sheep, golden eagle, and two Mexican species that reach their northern limit here—the Trinidad Merriam kangaroo rat and the barefoot gecko (*Anarbylus switaki*).

Numerous archeological sites are scattered throughout the wilderness and are evidenced by petroglyphs, stone tools, cooking hearths, agave roasting pits, pottery shards, stone mortars, and grinding holes. In the Davies Valley and Skull Valley areas, old aboriginal trails are still evident in areas of desert pavement.

Smuggler's Cave in the western portion of the wilderness is a hollow beneath a huge boulder that is associated with numerous historic wrong doings, including a hideout for robbers and a waystation for smugglers bringing in illegal workers from Mexico. The US Border Patrol still maintains surveillance of the area, so don't be surprised if you are contacted while hiking in the area. Davies Canyon on the northwest is a 5-mile-long valley with outcrops of agate, garnet, and petrified wood.

ACCESS

A number of now-closed, abandoned roads serve as "trails," although cross-country hiking is relatively easy if you are willing to scramble over granite boulders and maneuver down short, steep faces. Access to the western part of the wilderness is located off I-8 at the In-Ko-Pah Park exit. A steep, unsigned dirt road (covered with cement in the steepest pitches) winds up to a radio tower and provides access to the higher ridges by Smuggler's Cave and Valley of the Moon. I parked partway up this road and walked, but 2wd vehicles do negotiate this road.

To reach Davies Valley, take I-8 to the Ocotillo/CA 98 exit. Head south on County Road S2 for less than a mile to CA 98 then go east on CA 98 to Clark Road. Take the dirt Clark Road southwest to the wilderness boundary. The now-closed dirt track to Davies Valley serves as a hiking trail that meanders more than 7 miles into the central part of the wilderness.

Myer Valley lies in the north-central portion of the wilderness. Several palm oases dot the valley. Old roads, now closed, provide a network of "trails" into the region. It is possible to reach the valley if you are willing to scramble over boulders and up to the saddle above the valley. You'll probably need a map to guide

Jacumba Mountains

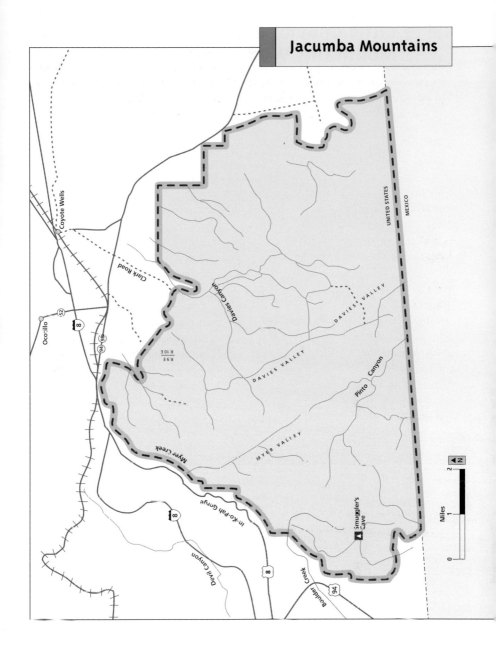

yourself across country. To reach the valley, take the Mountain Springs exit off I-8. Halfway between the east- and westbound lanes of the interstate, take a dirt road to the east 0.25 mile to the now-abandoned track of Hwy 80. Take the old highway east for 1.3 miles to the end of the road and park. Clamber down the slope to Myer Wash. Pass under I-8 via a culvert and scramble east over a saddle and into Myer Valley.

69 Little Chuckwalla Mountains Wilderness

Cholla cactus frames the Little Chuckwalla Mountains in Little Chuckwalla Mountains Wilderness.

LOCATION: Imperial and Riverside Counties; 25 miles southwest of Blythe, California

SIZE: 29,880 acres

ELEVATION RANGE: 600 to 2,100 feet

ADMINISTRATION: BLM Palm Springs Resource Area Office

MAPS: Desert Access Guide Parker/Blythe #16, Midway Well #21; AAA Imperial County

Little Chuckwalla Mountains Wilderness consists of rolling volcanic peaks in a generally northeast-southwest alignment. A network of washes radiates from the peaks, cutting small canyons and wide washes into the surrounding bajadas that slope away from the mountains. Bradshaw Trail forms the southern boundary of the area.

The area is a favorite of rock hounds and is known for minerals like selenite, banded agate, iris agate, jasper, calcite geodes, petrified wood, chalcedony, and moss plume agate.

Creosote bush and bur sage are the dominant plants in this sparsely vegetated area. A number of sensitive plants are reported from the area, including California snakeweed, Alverson's foxtail cactus, and barrel cactus.

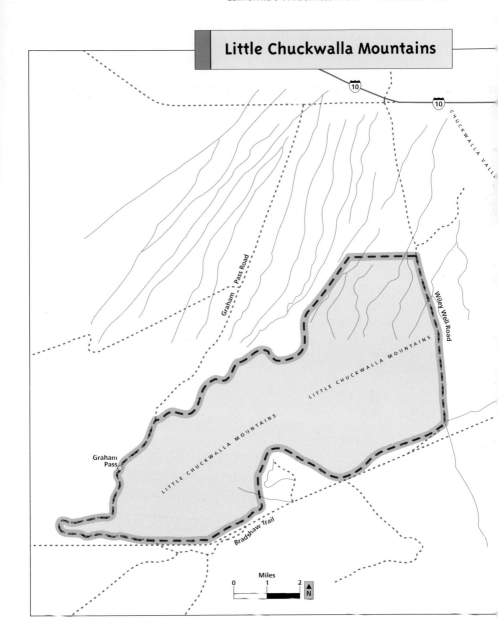

Little Chuckwalla Mountains

Wildlife include a small, relict herd of desert bighorn sheep. Rare species include Couch's spadefoot toad and the endangered desert tortoise. Tortoise densities of 50 to 100 tortoise per square mile are recorded for some parts of the wilderness.

ACCESS

A number of now-closed, old tracks penetrate the wilderness, providing "hiking trails," or one can simply take off across country from one of the roads that border the wilderness. One of the easiest access points lies along Graham Pass Road. This good gravel road forms the western border of the wilderness and provides egress to a region of rugged canyons and easy scrambles to peaks. To reach this road, take the Chuckwalla Road exit off I-10. Go 3 miles west to the turn for Graham Pass Road. You travel about 10 miles or so south along this road before you reach the western edge of the wilderness.

Bradshaw Trail forms the southern border of the wilderness and, like Graham Pass Road, hikers can simply park and walk north off the road into the wilderness. Bradshaw Trail can be reached by taking the Wiley Well Road exit off I-10. Continue south past Chuckwalla State Prison until you reach Bradshaw Trail some 8.7 miles from the interstate. At the intersection just beyond Wiley Well Campground, turn west on Bradshaw Trail. In approximately 5 miles you reach the southeastern corner of the wilderness, which Bradshaw Trail continues to border for another 12 miles.

Little Picacho Peak Wilderness 70

View of the rugged volcanic necks of ancient volcanoes in Little Picacho Peak Wilderness.

Little Picacho Peak Wilderness is one of the most striking wildlands in the California desert. The superlative qualities of the Little Picacho were recognized early on when the BLM rated the area's outstanding wilderness values as twelfth out of 137 wilderness study areas in the state of California. Little Picacho Peak Wilderness makes up the southern part of the 70-mile-long Chocolate Mountains, a range consisting of volcanic and metamorphic rock, with many colorful spires, broken canyons, and tree-lined washes. Topping out at 1,193 feet is Little Picacho Peak—the highest summit in the wilderness. Don't let the low elevation fool you. This is a region of rugged, steep mountains.

The Colorado River borders the area on the east, providing a diverse riparian habitat close to the river. However, most of the slopes are nearly devoid of vegetation, whereas the intervening plains are covered with desert pavement.

LOCATION: Imperial County; on the Colorado River 9 miles north of Yuma, Arizona

SIZE: 33,600 acres

ELEVATION RANGE: 200 to 1,193 feet

ADMINISTRATION: BLM El Centro Resource Area Office

MAPS: Desert Access Guide Midway Well #21; AAA Imperial County

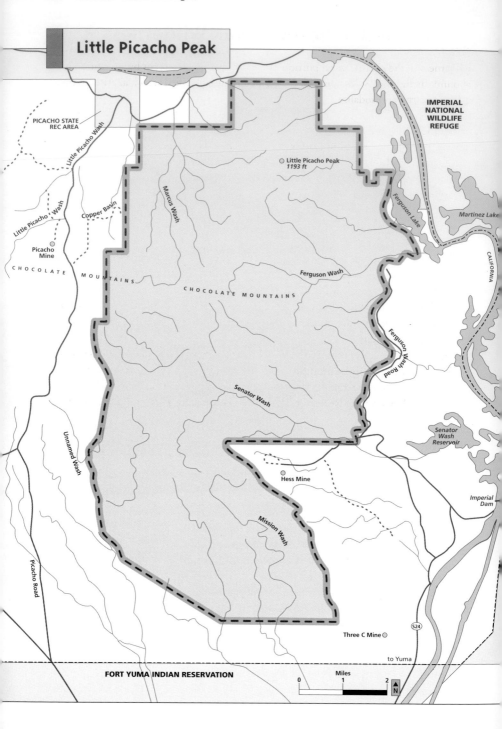

Little Picacho Peak

IMPERIAL
NATIONAL
WILDLIFE
REFUGE

PICACHO STATE
REC AREA

Little Picacho Wash

Little Picacho Peak
1193 ft

Marcus Wash

Ferguson Lake

Martinez Lake

Copper Basin

Little Picacho Wash

Picacho
Mine

CHOCOLATE   MOUNTAINS

CALIFORNIA

Ferguson Wash

CHOCOLATE MOUNTAINS

Ferguson Wash Road

Senator Wash

Senator
Wash
Reservoir

Unnamed Wash

Hess Mine

Imperial
Dam

Mission Wash

Picacho Road

Three C Mine

S24

to Yuma

FORT YUMA INDIAN RESERVATION

Miles

0   1   2

N

Evidence of past mining efforts are scattered about the wilderness. The old Hess Mine, with its abandoned machinery and structures, lies along the edge of the wilderness in the south-central portion of the area. Minerals sought by rock hounds abound, including geodes, chalcedony, banded agates, petrified wood, azurite, pyrite, calcite, quartz, and sodalite.

The washes are cloaked with a lush riparian woodland of palo verde, ironwood, mesquite, and smoke tree. A small herd of desert bighorn sheep roams the area. The spotted bat, a threatened species, is also recorded for the area. A diverse array of reptiles and amphibians are found here, including the Yuma king snake, Couch's spadefoot toad, the Rocky Mountain toad, the Great Plains toad, and the Colorado River toad.

ACCESS

The best access point lies along the eastern edge of the wilderness. From Yuma take County Road S24 northwest for 18 miles to Imperial Dam. At the dam turn left (north) onto Ferguson Wash Road. After driving some 3 miles north, Ferguson Wash Road forms the eastern border of the wilderness for the next 6 miles. Senator Wash heads west off this road and provides a good hiking route that runs 5 miles into the mountains.

Access is also provided from the Picacho State Recreation Area access road. The Picacho State Recreation Area, with its campsites, showers, and store, makes for a good base of operations for exploration of this wilderness. Hike up Railroad Wash in Picacho State Recreation Area, which eventually leads into the wilderness.

71 Mecca Hills Wilderness

Badlands near Painted Canyon in Mecca Hills Wilderness.

LOCATION: Riverside County; 15 miles southeast of Indio, California

SIZE: 24,200 acres

ELEVATION RANGE: 200 to 1,781 feet

ADMINISTRATION: BLM Palm Springs Resource Area Office

MAPS: Desert Access Guide Palm Springs #17, Chuckwalla #18; AAA Riverside County

Mecca Hills is a labyrinth of winding, eroded badlands and canyons upthrusted by the San Andreas Fault to create a wonderfully intricate maze. Sometimes called the Mud Hills, these slopes are nearly impossible to climb when wet. Fortunately, given the arid climate, this is not a major obstacle most of the time. Sandy washes with stands of smoke tree, ironwood, and palo verde cut through the hills. The Mecca aster—a species known only in this region and in Baja, Mexico—grows among these badlands. Bighorn sheep occasionally wander into the area. Box Canyon Road separates the wilderness into two units, with Hidden Spring Canyon to the south of the road and Painted Canyon to the north.

ACCESS

Leave I-10 at Indio and head south on Hwy 111 approximately 12 miles to Mecca. From Mecca go east on Box Canyon Road. Once you cross the Coachella Canal, there is a dirt road to the left that heads northeast to Painted

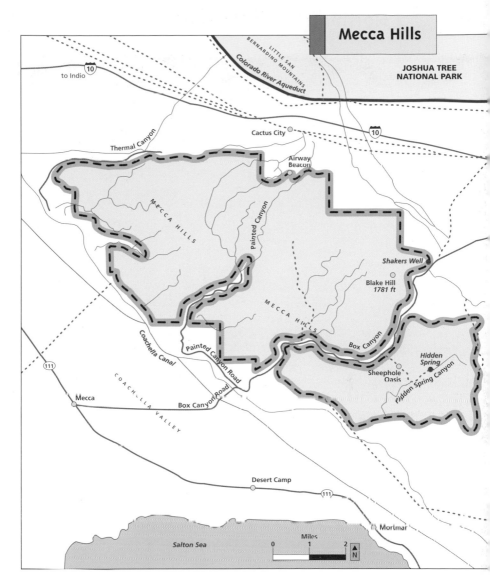

Canyon. If you are coming from the east, exit I-10 at the Cottonwood Springs exit and head south on Box Canyon Road approximately 14.5 miles to the turn for Painted Canyon. Travel about 3 miles to the entrance of Painted Canyon. The road ends another 1.7 miles further down. Once in Painted Canyon there are numerous hiking options. You just need to find your way through the badlands and the washes. Beyond the end of the road is a narrows called Ladder Canyon, named for the small ladders placed in the canyon to facilitate climbing up steep rocky sections. This hike offers a southwestern slot canyon experience.

Hidden Spring Canyon harbors a palm grove. A trail leads to the spring and palm grove. A signed trailhead for the canyon is located on the south side of Box Canyon Road.

72 North Algodones Dunes Wilderness

Sand dunes in North Algodones Dunes Wilderness.

LOCATION: Imperial County; 26 miles east of Brawley, California

SIZE: 32,240 acres

ELEVATION RANGE: 300 to 423 feet

ADMINISTRATION: BLM El Centro Resource Area Office

MAPS: Desert Access Guide Salton Sea #20, Midway Well #21; AAA Imperial County

The Algodones Dunes are what people think deserts should look like—a lot of sand that stretches off into the horizon. Camels and pyramids would not seem out of place here. Indeed, the Algodones Dunes spread over 1,000 square miles, making it one of the largest dune systems in the United States. The area was previously designated a National Natural Landmark and a BLM Outstanding Natural Area. Located along the eastern edge of the Imperial Valley, the Algodones Dunes rise to heights of 300 feet and are more than 5 miles wide and 40 miles long. The dunes continue south into Mexico. The dune system exhibits classic examples of the following kinds of dunes: transverse sief, parabolic, whaleback, barchan, and sand sheet. It is the only dune system in California with extensive whaleback dune development covering 20 percent of the area.

The dune system can be divided into two distinct regions. The western side of the system has larger, taller

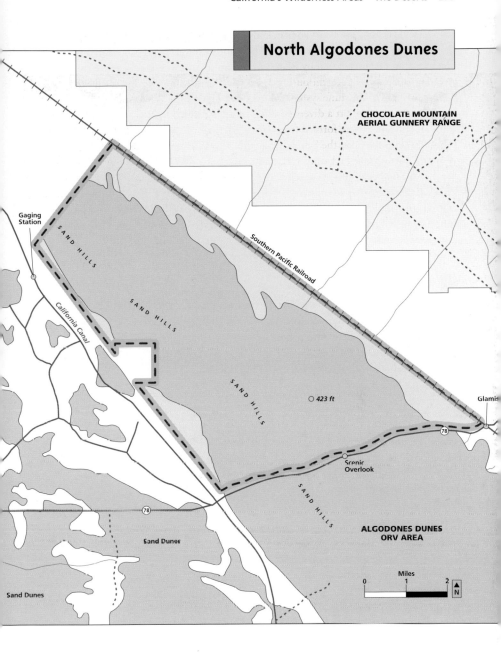

North Algodones Dunes

CHOCOLATE MOUNTAIN
AERIAL GUNNERY RANGE

Southern Pacific Railroad

Gaging
Station

SAND HILLS

SAND HILLS

California Canal

SAND HILLS

○ 423 ft

Glamis

78

Scenic
Overlook

SAND HILLS

78

Sand Dunes

ALGODONES DUNES
ORV AREA

Sand Dunes

Miles
0   1   2

N

transverse dunes composed of course sands. To the east lie smaller dunes made of finer sand particles. The western side of the dune system is nearly all sand, but the eastern section is interrupted by islands of mesquite, ironwood, palo verde, and smoke tree. The difference in vegetation is due to drainage. Streams flowing off the Chocolate Mountains east of the dune system are dammed behind the dune complex, creating small ponds that support a diversity of life in wet springs.

The dunes were formed from sands originally deposited in ancient Lake Cahuilla. The lake filled the Salton Trough, but it dried up around 1400 AD. Winds drove the former lake bed sands eastward to form the dune complex.

A number of unique species are reported in the dunes. They include Andrew's dune scarab beetle (found only in the Algodones Dunes) plus Pierson's locoweed, silver-leafed dune sunflower, and giant Spanish needle. Three wildlife species of special significance found in these dunes include the desert tortoise, the flat-tailed horned lizard, and the Colorado Desert fringe-toed lizard.

ACCESS

The easiest access is off Hwy 78, which forms the southern border of the wilderness. The dunes are obvious. Just pull off the highway and park. Be prepared to hike with lots of water. And a word of warning from experience: If it is even slightly windy, your footprints may be quickly obliterated and you may not be able to retrace your tracks back out of the dunes.

Orocopia Mountains Wilderness

Ocotillo frames Orocopia Mountains Wilderness.

Created by the San Andreas Fault, the Orocopia Mountains present a striking landscape with folded, faulted, and eroded valleys, canyon, and washes. The northern portion is dominated by open valleys and dissected ridges, whereas the southern portion boasts colorful eroded canyons.

Ironwood is found along washes and ocotillo is found along the mountain slopes. Creosote bush is found almost everywhere. A number of rare plants occur in the area, including Orocopia sage (known only in the Orocopia Mountains, Mecca Hills, and Chuckwalla Mountains). Two other rare species—Alverson's foxtail cactus and Orcutt's woody aster—are found here. A herd of bighorn sheep roam the mountains, and desert tortoise (an endangered species) is known to occur in the eastern portion of the area.

LOCATION: Riverside County; 20 miles southeast of Indio, California

SIZE: 40,735 acres

ELEVATION RANGE: Sea level to 3,600 feet

ADMINISTRATION: BLM Palm Springs Resource Area Office

MAPS: Desert Access Guide Chuckwalla #18; AAA Riverside County

Orocopia Mountains

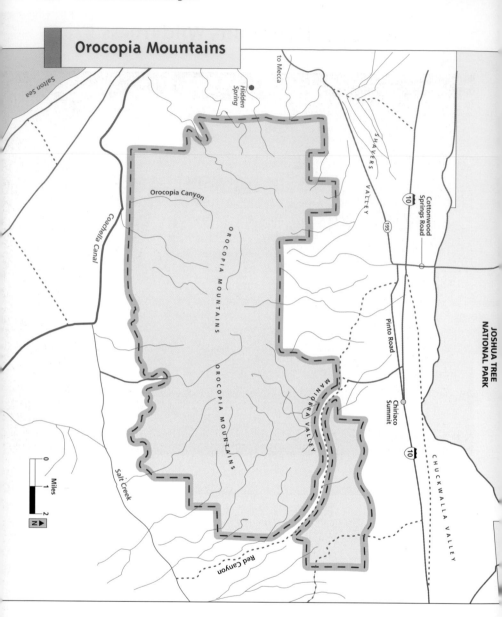

ACCESS

The easiest access is from I-10. Take the Chiriaco Summit exit and turn west onto
Pinto Road. Go 1 mile until you come to a dirt road that heads south to Maniobra
Valley. At a little over a mile you come to the boundary of the wilderness, although
the road continues for another 4 miles with the wilderness on either side. Orocopia
Canyon, in the southwestern corner of the wilderness, looks inviting on maps and
is worth a visit—if you can figure out how to get across the Coachella Canal.

Palo Verde Mountains Wilderness 74

Palo Verde Peak, Palo Verde Mountains Wilderness.

The Palo Verde Mountains Wilderness lies along the Colorado River south of Blythe. Although not very high, the rugged volcanic peaks—including Thumb Peak (elevation 1,375 feet), Flat Tops (1,604 feet) and the namesake Palo Verde Peak (1,795 feet)—all provide sharp relief to the landscape.

An abundance of gems and minerals—including geodes, banded nodules, jasper, and black agate—attract rock hounds to the area.

The mountains are rugged and the vegetation is sparse. Creosote bush grows in patches here and there, with broad expanses of desert pavement and bare rock dominating the landscape. Indeed, this is one of the most bleak wildernesses I have ever visited. There is, however, some relief from the austere landscape along the washes, where there is dense growth of palo verde, mesquite, and ironwood. The relatively rare California palm is found at Clapp Spring. Unlike most palm oases tucked away in canyons, Clapp Spring and its

LOCATION: Imperial County; 18 miles southwest of Blythe, California

SIZE: 32,310 acres

ELEVATION RANGE: 500 to 1,800 feet

ADMINISTRATION: BLM EL Centro Resource Area Office

MAPS: Desert Access Guide Midway Well #12; AAA Imperial County

palms exist in a relatively open landscape. Even rarer than palms—at least for California—are saguaro cactus, which grow along the southeastern margin of the wilderness.

Rarer wildlife species known to frequent the area include bighorn sheep and desert tortoise, as well as more common species such as burro, coyote, mule deer, and bobcat.

Considerable archeological evidence of past use by native Americans abounds, including cleared circles, rock rings, rock shelters, and trails.

ACCESS

To gain entry to the wilderness, take Hwy 78 south from Blythe. About 8 miles south of Palo Verde you can park and just walk west. The wilderness boundary is less than a half-mile from the pavement. Another option is to continue 12 miles south of Palo Verde on Hwy 78 then turn onto the gravel Milpitas Wash Road. Head north. The wilderness lies east of this road. Another access is from the old Palo Verde Road, which separates the wilderness into two segments. Again turn on Milpitas Wash Road, but less than 1 mile from Hwy 78 turn north onto old Palo Verde Road. In approximately 4 miles the wilderness is on either side of the road.

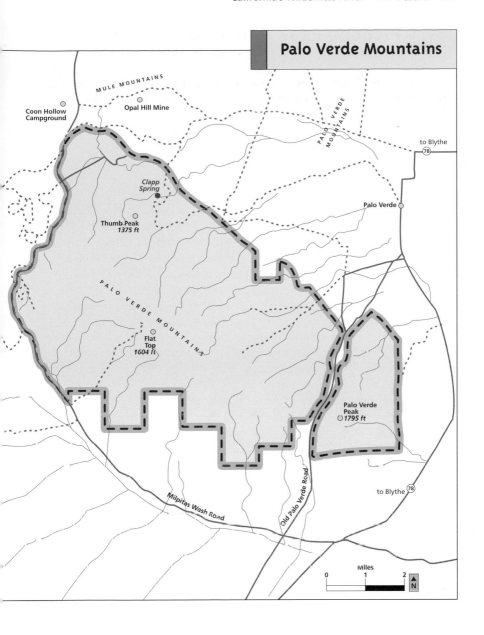

Palo Verde Mountains

MULE MOUNTAINS

Coon Hollow
Campground

Opal Hill Mine

PALO VERDE
MOUNTAINS

to Blythe
78

Clapp
Spring

Palo Verde

Thumb Peak
1375 ft

PALO VERDE MOUNTAINS

Flat
Top
1604 ft

Palo Verde
Peak
1795 ft

Milpitas Wash Road

Old Palo Verde Road

to Blythe 78

Miles
0   1   2

N

75 Picacho Peak Wilderness

Looking south from Picacho Peak Wilderness (which does not include its namesake, Picacho Peak). Picacho Peak is the large, blocky peak on the left-hand side of the photo.

LOCATION: Imperial County; 40 miles south of Blythe, California; 25 miles northwest of Yuma, Arizona.

SIZE: 7,700 acres

ELEVATION RANGE: 300 to 1,499 feet

ADMINISTRATION: BLM El Centro Resource Area Office

MAPS: Desert Access Guide Midway Well #12; AAA Imperial County, Colorado River Guide

Picacho Peak Wilderness doesn't contain Picacho Peak. The wilderness actually lies north of Picacho Peak, a well-known landmark in the Chocolate Mountains along the Lower Colorado River. Picacho Peak is a volcanic neck and, like its namesake, the rugged canyons and mountains that make up this wilderness are of volcanic origin. The wilderness is sandwiched between Gavilan Wash and Carrizo Wash — both of which have roads. The BLM in its original wilderness study of the area recommended that the wilderness be renamed Gavilan Wash Wilderness to reflect its location more accurately. Somehow this was overlooked when the area was designated, and the name Picacho Peak has remained.

The effective size of this wildland is greatly enhanced by the presence of other surrounding, protected lands: Picacho State Recreation Area borders the wilderness on the east and Indian Pass Wilderness lies directly to the north on the other side of Gavilan Wash. Several hiking routes into the wilderness start from Picacho State Recreation Area, including hikes to Carrizo Falls.

The wilderness is made up of three major landforms. In the northeastern corner of the wilderness there are open basins with large washes that cut through colorful volcanic tuff deposits. The western and central portions consist of basaltic mountains and culminate in 1,499-foot Mica Peak—the highest point in the wilderness. Further south of these mountains is a rolling benchland with narrow, vertical canyons. Gavilan and Carrizo Washes mark the boundaries of the wilderness on the north and south, and also provide good hiking routes into the wilderness.

Carrizo Wash has a natural rock basin below a 40-foot series of ledges known as Carrizo Falls, which only flows during cloudbursts. The water trapped in this natural cattail-lined tank provides a watering hole for many desert wildlife, including bighorn sheep.

Other animals likely to be seen in the wilderness include the Yuma king snake, Couch's spadefoot toad, the Rocky Mountain toad, the Great Plains toad, and the Colorado River toad. Common species like mule deer, bobcat, coyote, and wild burro also exist. The wilderness provides an exceptional habitat for the desert tortoise, which finds the soft volcanic soils perfect for construction of its burrows. The burrows are used by the tortoise to avoid summer heat and to hibernate during the colder months of winter.

Vegetation along the washes includes typical desert plant species such as creosote bush, ocotillo, and palo verde. One sensitive plant considered for endangered species listing—California ditaxis—is reported in Gavilan Wash.

Reflecting its proximity to the Colorado River and water, archeological sites are numerous. There are old Indian trails, cleared circles, rock shelters, bits of pottery, and inscribed cobbles (small cobblestones inscribed with miniature petroglyphs) found along ancient trails. Old mining prospects are also evident.

ACCESS

The easiest way to reach the wilderness is by way of Indian Pass Road to Indian Pass and Gavilan Wash, which lie at the northern border of the wilderness. You can reach Indian Pass Road from I-8 west of Yuma by taking Ogilby Road (County Road S24) 12 miles north to the turnoff for Indian Pass Road. It is 9 miles to Indian Pass. One can also access the wilderness by hiking from Picacho State Recreation Area. A dirt road within the recreation area crosses Carrizo Wash and you can follow this road upstream into the wilderness.

Picacho Peak

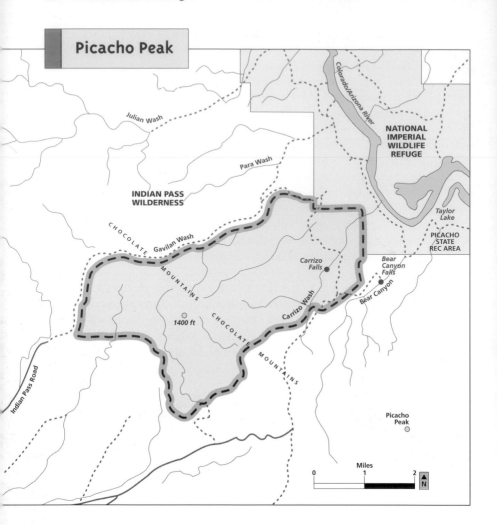

Julian Wash

Para Wash

Colorado/Arizona River

NATIONAL IMPERIAL WILDLIFE REFUGE

Taylor Lake

INDIAN PASS WILDERNESS

PICACHO STATE REC AREA

CHOCOLATE   Gavilan Wash

MOUNTAINS

Carrizo Falls

Bear Canyon Falls

Bear Canyon

CHOCOLATE

1400 ft

Carrizo Wash

MOUNTAINS

Indian Pass Road

Picacho Peak

Miles

0   1   2

N

Santra Rosa Wilderness

Cottonwoods along Horsethief Canyon, Santa Rosa Wilderness.

Santa Rosa Wilderness lies on the eastern slope of the Santa Rosa Mountains, one of southern California's Peninsula Ranges. Many geologists consider the Santa Rosas the southern continuation of the San Jacinto Range to the north. Toro Peak, just outside the wilderness, rises to 8,716 feet and is cloaked by magnificent forests of pine and fir—a striking contrast to most of the wilderness, which is largely a desert plateau vegetated with ocotillo, agave, creosote bush, cactus, and scattered stands of pinyon and juniper.

Besides the usual southern California wildlife of coyote, ringtail, mountain lion, and mule deer, the Santa Rosa Wilderness is home to the largest Peninsula bighorn sheep herd in the state. Good places to see these wild mountaineers are the aptly named Sheep Mountain as well as Martinez Mountain. Another unusual species found here is the desert slender salamander.

LOCATION: Riverside County; 7 miles south of Palm Springs, California

SIZE: 84,500 acres

ELEVATION RANGE: sea level to 8,700 feet

ADMINISTRATION: BLM Palm Springs Resource Area Office; San Bernardino National Forest

MAPS: Desert Access Guide Palm Springs #17, McCain Valley #19; AAA Riverside County

The area was originally set aside as part of the San Jacinto Forest Reserve, and was later combined with the Trabuco Reserve to form the Cleveland National Forest. In 1925 it was reassigned to the San Bernardino National Forest. The 20,160-acre Santa Rosa Wilderness was created in 1984 by the California Wilderness Act and was expanded with the addition of 64,340 BLM acres with the passage of the 1994 California Desert Protection Act. The formally protected lands now total 84,500 acres. These lands are immediately adjacent to some 87,000 acres of state wilderness in the Anza Borrego Desert State Park to the south. In addition, there are more than 140,000 additional BLM and Forest Service roadless areas, and if protected and combined with the adjacent state lands they could create a huge desert ecotone wildland of nearly 300,000 acres.

This is primarily a desert upland, but unlike most areas in the California desert there are a few permanent water sources. Most water access is via the Cactus Spring Trail, an old Indian trail that crosses several perennial streams that have lush, green riparian vegetation. This area is often replete with the sound of birdsong and it creates a stark contrast to the surrounding desert. If you bother to wander far off the trail, you aren't likely to encounter anyone else in this rarely used wildland.

Due the greater number of springs and streams, the Santa Rosa Mountains were a popular travel corridor for native Americans. There are numerous examples of roasting pits, milling stations, and rock art.

ACCESS

The most popular access is via the Cactus Spring Trail—the only official trail in the wilderness. It actually extends for 18 miles between Pinyon Flat on Hwy 74 and Martinez Canyon in the Coachella Valley. The most popular hike is the section between Pinyon Flat and Cactus Spring. To locate the trailhead, take Hwy 74 southwest from Palm Springs Pass to Pinyon Flat Campground just beyond the California Department of Forestry Fire Station. The trailhead is located on the south side of the road between these two landmarks.

The first part of the hike follows a confusing knot of old mining roads. Just keep in mind that the trail heads southeast, so bear in that direction. You pass an old dolomite mine and a sign indicating the way to the trail. Eventually you pass an official wilderness boundary sign and know you're on the right path. The trail works its way up and down along a draw to Horsethief Creek—a refreshing perennial stream lined by cottonwood. After leaving the stream, the trail is sometimes difficult to locate as it follows washes to Little Pinyon Flat and reaches Cactus Spring, which is usually dry. Look for cairns to mark the way beyond Horsethief Canyon.

Other potential hiking destinations for day hikers are Bear Creek, Lost Canyon Oasis, Guadelupe Canyon, and Devil Canyon—all southwest of the town of Palm Desert.

One of the most popular desert mountain ascents is 6,623-foot Rabbit Peak in the southeastern portion of the wilderness. Views from the summit include much of Anza Borrego Desert State Park and the Salton Sea. It is not a hike for the inexperienced. Not only is it a 12-mile round-trip cross-country trek, but since the start of the hike begins near sea level, the total elevation gain is 6,600 feet!

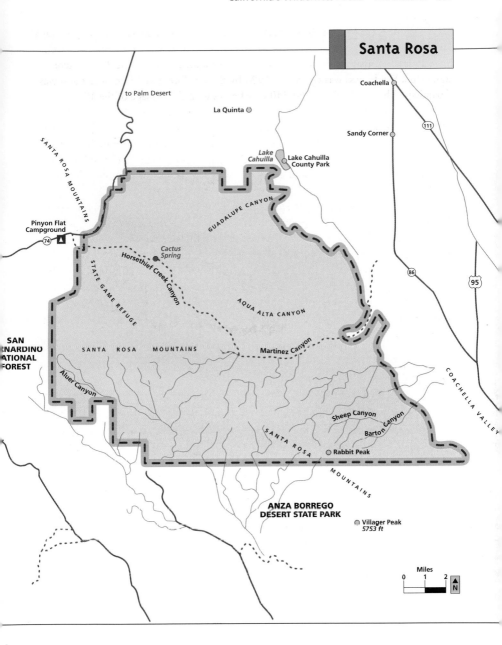

Santa Rosa

Most people attempting to climb this peak begin at Oasis off Hwy 86 just before it merges with Hwy 195. Head across the alluvial fans at the mouth of Sheep Canyon. Near the canyon entrance cross to the south side, where a poorly defined "trail" heads up the southeastern ridge of Rabbit Peak.

77 Sawtooth Mountains Wilderness

View of Sawtooth Mountains Wilderness from the Laguna Mountains.

LOCATION: San Diego County; 35 miles south of Borrego Springs, California

SIZE: 35,080 acres

ELEVATION RANGE: 1,400 to 5,600 feet

ADMINISTRATION: BLM Palm Springs Resource Area Office

MAPS: Desert Access Guide McCain Valley #19; AAA San Diego County

The granite spires of Sawtooth Mountains Wilderness lie immediately west of Anza Borrego Desert State Park, taking in the crest of the Laguna Mountains and the Sawtooth Mountains for which they are named. A tiny portion of the Tierra Blanca Mountains makes up the very easternmost segment of the wilderness. Despite its size, the amount of roadless terrain is greater than its acreage. To the east, state lands in Anza Borrego Desert State Park are protected as wilderness, and the adjacent portion of the Cleveland National Forest is also roadless and may be added to the wilderness system someday. As a consequence, Sawtooth Mountains Wilderness is actually part of a much larger wildland complex.

Relief between the valley and the peaks is quite substantial, and these mountains are steep! Ridges radiate east and north into the desert from the main crest of the Laguna Mountains, including Canebrake, Vallecito, Potrero,

Storm, and Inner Pasture Canyons. Ephemeral streams drain these valleys and canyons.

The biologic diversity of this wilderness is significant. For instance, one survey found more than 80 different species of flowering plant in 1 square mile. Astride the transition zone between the coastal vegetative zone and desert, this wilderness contains habitats for a number of rare or sensitive species. The highest and most westerly ridges have limited amounts of conifer, including some Coulter pine, oak, and chaparral species, whereas the lower elevations and more easterly valleys harbor species typical of the desert, including creosote bush. Several rare species are known to occur in this wilderness including Mount Laguna alumroot, *Astragalus douglassi* var. *perstrictus, Diplacus aridus, Ferocactus acanthodes* var. *acanthodes, Lupinus excubitus* var. *medius, Opuntia bigelovii* var. *hoffmanii, Delphinium parishii* spp. *subglobosum, Proboscidea althaeifolia,* and *Ayenia compacta* among others.

Unusual or rare wildlife include the willow flycatcher (a riparian species), the San Diego horned lizard (which lives among the granite boulders), the spotted bat, and the Peninsula bighorn sheep (which may be reintroduced to the region). Other species of concern to the California Department of Fish and Game that are known to occur in the wilderness include Cooper's hawk, golden eagle, and prairie falcon. A number of these species are listed or under consideration for listing as endangered species under the Endangered Species Act. Many of these plants and wildlife species are affected negatively by domestic livestock grazing, which still occurs in this wilderness.

Archeological sites are also abundant in the Sawtooth Mountains Wilderness. These include temporary campsites, seed-grinding stations, pottery scatters, rock art, and earthen ovens and roasting pits. The rock art is linked to rituals.

ACCESS

A number of options exist for entry to this wilderness. Old roads lead up a number of valleys and canyons including Potrero and Canebrake Canyons from County Road S2, which travels through Anza Borrego Desert State Park. However, you must skirt or cross private property to reach the public holdings beyond. The Pacific Crest Trail traverses the Laguna Mountains just to the west of the wilderness border. There are a number of signed trailheads for the Pacific Crest Trail from the Sunrise Highway. Several tributary trails lead off the Pacific Crest Trail to high overlooks for views of the wilderness including Garnet Peak and Stephenson Peak from Vista Point.

Experienced hikers may wish to try hiking cross country and downhill from the ridge into Sawtooth Mountains Wilderness (you follow deer trails through the chaparral). Such descents are possible from a number of points along the western edge of the wilderness. One route starts at Vista Point. From the point walk out along the ridge to Stephenson Peak. Work your way down the ridge, staying as high as possible until you can drop into Potrero Canyon, where there is an old "road" that is now a trail. This can be followed out across country to County Road S2.

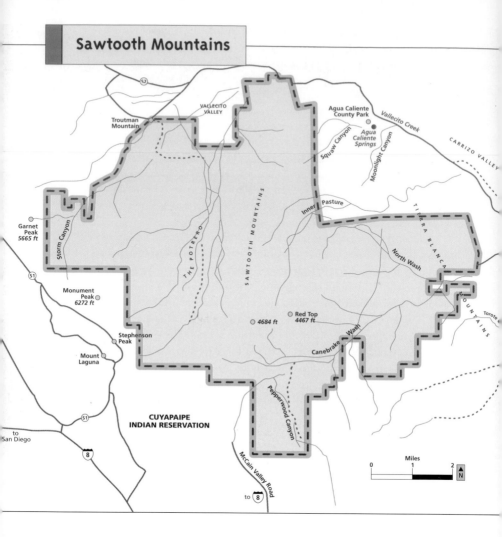

Finally, the Pepperwood Trail (which begins at the BLM's Cottonwood Campground on the McCain Valley Road north, off I-8) offers access to Canebrake Canyon. California bay, or pepperwood, is found along the upper portions of Pepperwood Canyon. The trail may be difficult to follow in places. To reach the trailhead, exit I-8 at Manzanita Boulevard, take Hwy 94 to McCain Valley Road, and follow that road 13 miles to the campground. From the campground head north on an old jeep road toward Pepperwood Canyon. The trail crosses a minor divide, and in about 3 miles it begins a steep descent into the upper part of the canyon. At about 4 miles you reach the canyon bottom, where there is often water, pepperwood (California bay), and cottonwood trees. Beyond this point the trail gets difficult to follow, but you can continue to Canebrake Valley within the wilderness if motivated.

Wash in Painted Canyon, Mecca Hills Wilderness.

Appendix A: For Further Information

**ANZA BORREGO DESERT
STATE PARK**
200 Palm Canyon Drive
Borrego Springs, CA 92004
619-767-4684

**BLM BARSTOW RESOURCE
AREA OFFICE**
150 Coolwater Lane
Barstow, CA 92311
760-255-8700

**BLM BISHOP RESOURCE
AREA OFFICE**
785 N. Main Street
Bishop, CA 93514
760-872-4881

**BLM CALIENTE RESOURCE
AREA OFFICE**
3801 Pegasus Drive
Bakersfield, CA 93308
805-391-6000

BLM CALIFORNIA DESERT DISTRICT
6221 Box Springs Boulevard
Riverside, CA 92507
909-697-5200

**BLM EL CENTRO RESOURCE
AREA OFFICE**
1661 S. 4th Street
El Centro, CA 92243
619-337-4400

**BLM NEEDLES RESOURCE
AREA OFFICE**
101 W. Spikes Road
Needles, CA 92363
619-326-2896

**BLM PALM SPRINGS RESOURCE
AREA OFFICE**
PO Box 2000
North Palm Springs, CA 92258
619-251-4800

**BLM RIDGECREST RESOURCE
AREA OFFICE**
300 South Richmond Road
Ridgecrest, CA 93555
760-384-5400

BLM YUMA DISTRICT OFFICE
3150 Winsor Avenue
Yuma, AZ 85365
602-726-6300

**CANNELL MEADOW RANGER
DISTRICT**
105 Whitney Road
Kernville, CA 93238
760-376-3781

DEATH VALLEY NATIONAL PARK
PO Box 579
Death Valley, CA 92328
760-786-2331

**IMPERIAL NATIONAL
WILDLIFE REFUGE**
PO Box 72217
Martinez Lake, AZ 85365
520-783-3371

INYO NATIONAL FOREST
873 N. Main Street
Bishop, CA 93514
760-873-2400

JOSHUA TREE NATIONAL PARK
74485 National Park Drive
Twentynine Palms, CA 92277
760-367-7511

**MOJAVE DESERT INFORMATION
CENTER**
PO Box 241
Baker, CA 92309
760-733-4040

MOJAVE NATIONAL PRESERVE
222 East Main Street
Suite 202
Barstow, CA 92311
760-255-8800

Appendix B: Acreage of California Desert Wilderness Areas

Anza Borrego Desert State Park	378,000 acres
Argus Range Wilderness	74,890 acres
Bigelow Cholla Garden Wilderness	10,380 acres
Bighorn Mountains Wilderness	39,185 acres
Big Maria Mountains Wilderness	47,570 acres
Black Mountain Wilderness	13,940 acres
Bright Star Wilderness	9,520 acres
Bristol Mountains Wilderness	68,515 acres
Cadiz Dunes Wilderness	39,740 acres
Carrizo Gorge Wilderness	15,700 acres
Chemehuevi Mountains Wilderness	64,320 acres
Chimney Peak Wilderness	13,700 acres
Chuckwalla Mountains Wilderness	80,770 acres
Cleghorn Lakes Wilderness	33,980 acres
Clipper Mountains Wilderness	26,000 acres
Coso Range Wilderness	50,520 acres
Coyote Mountains Wilderness	17,000 acres
Darwin Falls Wilderness	8,600 acres
Dead Mountains Wilderness	48,850 acres
Death Valley National Park designated wilderness	3,158,038 acres
Domeland Wilderness	130,986 acres
El Paso Mountains Wilderness	23,780 acres
Fish Creek Mountains Wilderness	25,940 acres
Fish Slough-Volcanic Tablelands Proposed Wilderness	25,000 acres
Furnace Mountains Wilderness	28,110 acres
Golden Valley Wilderness	37,700 acres
Grass Valley Wilderness	31,695 acres
Hollow Hills Wilderness	22,240 acres
Ibex Hills Wilderness	26,460 acres
Imperial Wilderness	15,056 acres
Indian Pass Wilderness	33,855 acres
Inyo Mountains Wilderness	205,020 acres
Jacumba Mountains Wilderness	33,670 acres
Joshua Tree National Park designated wilderness	585,040 acres
Kelso Dunes Wilderness	129,580 acres
Kiavah Wilderness	88,290 acres
Kingston Range Wilderness	209,608 acres

Appendix B: continued

Little Chuckwalla Mountains Wilderness	29,880 acres
Little Picacho Peak Wilderness	33,600 acres
Malpais Mesa Wilderness	32,360 acres
Manly Peak Wilderness	16,105 acres
Mecca Hills Wilderness	24,200 acres
Mesquite Mountains Wilderness	47,330 acres
Mojave National Preserve	695,200 acres
Newberry Mountains Wilderness	22,900 acres
Nopah Range Wilderness	110,860 acres
North Algodones Dunes Wilderness	32,240 acres
North Mesquite Mountains Wilderness	25,540 acres
Old Woman Mountains Wilderness	146,020 acres
Orocopia Mountains Wilderness	40,735 acres
Owens Peak Wilderness	74,640 acres
Pahrump Valley Wilderness	74,800 acres
Palen-McCoy Wilderness	270,629 acres
Palo Verde Mountains Wilderness	32,310 acres
Picacho Peak Wilderness	7,700 acres
Piper Mountain Wilderness	72,575 acres
Piute Mountains Wilderness	36,840 acres
Resting Spring Range Wilderness	78,868 acres
Rice Valley Wilderness	40,820 acres
Riverside Mountains Wilderness	22,380 acres
Rodman Mountains Wilderness	27,690 acres
Sacatar Trail Wilderness	51,900 acres
Saddle Peak Hills Wilderness	1,440 acres
San Gorgonio Wilderness	94,702 acres
Santa Rosa Wilderness	84,500 acres
Sawtooth Mountains Wilderness	35,080 acres
Sheephole Valley Wilderness	174,800 acres
Soda Mountains Proposed Wilderness	132,000 acres
South Nopah Range Wilderness	16,780 acres
Stateline Wilderness	7,050 acres
Stepladder Mountains Wilderness	81,600 acres
Surprise Canyon Wilderness	29,180 acres
Sylvania Mountains Wilderness	17,820 acres
Trilobite Wilderness	31,160 acres
Turtle Mountains Wilderness	144,500 acres
Whipple Mountains Wilderness	77,520 acres
White Mountains Proposed Wilderness	250,000+ acres

Index

George Wuerthner

George Wuerthner is an accomplished ecologist, writer, and photographer who has written 19 books, including *California's Wilderness Areas: The Complete Guide, Volume 1—Mountains and Coastal Ranges* (Englewood, CO: Westcliffe Publishers, 1997). Other titles authored by Wuerthner include *Yosemite—A Visitor's Companion, Yellowstone—A Visitor's Companion, Grand Canyon—A Visitor's Companion, Nevada Mountain Ranges, California's Sierra Nevada, Alaska Mountain Ranges, Oregon Mountain Ranges, Idaho Mountain Ranges, Texas' Big Bend Country, Southern Appalachian Country, Forever Wild—The Adirondacks, Maine Coast, Vermont—A Portrait of the Land and Its People, Yellowstone—The Fires of Change, Rooftop of America—Rocky Mountain National Park, Alaska,* and *Montana—Magnificent Wilderness.*

Prior to becoming a full-time freelance writer and photographer, Wuerthner worked as a backcountry ranger, biologist, botanist, high school teacher, college instructor, and wilderness guide. He makes his base in Livingston, Montana, adjacent to Yellowstone National Park.